MW00529583

Forgotten Founder

Forgotten Founder

The Life and Times of Charles Pinckney

Marty D. Matthews

University of South Carolina Press

Published in Columbia, South Carolina, by the
University of South Carolina Press

Manufactured in the United States of America

08 07 06 05 04 5 4 3 2 1

Library of Congress Cataloging-in-Publication Data

Matthews, Marty D., 1961–
Forgotten founder : the life and times of Charles Pinckney / Marty D. Matthews.
p. cm.
Includes bibliographical references and index.
ISBN 1-57003-547-4 (cloth : alk. paper)
1. Pinckney, Charles, 1757–1824. 2. Legislators—United States—Biography.
3. United States. Congress. Senate—Biography. 4. United States. Constitution—Signers—Biography. 5. Governors—South Carolina—Biography. 6. Diplomats—United States—Biography. 7. Diplomats—Spain—Biography. 8. South Carolina—Politics and government—1775–1865. I. Title.
E302.6.P54M38 2004
973.4'092—dc22

2004002626

For Marta and Uncle Nick

Contents

Illustrations

Acknowledgments

I started this work as my dissertation under the direction of Constance B. Schulz, mentor and friend. Her advice and contributions have been invaluable, and I begin by acknowledging and thanking her. I also appreciate the input of Robert Weir, Walter Edgar, Charles Kovacik, Lawrence S. Kaplan, Robert Weyeneth, and Kevin Gannon, all of whom read the entire draft or major portions thereof.

Original funding was provided by the National Park Service. I am especially grateful for the assistance of Rick Hatcher and Carlin Timmons of Charles Pinckney National Historic Site and archaeologist Bennie Keel for their assistance, advice, and support as the project progressed. Coxey Twogood of Independence Hall provided valuable information as well as a nice place to stay while I conducted research in Philadelphia and New York. I also thank the Friends of Snee Farm for their efforts to assure Charles Pinckney's legacy is not forgotten.

The staffs of several libraries have been quite helpful, especially Robert Mackintosh of the South Carolina Department of Archives and History and Robin Copp at the South Caroliniana Library, both in Columbia. One of the first places I conducted research for this project was the Duke University Library Special Collections. Their generosity and help remain vivid in my memory. The Charleston Library Society and South Carolina Historical Society facilitated additional research and allowed me to try out my ideas on interested audiences. And Peggy Clark and C. James Taylor at the Laurens Papers were also invaluable allies. I also thank my editors at the University of South Carolina Press, Alex Moore and Scott Burgess, for their advice and patience as I completed the manuscript.

My family and friends have been very supportive, especially my mother and father and Robert and Sigrid Jordan. My uncle, Professor Nicholas Aaron Adams, died before this manuscript was completed, but he was a constant source of encouragement and inspiration for much of my writing.

Most importantly I thank my wife, Marta, for making this project possible. I would never have completed it without her assistance and support. And though it has become somewhat contrived, I cannot think of a better way to say this: all of the good things about this work I owe to the above-mentioned individuals and many others; any deficiencies are mine alone.

Introduction

In the 1920s, a little over one hundred years after Charles Pinckney's death, an interesting correspondence occurred in the state of South Carolina. W. E. Bowen, a resident of Greenville in the western part of the state, wrote to the state historian A. S. Salley Jr. in Columbia. Bowen had recently read *The Mystery of the Pinckney Draught* by retired United States justice C. C. Nott, which assessed Pinckney's contribution to the United States Constitution. Nott's book quoted an 1866 article from *DeBow's Review* stating that Pinckney's grave at Snee Farm, one of his family's plantations in Mount Pleasant, was unmarked. When he finished Nott's book, Bowen became interested in placing some type of marker on Pinckney's grave.

In his reply, Salley concurred that Pinckney was buried at Snee Farm and suggested Bowen write its owner, George F. von Kolnitz, for further details. Bowen wrote, and von Kolnitz answered that he did not actually own Snee Farm but land adjacent to it. He also stated that he too had heard Pinckney was interred at Snee Farm, although he did not know the exact location. He also informed Bowen that a stone commemorating Pinckney stood at nearby Christ Church.

Bowen next turned to University of South Carolina historian J. Rion McKissick. McKissick informed him that he did not know the exact site of Pinckney's grave but would try to determine the location by examining contemporary newspaper accounts of the burial. Bowen also corresponded with three of Pinckney's descendants: Lawrence M. Pinckney, Charles Cotesworth Pinckney, and Josephine S. Pinckney. All three replied that they were not sure of the exact location of the grave. Bowen tracked down and wrote to the actual owner of Snee Farm, O. D. Hamlin. Within a few days Hamlin responded, verifying that Pinckney was buried on the land under a grove of trees near the main house. He also confirmed that the grave was unmarked, the stone having been sent to Christ Church several years earlier as a permanent and more public tribute to Charles Pinckney. It appeared that Bowen's mystery had been solved.

But not quite. Bowen, aware that Pinckney's father was also named Charles, wrote again to Hamlin seeking to confirm that the grave belonged to Governor

Charles Pinckney—the son—and not the father, a colonel in the South Carolina militia. Julia Hamlin answered Bowen's letter stating that his hunch was correct. According to her, the stone at Christ Church actually belonged to the elder Charles Pinckney. She also stated she had always heard that the younger Pinckney had been buried in the graveyard at St. Philip's Church in Charleston. Bowen wrote again to Salley, who had by this time also learned that the stone at Snee Farm belonged to Pinckney the father. He had also discovered a description of the St. Philip's graveyard that indicated Gov. Charles Pinckney had been buried there. Despite the confusion, Bowen would not be deterred.

He next turned to Theodore Jervey, author of a biography of Pinckney's son-in-law, Robert Y. Hayne. Jervey replied that he had also heard that Pinckney was buried at St. Philip's Church in an unmarked grave. Seeking further confirmation, Bowen wrote to members of the history departments at Furman University, the College of Charleston, and the University of South Carolina. His efforts were in vain. Two recipients responded they did not know the location of the grave, and the third never replied. But, at the suggestion of one of the respondents, Bowen soon wrote to Joseph W. Barnwell in Charleston. Barnwell, president of the South Carolina Historical Society, replied that he believed Pinckney was buried at Christ Church. Bowen found himself back in Mount Pleasant where his search had begun.

At the suggestion of Theodore Jervey, Bowen had also written to Langdon Cheves, a descendant of one of Charles Pinckney's protégés. Cheves had also been searching for the grave. He replied that he had ascertained through his own equally complicated and extensive series of correspondence that the stone at Snee Farm marked nothing. It apparently had been commissioned by Gov. Charles Pinckney for his father's grave. When errors were discovered in the engraving he ordered a new one, which was placed on the colonel's actual grave in St. Philip's graveyard. The original was sent to Snee Farm, leading to the erroneous assumption that the son had been buried there. From there it eventually was erected at Christ Church.

According to Cheves, the younger Pinckney was, in all likelihood, buried in an unmarked grave near his father at St. Philip's. He had consulted Pinckney's will, which directed that he be buried beside his daughter at the Circular Congregational Church in Charleston. However, Charleston Board of Health records confirmed that, contrary to his wishes, Pinckney had been interred at St. Philip's. One source told Cheves the will might not have been read until after Pinckney had been buried.

Nearly six months from the time of his original query regarding the grave, Bowen decided to drive from Greenville to Charleston and visit St. Philip's

Church. He drove across South Carolina, passing from the hilly upstate into the midlands—the former backcountry—and through the state capital at Columbia. He continued southeast, crossing into the coastal plains or lowcountry region of the state until he arrived in Charleston. His drive probably took him at least a day, road and automobile conditions being what they were in the 1920s. Both the time it took to make the trip and the direction in which he traveled were in sharp contrast to a journey Charles Pinckney had taken nearly 150 years earlier.[1]

Pinckney was born in the city where Bowen arrived. He grew up there and on his father's various plantations in the lowcountry. While still a young man he made his first moves toward the sparsely settled backcountry, acquiring land on the Congaree River just below the fall line. On that property he established a political base where he would seek to unite the state's coastal lowcountry with the inland backcountry. In doing so, he became a major transitional figure in the history of both his state and his nation.

South Carolina was a major player in United States history from the colonial era until it seceded from the Union in 1861. Changes that eventually propelled it to take that fateful step occurred toward the end of the eighteenth century and at the beginning of the nineteenth. A thriving economy in the east, based on production of rice and indigo, was replaced by an equally thriving one in the west, bolstered by King Cotton. The political power of the lowcountry Federalists was usurped by Jeffersonian Republicans more likely to reside in the interior of the state. Lowcountry Federalists touting the benefits of a strong federal government were replaced first by Republicans who recognized powerful central government as a threat and then by overzealous states righters who eventually decried it as the end to their way of life.

In all of these areas Charles Pinckney played a key role. He was born into the upper echelon of the Charleston lowcountry elite. Eventually he forsook that heritage, broke with his family, most of whom were staunch Federalists, and supported Thomas Jefferson in the crucial election of 1800. Critics called him "Blackguard Charlie." He began growing and exporting cotton from his backcountry plantations during the last years of the eighteenth century, just as that staple began to eclipse the rice and indigo grown along the coast. He coupled the growing economic power of the upstate with his own political talents to create a coalition that transformed South Carolina and set the stage for the rhetoric—much of which he helped originate—that led to threats of secession from the Union.

Pinckney's status as a major transitional figure in postrevolutionary and early antebellum South Carolina alone places him high on the list of important United

States founding historical figures. But there is more. He played a major role at the Constitutional Convention of 1787, laying one of the few completed plans of government before that body at the outset of its term in Philadelphia. Over time, this Pinckney draft of a constitution would play a leading part in controversy that swirled around him, giving his political enemies ammunition and perplexing historians for nearly one hundred years. It is this contribution to the Constitutional Convention that most historians have examined. But, regardless of whether they added to or detracted from Pinckney's reputation, these assessments have overshadowed achievements that were perhaps even more important to the formation of the early republic and that set the stage for events leading to the ultimate test of that republic.

Charles Pinckney was an avid proponent of civil rights for white men. While he recognized the need for a stronger government than that which existed under the Articles of Confederation, he also recognized its dangers. The draft of a constitution he laid before his fellow delegates in Philadelphia contained a bill of rights to protect citizens from an overbearing federal government. He was a staunch defender of freedom of the press and freedom of speech and just as ardent an advocate of religious tolerance.

He was also a leading reformer in his state, especially in its backcountry. He recognized the importance of an effective judicial system in order that the state's inhabitants could have faith in its laws. He also sought to implement penal reform, eliminating corporal punishment and restricting capital punishment to only the severest of offenses. Recognizing the importance of an educated electorate in his vision of a society where even the lower classes could eventually participate, he advocated public education at both the primary and secondary levels. While evidence is slim that he knew and corresponded with artisans and mechanics on a personal basis, his concern for them and their lot is evident by the reforms he advocated while governor of South Carolina and while serving in the state legislature. And though he was not in favor of universal white manhood suffrage, the ideology he espoused would help lead to it.

Charles Pinckney was a man and product of his time and place. As a southern planter, the benefits, rights, and opportunities he believed to be indispensable for white men were not applied to women nor to the slave labor force that supported him and his society. Women would have their place in Pinckney's vision, but it was limited to the domestic arena in which they traditionally operated during the time period. And there was only one place for blacks in South Carolina during Pinckney's life: bondage.

The economic realities of his time also plagued Charles Pinckney. While many of his personal debts were inherited, most seemed to have been caused by too much attention to public political affairs at the expense of his own financial ones. Still others came about from mishandling of his finances by a trusted relative. But like his contemporary Thomas Jefferson, he appeared to live far beyond his means, surrounding himself with the finest accoutrements and his beloved books. In the end his debts became so overwhelming, he turned to friends to assist him and protect his estate for his children.

This book will attempt to address the various aspects of Charles Pinckney's public life and, as much as is possible, his personal affairs as well. Chapter 1 traces his life from birth until his return to the state following the American Revolution. His life experiences during that impressionable period forged an ardent patriot and defender of freedom. But the actions of his father placed a burden on him that he would spend much of the remainder of his life trying to overcome. Chapter 2 deals with his early political years, first within his state and then at the Confederation Congress, where he grew frustrated at the near powerlessness of the central government. He made a reputation for himself as bright and articulate and made new friendships, including one with James Monroe, that would last a lifetime. Unbeknownst to him, however, a letter written in haste would impugn him in the eyes of James Madison, who relayed his impression to others, thereby maligning Pinckney, even after his death.

The next four chapters follow Pinckney's rise to the pinnacle of his political career. Chapter 3 is an assessment of his performance in the Constitutional Convention. It focuses to some extent on his Pinckney draft and also on his contributions in the Committee of the Whole during that body's deliberations. His nationalist oratory, foreshadowing many of the themes that eventually took center stage in Jacksonian American political ideology, became especially important. Chapters 4 through 6 follow Pinckney as he returned to South Carolina, started his own family, and began building a political coalition that extended across economic, regional, and generational lines. These efforts ultimately succeeded in uniting South Carolina and changing the ruling party both within the state and at the federal level. As head of that party in South Carolina, Charles Pinckney assured the ascension of Jeffersonian Republicans to political power during the crucial "Revolution of 1800."

As a reward for his efforts during the election of 1800, Thomas Jefferson named Charles Pinckney ambassador to Spain. Chapter 7 documents his term abroad, recognizing both the continued friendship between him and James Monroe and the enduring animosity of James Madison. Madison's continued ill will erroneously painted Pinckney as an inept representative of the United States, not only to his contemporaries but also to many subsequent diplomatic historians. Chapter 8 examines his plight upon returning home to South Carolina in

1806. While he faced financial ruin in his personal life, many of the reforms he had advocated for years in his home state came to fruition.

Chapter 9 describes Pinckney's last appearance in the public arena as a member of the United States House of Representatives during the Missouri controversy of 1820. In impassioned speeches to his fellow congressmen, he laid the groundwork for states' rights ideology that eventually dominated South Carolina and her southern neighbors. His oratory once again presciently foreshadowed changes in southern political ideology. Little could he know, however, upon his return to Charleston, where he died a few years later, that his last public statements and the eloquence for which he was so well-known would eventually inform ideas that would nearly destroy the Union he had worked so hard to create.

This biography also examines Pinckney's relationships within the South Carolina community in the contexts of race, class, and gender, describing how all worked together to create the republican society Pinckney idealized. In his vision, classes might not have been equal, but the opportunity for advancement for the lower classes was of prime importance. Gendered notions of society, especially as they related to households of the yeoman and the elite, became extrapolated to the public arena and played an equally important part in his ideal. Finally, issues of race literally and figuratively underpinned the entire southern community in which Charles Pinckney lived.

Historian Joseph Ellis has described the founders of the early republic as "a relatively small number of leaders who knew each other, who collaborated and collided with one another in patterns that replicated at the level of personality and ideology the principle of checks and balances imbedded structurally in the Constitution." Charles Pinckney certainly fits that definition. He knew and corresponded with most of the other important men of his day. He collaborated with some, like Jefferson and Monroe, and collided with others, like his Federalist cousins and Madison. He exercised very real power and authority both in South Carolina and in the seats of the national government.[2] He also exercised considerable political influence because of his oratory skills. Therefore, when quoting from his speeches, I have tried to present them in as readable a manner as possible. I have imposed on them modern punctuation and spelling conventions in order to make his eloquence as an orator better understood and appreciated. I have left most other quotations as I found them unless unfamiliar capitalization, punctuation, or spelling hindered readability.

These public speeches are perhaps the most accessible aspects of Pinckney's life, but his personal story is not easily told. Very little of his private correspondence remains. In one excellent assessment of him, the late Mark D. Kaplanoff examined "Charles Pinckney and the American Republican Tradition," concluding, among other things, that no biography of Pinckney could probably ever be written due to the scarcity of documentation. Only a year later, preeminent South Carolina historian George C. Rogers disagreed. He believed that the study of South Carolina history stood "on the eve of a great breakthrough" and voiced his opinion that a biography only awaited someone to take up the pen and the task.[3]

Despite Rogers' optimism, large portions of Pinckney's life are gone. Absent the miraculous finding of some lost treasure trove of yellowed Pinckney diaries or correspondence in a dusty lowcountry attic, they will probably never be fully reconstructed. W. E. Bowen's quest for his grave is but one instance of what appears to be the fates conspiring to obliterate the memory of Pinckney's role in the formation of the United States. Even a recent undergraduate history textbook omitted his name as one of South Carolina's signers of the Constitution. But the important transitional role Pinckney played within his home state and on a national level—from making major contributions at the Constitutional Convention to inspiring a new generation of states' rights advocates—requires that an attempt be made to examine his life.[4]

And so, with the optimism of George C. Rogers, the prudence of Mark D. Kaplanoff, and the tenaciousness of W. E. Bowen, Charles Pinckney's story begins.

Prelude

A Formidable Ancestry

In early 1692, the fledgling province of South Carolina was less than twenty-five years old, even though Europeans had first explored the region more than 150 years earlier. Summers were hot and humid in the colony, and although winters were more bearable, early settlers suffered from pestilence and disease all year long. The largest settlement, Charles Town, at the confluence of the Ashley and Cooper Rivers, was only a small English outpost in a great American wilderness. In time, the area would become one of the richest and most cultured spots on the continent. But when Thomas Pinckney arrived from Jamaica in April, such a status lay far in the future.

Pinckney played a major role in this journey to prosperity. He had been born in Bishop Auckland, County Durham, England, and by the time he was twenty-two had made his way to Jamaica to seek his fortune in sugar. He soon discovered fortune could be more easily obtained sailing in a privateer against ships of France, which was then at war with England. On one such voyage, a French ship was taken, returned to Port Royal, and delivered by a court of admiralty as a prize to her purchasers, who rechristened her the *Loyal Jamaica.* Pinckney then signed on to privateer with her, and by April of 1692 the ship had made its way to Charles Town.[1]

Because residents of the port city feared piracy and because Pinckney and his compatriots had quite a bit of money with them when they arrived, there was some apprehension about the crew's true business. But after receiving assurances that they were not pirates, the town allowed Pinckney and his mates to remain so long as two reputable citizens agreed to post bond for each of them. Sir Nathaniel Johnson, also of County Durham, England, and Francis Noble agreed to post Pinckney's bond, and soon the former privateer had settled in town.

Within a short time, Pinckney became a prominent merchant and influential member of the community. By September of the same year, he had married Grace Bedon, daughter of George and Elizabeth Bedon, both of whom had been a part of the original permanent settlement of the colony twenty years earlier. He bought several lots in town and acquired a 480-acre plantation north of the city named Fetteressa. For a time, all seemed well for the young settler who had arrived in town under clouds of suspicion. But within five years the harsh climate and associated disease claimed Grace. He also received news that his mother, father, and eldest brother all had died at their homestead in Bishop Auckland. Weighed down by the burden of so many deaths in such a short period of time, Pinckney decided to sail home to England to see his surviving family. During this visit home, Pinckney was introduced to a neighbor's daughter, Mary Cotesworth. Within a short while, the two were married, and shortly afterwards Thomas returned to Charles Town with his new bride.

Over the next three years, Pinckney added further to his holdings, buying one of the first wharfs to be built on the lower bay. Mary bore three sons—Thomas, Charles, and William. But in 1705, the harsh climate claimed the family patriarch: Thomas died of yellow fever, a common ailment in the mosquito-infested lowcountry. Pinckney had been in Charles Town a little over ten years and had amassed quite a fortune. His landholdings, merchant interests, and wharf had proven lucrative and left his family fairly wealthy and prominent members of the Charles Town society. Thomas, the son, became a mariner but died while trading in Nassau in 1733. Charles, named for his mother's father, Charles Cotesworth, became one of the most prominent members of the colony. After losing his first wife, he married Eliza Lucas in 1744. The two produced three children—Charles Cotesworth, Thomas, and Harriott—all of whom continued the prominence that had become associated with the Pinckney family name.[2]

William, the youngest son of Thomas and Mary, succeeded his father as merchant and manager of the wharf. In 1735, he and his brother helped organize the first fire insurance company in America, the Friendly Society. The endeavor proved to be quite progressive but not nearly as profitable. In November of 1740, fire swept through Charles Town, causing such extensive damage that the Friendly Society could not meet its claims and went bankrupt. William had not been as economically stable as his brother and suffered more heavily from his loss. As a result, he and his wife, Ruth Brewton, daughter of prominent Charles Town banker Miles Brewton, became unable to care for their child, a son named Charles who had been born in 1731, and sent him to live with his uncle and namesake. The uncle had not yet become a father and treated his nephew as one of his own. In fact, even though three children were eventually born to Charles and Eliza, William and Ruth's son began calling himself "Charles Pinckney, Junior."[3]

Upon reaching maturity, Charles Junior decided to study law, and his uncle Charles and aunt Eliza agreed to fund his education. Although Charles' marriage to Eliza and the subsequent births of their three children prevented Charles Junior from becoming his uncle's sole heir, Eliza wrote that he stayed on with his cousins, pursued his studies, and "never show[ed] disappointment at his missed fortune." In July of 1752, a few months after turning twenty, he was admitted to the South Carolina bar. Things began to happen rapidly for the young lawyer. He married, bought a plantation northeast of Charles Town, had a son, and entered politics all within about two and one-half years.[4]

On 2 January 1753, Charles Junior married Frances Brewton, his first cousin and daughter of Robert Brewton. A little more than nine months later, she gave birth to a son whom they named Charles. But the baby died in only a few weeks. In 1754, they purchased a plantation from John Savage in Christ Church Parish, northeast of Charles Town, across the Cooper River. Pinckney called his small plantation Snee Farm, the name being derived from an old Irish word meaning "bountiful," and used it to win a seat in the South Carolina Royal Assembly as representative from the parish. From that point on, Pinckney served in every term of the assembly until its demise. He and Frances also maintained a home in town on Queen Street and began purchasing other properties throughout the colony.[5]

Like Charles, Frances was also the granddaughter of banker Miles Brewton. Her brother, also named Miles, became and remained a merchant, despite marrying into one of the leading planter families, the Izards. Many merchants used capital obtained from their trading endeavors to purchase land and become planters, eventually divesting themselves of their business pursuits. But others did not. Instead, they married into planter families and retained what they viewed to be more reliable sources of income. When Charles married Frances he united the Pinckneys, who by that time had become known as a planter family, to the Brewtons, who were associated with the merchant class. This unification of the various interests in the lowcountry society became an important component of the harmony among the citizens of lower South Carolina. This harmony enabled them to mount an effective front against the British during the Revolution and to maintain a semblance of stability throughout most of the state afterwards.[6]

Charles and Frances' marriage proved to be quite harmonious as well. Over the next several years, eight children arrived at regular intervals, with two dying in infancy. Two daughters, Mary and Rebecca, and three sons, Thomas, William Robert, and Miles Brewton, lived to adulthood. On 26 October 1757, a fourth son was born. In May, Charles and Frances baptized him at St. Philip's Church and christened him Charles. He was the fifth male in the family to bear the name since Thomas Pinckney arrived in 1692. His father's continued involvement in civic and political duties inspired the youngster as he grew older.

Impressions made on him during his youth secured his own desire for success in his life, his colony, and, within a few years, both his state and his nation. His family's wealth and lowcountry political and familial connections would enable him to obtain that success. But on that cool fall day of his baptism, no one had any idea that this Charles would rise to become one of the most influential and important figures of his time.

One

Forging the Founder

Very few places on the American continent could match Charles Town for vitality and excitement in 1757, the year of Charles Pinckney's birth. In terms of its economy, the year lay almost directly in the middle of the period that George C. Rogers Jr. called the city's "golden age of commerce," from the 1730s to the 1820s. Merchants, doctors, lawyers, seamen, artisans, and planters who kept "town houses" within the city's walls all contributed to the vibrant society. Politically speaking, white males long had enjoyed large amounts of discretion in the way they chose to govern the colony, due to the British policy of salutary neglect. The crown simply took the position that "Government should be as Easy and mild as possible." But after 1748, it began to assert more power over the Royal Assembly, causing resentment among many of the colony's inhabitants.[1]

Culturally speaking, the diversity of the lowcountry was astounding. The various ethnic, racial, and religious groups created a special blend of influences that colored lowcountry life with a mélange unseen nearly anywhere else in the British colonies. African slaves had created their own Gullah culture, a unique blend of West African and European customs and language. This culture did not stay within its own racial boundaries but readily diffused into much of the white population as well. French Huguenots, Scottish Presbyterians, German Quakers, Anglicans, Congregationalists, Roman Catholics, and Jews all contributed to the culture of pre-Revolutionary Charles Town. Still, the English made up nearly 80 percent of the lowcountry's white inhabitants. The other large population group consisted of the African slaves. Thus, Anglo and African culture influenced society more keenly than their counterparts.[2]

Charles Pinckney grew up in this spirited place. The impressions made on him during his youth in Charles Town imbued him with a sense of his own destiny and that of his home and, eventually, nation. His father's example instilled in him the importance of representing his fellow citizens in various government bodies. His own experiences during the Revolution ignited in him a patriotic ardor not easily extinguished and one that burned all of his adult life.

His eventual exile to Philadelphia after his capture by the British at the fall of Charles Town first appeared to be an unfortunate sidetrack, but actually allowed him to establish interstate ties that assisted him as he made a move to the national political arena. But the shame he felt over his father's decisions regarding the patriots' cause, along with resulting economic hardships, tainted him permanently both financially and, perhaps even more importantly, psychologically.

His parents' participation in the cultural development of white society in the South Carolina lowcountry probably made one of the earliest influences on the young Charles. Many of the community's wealthy and educated citizens, protective of the English-flavored society they were attempting somewhat futilely to recreate, belonged to organizations such as the Charles Town Library Society, chartered in 1748 by its organizers "to keep their descendants from sinking into savagery." "Charles Pinckney Junior," as he inscribed some of his earliest books, and his wife, Frances Pinckney, belonged to the society from 1770 until his death, and he served as its vice president for three years. Their son would eventually become a member as well. Both father and son enjoyed books and had substantial libraries that they passed to each succeeding generation. The son, however, added more volumes to the collection than any of his forebears or progeny, and his interests ranged from the classics to political theory to world religions to astronomy—a sharp contrast from what many colonial South Carolinians had read and much more akin to the cosmopolitan interests of someone like Thomas Jefferson.[3]

Charles' family played a major role in other aspects of Charles Town society as well. Both parents were members of prominent lowcountry families, the Pinckneys and the Brewtons. In addition to his duties as assemblyman and vice president of the library society, the elder Charles involved himself in many other endeavors. He practiced law. He ran five plantations around the state, including one at the Congarees, one in the Ashepoo-Combahee-Edisto River Basin, one in St. Bartholomew's Parish, and Snee Farm in Christ Church Parish. He belonged to the Masons, the South Carolina Society, and the Saint Andrews Society.[4]

Charles' mother, Frances, according to South Carolina law, was a *femme covert,* or, legally speaking, she was "covered" by her husband. He assumed control of any and all property brought with her into their marriage unless other arrangements had been made previously. Most women in eighteenth-century Charles Town had little legal or civic power. But they did exercise a great deal of influence and power at home and in running the plantations. Considering the importance of successful plantations to the economic infrastructure of the lowcountry, women like Frances Brewton Pinckney exercised considerable power and influence beyond the restrictions placed on their sex by law. Evidence is scarce regarding Frances' day-to-day activities, but she, like her in-law Eliza Lucas Pinckney, probably played an active role in managing both the house in Charles Town and the various plantations, especially Snee Farm, where she appears to have lived after her husband died in 1782.[5]

Snee Farm also provided the political base from which the elder Charles operated during the first few years of his public service. In the twenty-first and twenty-second sessions of the assembly (1754–60), he represented Christ Church Parish. Within a few years, after he made a name for himself, South Carolinians routinely elected him from the much more competitive St. Michael's and St. Philip's districts of peninsular Charles Town. He served as justice of the peace for Berkeley, Colleton, and Charles Town Districts and vestryman for both St. Philip's and St. Michael's Parishes. He also joined the militia, where he ascended to the rank of commander. For some reason, however, a lesser title stuck with him, and Charles Pinckney Junior became known as Colonel Pinckney to distinguish him from his various namesakes.[6]

By 1765, Charles Town and the rest of the colony relied heavily on trade going through London for its wealth. In March, when Parliament passed the Stamp Act, which placed a tax on public documents, many of the colonists felt betrayed. Events moved quickly during the latter part of the year. In early October, Christopher Gadsden, John Rutledge, and Thomas Lynch traveled to New York, represented South Carolina at the Stamp Act Congress, and returned home with a report, which met the overwhelming approval of most of the port city's residents, stating that taxation could only be imposed by a colonial assembly. Gadsden was one of the most radical and outspoken of the revolutionaries. Some moderates, such as Charles Pinckney's future father-in-law, merchant Henry Laurens, found themselves forced into becoming more active supporters of the cause when events ensued that propelled them both figuratively and literally into the thick of things. A riot broke out when a group of colonists, suspecting him of hiding some of the hated British stamps, surrounded Laurens' home. By the time the mob dispersed and the crisis subsided, Laurens had seen firsthand the depth of emotion the issue had caused. He became one of the staunchest supporters of the growing rebellion against the Crown.

When the Stamp Act took effect in November, the port of Charles Town all but closed completely. On 29 October, Colonel Pinckney and his fellow representatives in the Commons House of Assembly voted near unanimous approval of the report brought from New York by Gadsden, Rutledge, and Lynch. The atmosphere in Charles Town verged on chaos. Mobs virtually ruled the streets, rioting and holding mock funerals for "Liberty." In addition, at the end of the year, the threat of a Christmastime slave insurrection arose, instilling more fear into many of the white inhabitants. Almost as quickly as they arose, however, the apprehensions subsided. The insurrection never occurred. The Crown repealed the Stamp Act in 1766. When the news reached Charles Town in May, the riots turned from anger to celebration. Such excitement must have made a strong impression on nine-year-old Charles Pinckney, whose father had proved his loyalty and devotion to the resurrection of "Liberty" by standing steadfast with fellow assemblymen who favored continued autonomy for the colony.[7]

In December, Charles' grandfather died. Despite his economic troubles early in life, William Pinckney had long held the important position of commissary general, making sure the colony was protected by a well-equipped militia. He had lived to see Charles Town—or Charlestown, as inhabitants now referred to it—grow into one of the most cosmopolitan, sophisticated, and wealthiest cities on the continent. He had seen his son assume an instrumental role in the colony's development. But he did not live to see the even more sweeping changes that were about to take place in that colony or on the continent.[8]

Despite the relative calm that fell over Charlestown and the surrounding lowcountry, lawlessness in the colony's backcountry—that area roughly northwest of the coastal plain—began to increase. While many citizens in the lowcountry either ignored or did not know of the turmoil in the upstate, others like the Reverend Charles Woodmason, expressed concern for the area's inhabitants by becoming one of their most ardent supporters and spokesmen. This intracolony strife also occupied the attention of the Charlestown government and Colonel Pinckney, especially during the summers of 1766 and 1767, as gangs of bandits roamed the backcountry, robbing and pillaging. Violence was common. Formally sanctioned justice was rare.[9]

In order to assess Charles Pinckney's eventual role in unifying the upper and lower regions of the state, it is important to understand the divisions that existed between the two and the conflict that developed over those divisions. Colonists in the backcountry resented what they perceived to be a lack of attention given their region by the assembly in Charlestown. In order to protect themselves from anarchy, they formed their own local vigilante groups. These local groups eventually joined one another and became known as Regulators. Along with physical power exercised over outlaws, the Regulators also succeeded in obtaining a small measure of political power. The House of Commons eventually deputized many of them as Rangers, giving them the legitimate political authority to clean up the licentious elements of the backcountry. They also made inroads into the assembly by intimidating election representatives in several polling places and voting themselves into the House of Commons. The royal governor denied their victory its possible fruits when he adjourned the assembly in November of 1768 for protesting the Townshend duties.

Within a year, the Regulators had begun to use measures that were viewed by many as too extreme, angering more moderate residents of the upstate. These residents formed a group to counter the Regulators. Calling themselves the Moderators, they sought to temper the vigilantes' cruelties. In March of 1769, the two groups narrowly avoided an all-out battle, eventually agreeing to a truce and going their separate ways. Over the next couple of years, most of the groups' activities petered out as their objectives began to be met: lawlessness in the backcountry had been squelched along with the extreme reaction of the Regulators. By 1771, the turbulence had subsided, and many of the Regulators who had been formally charged with cruelties were pardoned by Governor Montagu. The lowcountry elite were glad to have the problems of the back-country resolved for a while, viewing the activities of many of the region's inhabitants as direct threats to harmony in the colony. The conflict between the two areas existed for years and would remain until Charles Pinckney—just a youth when the Regulators and Moderators clashed—began making decisive efforts on behalf of the backcountry during the latter part of the century.[10]

As tensions within the colony subsided, those between the colony and the Crown increased, despite the Stamp Act's repeal in 1766. In 1768, Colonel Pinckney helped draft and signed a letter to colonial agents in England urging repeal of the Townshend duties, which, among other things, placed a duty on tea, glass, and paper and used this revenue in part to pay royal governors, judges, and other appointees. In the past, the colonial assembly paid royal appointees and thus had the power of the purse over them. Colonists were especially incensed at this feature of the duties and did everything in their power to have them go the way of the Stamp Act before them. The colonel had also been a staunch proponent of resolutions supporting the Massachusetts Circular Letter, which decried the Townshend duties. In fact, it was passage of these resolutions that brought about the suspension of the assembly by the governor just as the Regulators were starting to make their inroads.[11]

Two years later, in 1770, the colonel was elected chairman for the day at a meeting of South Carolinians under the Liberty Tree. On a hot, humid summer day, the group gathered under the large oak in Charlestown where Christopher Gadsden had spoken during the celebration after the repeal of the Stamp Act. As chairman, Colonel Pinckney led the group in passing resolutions suspending trade with Rhode Island and shunning neighboring colony Georgia. Rhode Island had been guilty of violating an agreement not to import British goods. Georgia, the Carolinians believed, was not acting with sufficient zeal in the "Preservation of American Rights" and should be "amputated from the Rest of their Brethren, as a rotten part, that might spread dangerous infection."[12]

Tensions increased, and on 6 July 1774, a group of 104 South Carolinians from across the colony met in Charlestown. Despite differences between the upper and lower echelons of society, the delegates elected five men to attend the First Continental Congress in Philadelphia: Gadsden, Lynch, and Rutledge, who had attended the Stamp Act Congress, along with Rutledge's brother Edward and Henry Middleton. Merchant representatives, who often felt the pinch of nonimportation more than other groups in the colony, supported Colonel Pinckney as one of the five. They viewed him as more moderate than either Gadsden or Lynch, quite possibly because of his familial ties to Miles Brewton, whom they also backed. The group also elected a general committee to handle the urgencies foreseen by what many believed to be "the dangers impending." The colonel was elected to head the committee, which consisted of ninety-nine members: fifteen artisans, fifteen merchants, and sixty-nine planters. Despite a more moderate influence steering the committee, the merchants were often disappointed, as the radicals would succeed in advancing their aims over and above those of the others.[13]

In January of 1775, the extralegal First Provincial Congress formed, and it quickly named Colonel Pinckney its president. The body consisted of 187 delegates, with the number of representatives from the lowcountry outnumbering the backcountry, which was actually more populous in terms of its white inhabitants, 132 to 55. His role as president of the Congress appears to have been a high-water mark for the colonel's participation in the rebellion. Although he was viewed as more moderate than many of his lowcountry neighbors, his enthusiasm remained unquestionable until the middle part of the 1770s. At the second session of the Congress in June, only a few days after the colony learned of the Battle of Lexington, Henry Laurens replaced the colonel as president. Pinckney did take part in a deputation of leading citizens who called on the last royal governor, William Campbell, on 21 June. They presented Campbell with a list of grievances and explained the formation of the Provincial Congress. They included a not-so-veiled threat: "Conscious of the Justice of our cause, and the Integrity of our Views, we readily profess our loyal Attachment to our Sovereign, his Crown and Dignity: And trusting the Event to Providence, we prefer Death to Slavery." The colonel obviously supported such language and continued to serve in the militia, but he began to side with more conservative elements and, according to South Carolina historian George C. Rogers, became more and more "reluctant to cut the tie with England."[14]

In September, Governor Campbell, fearing for his safety, fled Charlestown for a British ship anchored in the harbor. Within two months, backcountry Tories attacked patriots at Ninety-Six, and blood was spilled. The Revolution had come to South Carolina. Christmas of 1775 was the last time the Pinckney family would enjoy peace. As they spent the holiday at Snee Farm, their time together was cut short when the colonel was called back into town. Two British frigates had been spotted just off Charlestown harbor, and fears among the city's patriots began to increase. Most officials believed a successful defense could be mounted against the ships, but more disturbing were apprehensions that loyalists within town would set fire to the city while the militia dealt with the threat posed by the enemy vessels. By mid January, Colonel Pinckney began dispatching members of the militia throughout the city to guard against such an insurrection. When the British ships eventually sailed, work began on fortifications at Sullivan's Island at the mouth of the harbor. From that point on, any British ships threatening the town would have to sail past the fortifications on the island, and local militia leaders like the colonel believed the best place to stop the invaders would be there.[15]

In March, the Second Provincial Congress enacted South Carolina's first constitution and formed the first General Assembly or House of Representatives. The colonel, in addition to his militia duties, served as a representative from St. Philip's and St. Michael's Parishes. However, he soon resigned his seat to devote more time to his military commitments. Within three months Charlestown harbor came under fire at Sullivan's Island. Troops stationed at the uncompleted fort hastily reinforced its walls with logs of palmetto trees growing nearby. The spongy wood repelled British cannonballs and enabled the patriots to defend both the harbor and the city. The colonel and his eighteen-year-old son watched apprehensively from town as the engagement raged and joined in with the cheering when the altercation ended in victory for the South Carolinians.[16]

When the Declaration of Independence was signed on 4 July 1776, the younger Charles Pinckney was only a few months shy of his nineteenth birthday. Nothing is known of his elementary education, but someone, probably a family member, prepared him well enough that he planned to continue his schooling at the Middle Temple in London, like many of his contemporaries in Charlestown. He enrolled in 1773, but the events transpiring between the colonies and England prevented him from attending. While his father busied himself with colonial affairs, Charles began studying with Dr. David Oliphant of Charlestown. Oliphant, born in Scotland in 1720, had studied medicine before migrating to South Carolina in the late 1740s. He opened a medical practice and became a planter and a private tutor. In 1773, when Charles began studying with him, Oliphant served as a member of the Royal Assembly with Colonel Pinckney and attended meetings of the library society with him. Oliphant also became one of the ninety-nine members of the General Committee headed by the colonel. He eventually served in the Provincial Congress and the First General Assembly but resigned (coincidentally) on 4 July 1776 to become director of hospitals for the Southern Department of the Continental Establishment. By that date, Charles had probably completed his studies with Dr. Oliphant and was reading law with his father.[17]

Another prominent physician who would eventually play a major role in Charles' life wrote a letter of introduction for him on 6 August. Charlestown had just received word of the signing of the Declaration and was in a jubilant mood. Pinckney was planning to visit the city where the signing had occurred. Dr. David Ramsay, a native of Lancaster, Pennsylvania, had studied under Dr. Benjamin Rush after graduating from the College of New Jersey at Princeton in 1765. On Rush's advice, Ramsay headed to Charlestown where he established a practice and became actively involved in politics. By 1776, he won election to the Second General Assembly and probably met Charles through his father. Both the colonel and Dr. Ramsay served as representatives from the two Charlestown parishes of St. Philip's and St. Michael's. Ramsay wrote a letter of introduction to his mentor, Dr. Rush, in Philadelphia. It is one of the first descriptions of Charles Pinckney and, although quite normal in its style and substance, indicates the degree of standing of both the Pinckney men. "Give me leave to introduce and recommend to you the bearer Mr. Charles Pinckney, a youth of merit and education," he began and concluded by adding, "His father is one of the first characters in the province, and holds some of the first places in the gifts of his country."[18]

By early September, Charles and a few of his friends had arrived in Philadelphia. While there, he paid a visit to his half-uncle, Robert Brewton. The two probably discussed the death of Robert's half-brother and Charles' uncle, Miles Brewton, and the legal status of his estate. Brewton and his family had been lost at sea on a voyage to Philadelphia nearly a year earlier. Settlement of his considerable estate remained pending. Charles also relayed other family news and firsthand accounts of events in South Carolina relating to the Revolution. Before leaving, he and his friends considered another serious matter: smallpox. Charles had never had the disease, and the colonel had sent a letter to Robert Brewton writing, "If he and his friends think it most advisable he should be inoculated, we, that is his mother and self leave it entirely to him." Charles and his friends could have consulted with Dr. Rush on the issue, hence the letter of introduction from Ramsay. Whether any decided to undergo the somewhat risky procedure remains unknown.[19]

While Charles visited Philadelphia, the South Carolina General Assembly met and indicated its support for the Declaration of Independence. Afterwards, the state entered into a two-year period when the feelings of the populace towards the Revolution have been described as "border[ing] on apathy." The assembly drew up a new constitution to replace that of 1776 but delayed ratification of the document by almost a year so that it could be communicated across the state. Like its predecessor, it did not benefit the backcountry nearly so much as it did the lowcountry. It did not require proportional representation; property requirements effectively excluded many of the less wealthy planters in the upstate; and Charlestown received two senators, whereas other districts received only one. The rift between the two regions continued, but when the constitution was ratified in March of 1778 there was one benefit to the mostly non-Anglican inhabitants of the backcountry: over the objections of many of the elite conservatives, the Church of England was disestablished in the state.[20]

While South Carolina enjoyed a respite from the Revolution, other parts of the new country were fully engaged. Shortly after Charles and his friends left Philadelphia, the city fell to the British in September 1777. But less than a month later, the American defeat of the British at Saratoga inspired hope in the former colonists. When news of the outcome reached Paris, the French agreed to an alliance with the infant United States, eventually insuring the Revolution's success. But the victory at Saratoga, the French alliance, and the subsequent withdrawal of British troops from Philadelphia portended bleak events in South Carolina. The British were about to refocus their war aims southward.

As the flames of war threatened much of the North, Charles and his family suffered flames of their own. On 15 January 1778, a fire broke out in a kitchen or bake house near the intersection of Queen and Union Streets in Charlestown. Aided by a blustery north wind, the fire swept through the city, doing extensive damage and destroying the Pinckney family mansion on Queen Street. Among the many other buildings damaged, the Charlestown Library Society and its extensive collection of books and scientific equipment was destroyed. On the following day, Charles and his family joined the throngs of other Charlestown citizens who walked the streets, dazed by the "smoking ruins, and the constant falling walls and chimneys."[21]

As the town and its citizens began the long road to recovery, the General Assembly attended to its business. In March, it enacted the new constitution and elected Rawlins Lowndes its president. John Rutledge had been president of the assembly but resigned because he could not support the new constitution. Although he expressed reservations about the undemocratic way in which the document was written and ratified, the real reason he stepped down appears to be his reluctance to accept as final the breach with the British. The colonel, by now back in the political realm and serving in the assembly, expressed his disappointment at Rutledge's resignation but support for the man himself by adding an amendment to a resolution of appreciation for his services. It prevented Rutledge from being sanctioned for his opposition to the constitution. By doing so, the colonel further identified himself with those who appeared to be having second thoughts about the Revolution. And while Rawlins Lowndes as president may have also been conservative, the vice president, Christopher Gadsden, was anything but.

Despite the political differences in the assembly, all of its members had at least one thing in common. On 28 March they, along with every other male citizen over the age of sixteen, were to gather at various places to swear an oath to the state, in accordance with a provision in the new constitution. Anyone not taking the oath had sixteen days in which to leave South Carolina. Although revolutionary fervor had ebbed and the law was ignored by many and not enforced by others, a number of citizens who maintained loyalty to the Crown departed, surrendering all of their real and much of their personal property. But if indifference had been the rule—on most occasions the assembly failed to have a quorum in attendance and could not even meet!—it would soon be replaced by concern and apprehension. As the loyalists fled, they left behind a town that would soon lie directly in the path of an invading British army. In November, His Majesty's troops, under the command of Lt. Col. Archibald Campbell, landed on the coast of Georgia with the aim of sweeping northward.[22]

While Georgians faced the invading army, South Carolinians faced an election. On a cool, stormy day in late fall 1778, Charles Pinckney and his overseer made their way from Snee Farm to nearby Christ Church to cast their votes in the election. For the first time, Charles had decided to follow in the footsteps of his father and run for public office from the parish. When he and the overseer arrived at the church, they found that the weather and general apathy amongst the state's inhabitants had kept many from the polls. In fact, as the day progressed, no one except Pinckney and his overseer voted. As a result, the twenty-one-year-old won his first seat to public office in the newly formed senate. On the day of the body's first meeting, Christopher Gadsden addressed the circumstances of the young senator's election. "Mr. Speaker," he stated in front of the rest of the senators, "I congratulate the house upon having a young gentleman of talents and fortune come among us; and sir, what adds greatly to the interest upon this occasion, I understand the gentleman has the unanimous vote of his constituents."[23]

The colonel had also been elected to the senate from the Charlestown parishes, although by no means unanimously. He was promptly elected president, and soon the body began to deliberate on filling the office of the state's first nonroyal governor. On 5 February 1779, even though he had resisted the 1778 constitution, the honor went to John Rutledge, mainly because of his strong interest in the military condition of the state. As president of the General Assembly in the summer of 1776, he had been instrumental in the fortification of Sullivan's Island and the defense of the city from the British armada. Soon afterwards, he helped squelch a Cherokee uprising in the backcountry that many blamed on British agitation. This military prowess stood him in good stead with the senate for dealing with the approaching threat of Campbell's troops to the south.[24]

The condition of the militia was also an issue that had to be dealt with in terms of its preparedness to meet the British forces. The colonel, as president of the senate and member of both the Privy Council and militia, corresponded with Gen. William Moultrie on the subject, including the South Carolina Volunteers, in which the young Charles enlisted and served as lieutenant. Moultrie, who as a colonel had helped repel the initial British attempt to take Charlestown at Sullivan's Island, was now in charge of the First and Second South Carolina Regiments and constantly lamented the lackluster nature of the militiamen. He noted to the colonel that even the most severe infraction of regulations resulted in only the most lenient punishment and urged the assembly to pass a stronger militia bill. Colonel Pinckney was reluctant to infringe on the liberties of volunteers, causing Moultrie and the colonel's cousins Thomas and Charles Cotesworth Pinckney, both commanders in the regular army, to question his stance. The three believed that sacrifices of liberty in the short term would secure more lasting freedom in the long run.[25]

The colonel may have been zealous regarding the liberty of his fellow militiamen, but he could not maintain his ardent passion for the cause of the Revolution. In September, when the militia headed south to reinforce the regular army at Savannah, he decided to remain in Charlestown and pay attention to his duties in the senate and Privy Council. Young Charles, however, looking forward to his twenty-second birthday, heeded the call and set out towards Georgia. When he arrived just outside of Savannah, he found the British-occupied city already under siege at the hands of the French admiral Comte d'Estaing. D'Estaing had landed troops south of the city on 14 September and promptly issued demands for surrender. The British commander, Maj. Gen.

Augustine Prevost, asked for and received a delay of twenty-four hours as he anticipated reinforcements at any moment. Once this support arrived from Beaufort, Prevost let it be known he would not surrender the city.

On 23 September, the Americans joined forces with the French. On 4 October, the bombardment of Savannah began. The delay of nearly three weeks from the time of the demand for surrender to the actual attack had given the occupying army time for both the arrival of reinforcements and the construction of stronger fortifications to repulse the firepower of the patriots and their French allies. As a result, the city remained in the hands of Prevost's army. After five days, the French commander's patience reached its end. Despite Continental general Benjamin Lincoln's opinion that a slow advance towards the enemy lines would be more effective than a sudden attack, Comte d'Estaing decided upon the latter.[26]

Lieutenant Pinckney probably slept briefly, if at all, on the night of 8 and 9 October. By one o'clock in the morning the armies began to move. The attack was scheduled for three hours later at four. When the assemblage of forces took longer than anticipated, the French commander once again showed his impatience: he started the attack before all of the troops had even arrived. This premature charge proved short-lived. Charles watched in horror as the British fire mowed down the first line of French troops. When the reinforcements began their charge, they faced the same withering fire. Filled with apprehension, excitement, and probably a lot of dread, Pinckney's unit began to move.

The American charge was led by the calvary of Count Casimir Pulaski, a Polish officer recently sent south by Gen. George Washington to assist the southern army. Within a short time, the Charlestown militia's first battalion found themselves in the heat of the battle, at the bottom of a trench where, according to eyewitness Thomas Pinckney, they sustained "much slaughter." Pulaski himself had to be carried from the field, his wounds proving mortal. Comte d'Estaing sustained a shot in the arm. The French suffered more than six hundred casualties, while the Americans sustained more than two hundred. The fire of the battle and the sight of his friends and acquaintances wounded, dying, and dead all around him helped forge Charles Pinckney, from that moment forward, into one of the staunchest defenders and advocates of his young country.

For fifty-five minutes the battle raged as one line after another attempted an assault against the entrenched army of General Prevost. The British continued their rebuff of the American forces, eventually forcing them to withdraw. Col. Charles Cotesworth Pinckney's previous doubts concerning his militia's readiness was put to rest. He wrote his mother, Eliza Lucas, that they performed "exceedingly well." Despite concerns expressed to his father by General Moultrie,

Lieutenant Pinckney's men and the rest of the militia, according to David Ramsay writing some years later, performed with an "alacrity" worthy of praise.[27]

Despite this alacrity, the assault ended in a failure and most members of the militia headed immediately home. Young Charles probably made his way back to Charlestown in a state of near shock. The high hopes he and his comrades had enjoyed had been dashed in a matter of weeks. It appeared the British invasion would succeed. If so, he could be certain that he and nearly every member of his family would be tried and possibly hanged for treason. All of these things probably ran through his mind as he trudged back home, weary, dirty, and full of despair at the loss of the engagement and of the friendships of those who had perished.

Even though his family was lucky to have Charles return in time to celebrate Christmas, the work of the assembly once again shortened what few holiday festivities there were, and the ominous threat of the British army just down the coast overshadowed them. News arrived that Sir Henry Clinton and over eight thousand troops from the north had arrived as reinforcements. Charlestown had little means of defense for an army that large. And the British would not make the mistake of a sea assault again. This time, they approached the city by land, hoping to cut the inhabitants off on the narrow peninsula the town inhabited.[28]

On the first day of 1780, the General Assembly met and wasted no time preparing to face the invaders. Charles Pinckney took his seat in the chamber. Looking around him, he saw his father, the president; cousins Thomas and Charles Cotesworth Pinckney; and General Moultrie. Henry Laurens, president of the Continental Congress, in town for the holidays from Philadelphia and about to leave for Europe, paid a visit. Reports of smallpox in Charlestown and the completion of rounds by circuit court justices, many of whom were assemblymen, contributed to a delay in the arrival of many of the delegates. When a quorum finally met on 26 January, Governor Rutledge relayed bad news to the body: the embarkation of the British fleet commanded by Sir Henry Clinton from New York to South Carolina. In early February, it arrived on John's Island, just south of town.[29]

On 12 February, the day after Clinton's troops landed in the state, the assembly adjourned for the last time, but not before granting very broad powers to the governor and resolving "that the State and capital should be defended until the last extremity." Events moved quickly over the next three months. By the end of March, Charlestown was surrounded on all sides, land and sea. Meanwhile, Banastre Tarleton's cavalry swept though the middle of the state, assuring there would be no escape route to the north for any Continental troops who happened to elude their British counterparts. With much of the backcountry in the hands of the British, the city of Charlestown surrounded, and the noose around its slender-necked peninsula tightening, Governor Rutledge and General Lincoln agreed that the state's executive and a select group of men from the Privy Council should leave the city before its impending fall to preserve a viable state government. The colonel was among those chosen.[30]

On 13 April, while the colonel prepared to leave the city, his son joined the rest of his militia unit on guard at the South Bay in lower Charlestown. The day had broken bright and fair, but the sun had only risen a short way into the South Carolina sky before its rays were blotted out by the smoke from hundreds of British shells falling into the city. At noon, the colonel, Governor Rutledge, Daniel Huger, and John Lewis Gervais left the beleaguered city in order to maintain the patriot government. Before leaving, the colonel may have hurried to where his son was posted a few blocks away to bid him farewell and Godspeed. It would be the last time the two would meet. The strange twists caused by the Revolution would soon drive a geographical, political, and, finally, mortal divide between the two. While his father and the other members of what was to be the provisional government crossed the Cooper River to the north, Charles Pinckney remained behind and watched as British shot rained down on the port city. There was nothing he or anyone else could do but wait for the inevitable.[31]

Within days, on 6 May, the state suffered a severe psychological blow. The symbol of its resistance to the Crown, the newly named Fort Moultrie on Sullivan's Island, which had been impervious to British attack only a few years earlier, was surrendered without a shot. Three days later, the enemy again lobbed explosives into Charlestown, and the city found itself under renewed British bombardment. Charles, worried for his family with whom he now had little if any contact, watched as the city endured even more destruction at the hands of Clinton's army. On 9 May, the British lobbed almost two hundred artillery shells into the besieged town. The explosions produced a "glorious sight" in the sky above, contrasting sharply with the "horror" in the streets below. The end came on 12 May. General Lincoln asked for terms and surrendered Charlestown to the British. Charles Pinckney—political rebel against the king of England and armed resistance fighter against His Majesty's troops—was now in enemy hands.[32]

Like most of his fellow militiamen, he was paroled to his home in Charlestown. Many of the Continental officers were held at Snee Farm in Christ Church Parish. Others were not as fortunate. The more radical leaders of the patriot cause were confined first in the dungeon of the Charlestown Exchange and then on British prison ships in the harbor to await exchange or parole. Eventually, they would be sent to Saint Augustine, Florida, where decisions regarding their fate would delay their release for over a year. Charles was probably thankful that he, as an officer in the militia, did not suffer the same fate. But things would change for him in a few months.

In June he heard news that must have caused him a great deal of anxiety and concern. The British now controlled virtually the entire state. The four men who had left the city a month earlier had no place within the state where they could maintain a seat of government while British forces occupied Charlestown. They either had to leave the state to avoid capture and possible hanging for treason or return to the enemy, betraying the American cause. Gov. John Rutledge fled to North Carolina. John Lewis Gervais traveled to Williamsburg, Virginia. But Daniel Huger and Colonel Pinckney accepted the British offer of protection. The British did everything in their power to try and persuade Charlestonians to renounce the patriot cause. It seems almost certain they would have taunted Charles over the colonel's decision to abandon the struggle and encouraged him to do likewise. But he held firmly to his convictions and refused to follow the example set by his father.[33]

Charles was not alone in resisting the urging of the British. In fact, most South Carolinians' apathy towards the Revolution disappeared once they found their homes at the mercy of a marauding army, and they more actively resisted His Majesty's troops. While the occupiers held fast to the port city, in other parts of the state they had begun encountering problems. The "Swamp Fox," Gen. Francis Marion, hiding out in the woody marshlands, waged a successful guerilla war against the British. He and "Lighthorse Harry" Lee recaptured Georgetown in January 1781. In April they enjoyed victories on the Santee River, and in May, Lee took Fort Granby near the future state capital of Columbia on the Congaree. Also in May, just south of Fort Granby, Gen. Thomas Sumter, the "Gamecock," reclaimed the town of Orangeburg for the patriot cause. Because of such resistance and victories, the British authorities decided to teach the general population a lesson by making an example out of those who had fought in the militia and were presently paroled in Charlestown. On 17 May, in clear violation of the terms of Lincoln's surrender, Charles and his fellow militiamen on parole in Charlestown were rounded up and placed aboard two British prison ships far out in the Charlestown harbor. British prison ships had become notorious, especially in New York, for the manner in which occupants were treated. Confinement was crowded, filthy, hot, and disease ridden. Smallpox was rife. One indicator that Charles actually received an inoculation while in Philadelphia is that he did not catch the dreaded disease and die like so many others. Since the British first occupied Charlestown, almost one-third of those held captive—in excess of eight hundred men—died as prisoners of the British.[34]

Pinckney's imprisonment in such quarters could not dampen his Revolutionary fervor. He had seen men die all around him at Savannah. He had seen his father flee the city of his birth in order to maintain civil government. He had watched as the British reduced the city to rubble. As he stewed in the crowded *Pack Horse,* he thought about all he had witnessed, and his resolve increased. Within days of being crammed in the prison ship with 129 others, he and five of his compatriots became active in a campaign to have their fellow prisoners, as well as those in the *Torbay* alongside, removed from their horrible plight. They wrote a letter to British colonel Balfour regarding the inhumane conditions in which they were being made to reside and their desire to be exchanged for British prisoners. They described "a most injurious and disagreeable confinement" and stated that their "only crime if such can possibly be termed by men of liberal ideas is an inflexible attachment to what they conceive to be the rights of their country." In answer to those who would enjoin him and the others to renounce the patriot cause, the letter concluded, "The idea of detaining in close custody as hostages a number of men fairly taken in arms and entitled to the benefits of a solemn capitulation is so repugnant to the laws of war and the usage of civilized nations that we apprehend it will rather be the means of increasing the horrors than answering the purposes of humanity you expect." The prisoners also wrote to Gen. Nathanael Greene, stating their disappointment that, should they die, "their blood could not be disposed of more to the advancement of the glorious cause to which they had adhered."[35]

Over a month passed before their captors finally exchanged the prisoners on 22 June and sent them north. For those who were in St. Augustine, the word of exchange would not arrive until 7 July. Like many others, Charles was sent to Philadelphia, where he met his cousins Thomas and Charles Cotesworth, who had arrived earlier with the other exchanged Continental officers. He found a place to reside at Mrs. McFunn's boardinghouse on Second Street, a few blocks northeast of the Statehouse where the Declaration of Independence had been signed only a few years earlier and where he would play a major role in the coming years. He and fellow South Carolinian Arthur Middleton and his family enjoyed themselves and Mrs. McFunn's generosity to her southern boarders. Middleton, one of the most radical of the Carolinians, was the author of the South Carolina bill that required loyalists to leave the state. He had also been a member of the Continental Congress in 1776, signing his name to the declaration drafted only a few blocks away.[36]

Over the next few months, Charles found himself quite content in the cosmopolitan and peaceful atmosphere of Philadelphia. Along with the Middletons and his cousins, he fraternized with Pierce Butler and his family. Butler had been in charge of organizing the South Carolina militia in which both

Charles and the colonel served. He was present with Charles at the fall of Savannah, but he left South Carolina after the capture of Charlestown and joined Horatio Gates' army in North Carolina. There, he supervised British prisoners held in Salisbury. By mid 1781, he too had reached Philadelphia, and, with the Pinckneys and his wife's family, the Middletons, the group of South Carolinians maintained ties that would have perhaps otherwise been disrupted by the war. Neither Charles nor Pierce Butler had any idea of the roles they would play in Philadelphia in the coming years.[37]

By the end of 1781, the ragged armies in South Carolina under Sumter, Marion, and Lee had been so successful that Gen. Nathanael Greene moved back into the state. Patriot assemblymen, excited and enabled by the year's victories, met on the Edisto River for the Jacksonborough Assembly—the first time a formal legislative body composed of patriots had met since the assembly adjourned just prior to the fall of Charlestown. One of the first acts of the new assembly concerned punishment of loyalists and those who had sought protection under the Crown. Former patriot, assembly president, Privy Council member, and militia officer Colonel Pinckney was not exempt from the sanctions. In fact, when he took protection from the British after the fall of Charlestown, he was by no means alone. He was in the company of men from some of the best families in the state, politically, financially, and socially: former governor Rawlins Lowndes; the richest man in the state, Gabriel Manigault; Arthur Middleton's father, Henry; Daniel Huger; and fellow militia member Col. Isaac Hayne, who eventually renounced protection and was executed; as well as many others who deserted the American cause. According to one historian of the city of Charleston, the actions of the members of the Jacksonborough Assembly were "motivated by revenge, retaliation, and self-interest, affect[ing] the political life of Charlestown for years."[38]

Henry Middleton escaped the assembly's wrath completely, probably because prior to taking protection he helped subsidize the war effort in the state. It spared others who had accepted British protection from outright confiscation of their property, imposing instead a fine, or amercement, as punishment. Colonel Pinckney's estate was amerced, largely due to the efforts of Christopher Gadsden, who leveled "petty and personal charges" at his old acquaintance. Gadsden had a reputation for being a zealous revolutionary, looking, according to one assessment, on "any object of British moderation and measure with a suspicious and jaundiced eye." Furthermore, his personality was erratic. He alienated family and friends time and time again, legitimizing the views of his enemies. Instead of accepting protection, he spent almost a year as a prisoner of war, much of the time in the dungeon of the Charlestown Exchange Building. When he returned to South Carolina after his parole, he brought with him resentment and contempt for those who had turned their backs on the patriot cause. One of the moderates whose actions seemed to upset him most of all was Colonel Pinckney, and he led the charge against his former ally. Only one member of the assembly spoke out in favor of the colonel. John Sanford Dart attempted to excuse his conduct, stating that the only reason Pinckney returned to Charlestown was to get food for his wife, Frances. That the wife of the wealthy planter, assemblyman, and militia officer was so badly in need of food he would become a traitor to his country was too unbelievable for most of the other representatives at Jacksonborough.[39]

While Gadsden and the others dragged his father's reputation through the mud of the Edisto, Charles remained in Philadelphia. As word arrived that most of the state, with the exception of Charlestown, was out of British hands, South Carolinians began making plans to head home. Thomas Pinckney left in January and his brother, Charles Cotesworth, in February of 1782, although neither had been formally exchanged. By April, Cotesworth was camped with General Greene's army up the Ashley River, several miles from Charlestown at Dorchester. On 24 April he wrote his brother-in-law, Arthur Middleton, back in Philadelphia, expressing his opinion that his young cousin should be preparing to head back home. Colonel Pinckney remained under protection, and Cotesworth apparently believed the younger Charles should have been in the state to protect the interest of his father's and his own future estate at Jacksonborough. On 24 June, in another letter to Middleton, Cotesworth wrote that he hoped Charles had left Pennsylvania for his home state, "where he ought to have been nine or ten months ago."[40]

In April, the assembly issued an order requiring anyone who had sought protection and remained in Charlestown to leave that city immediately or else face confiscation or amercement of their property. The colonel refused to heed the warning, and his estate was amerced at 12 percent. It is possible that had his son not shown himself to be a true patriot by fighting at Savannah, serving time as a prisoner of war, and subsequently representing his fellow prisoners on the *Packhorse* and *Torbay* in letters to Balfour, the entire estate could have been seized.[41]

Shortly after receiving word of the amercement, the colonel wrote a poignant letter to his cousin, Charles Cotesworth. The two had grown up together and were more like brothers than cousins. Admitting that he wrote with a "disturbed mind and uneasy conscience," he began by stating he would have written sooner had he not heard that Cotesworth had an "aversion to what are called *Protection Men.*" Assuring his cousin that "tho absent from you in person [I am] always near," he went on to state that he was glad many of his friends had not suffered as extremely as he had, but expressed his confusion over being singled out for such severe treatment. He stated he dreaded "as a burned child fears the fire" any further action that might be taken against him or his family and begged his cousin to do what he could to prevent it by appealing to his friends. "I really think I still must have some few friends," he wrote. In closing, he expressed his regard for Governor Rutledge and even Christopher Gadsden, who had spoken out so bitterly against him.[42]

In his reply, Cotesworth stated he would do what he could to assist his cousin but urged him to leave the British and come out of Charlestown. By 13 August, the colonel had heeded his cousin's advice. He and Frances made their way up the Ashley River to St. Andrew's Parish. Feeling better emotionally at finally coming to terms with his disloyalty and facing old friends and family once more, his physical condition began to decline. On 22 September, Cotesworth informed his sister, Harriott, that the colonel had died that morning: "Give vent to your tears for he was a man of worth."[43]

In Philadelphia, ignorant of his father's death, Charles began making plans to travel to Europe. The Revolution had interrupted his plans for education at the Middle Temple in London, but his desire to travel abroad remained. He spent much of his time during the summer and fall of 1782 preparing for this trip and sowing "wild oats." When he received word that his father had died, he put his travel plans abroad on hold and began to plan to return to South Carolina to help his mother settle the estate.[44]

The British finally evacuated Charlestown in December, and the former exiles returned triumphantly. Colonel Pinckney's body, temporarily interred in St. Andrew's Parish, was moved to St. Philip's in town. By April of 1783 Charles had arrived back in the city also, residing at 2 Orange Street and helping his mother with the estate. In June, his younger brother, Miles, left on the trip to London that Charles had so longed desired. Charles, on the other hand, began another phase of his public career. He would wet his feet in the political climate of his young state. Then, in only a few years, he would emerge on the national scene, where he would make more contacts and gain more experience that would propel him into the ranks of the nation's founding fathers. His experience as a child and young man in South Carolina had forged an adult especially suited for public service. Ardent in his passion for his state and the new nation, but in some ways hampered by the shame associated with the actions of his father towards the end of the Revolution, he would strive to use the attributes gained in Revolutionary America to overcome any shortcomings.[45]

Two

Forward to the National Stage

From the time he returned home, Charles Pinckney began his rise in prominence first in his own state and then on a national level. His friends and family connections continued to serve him well in South Carolina politics, and he would soon be elected to national political office for the first time. During his three years in the Confederation Congress, he established a reputation as one of its brightest and most eloquent members. He was in the vanguard of those calling for a more powerful central government, to be brought about by a constitutional convention if necessary. And in a brief, somewhat irrational act, caused by tension between the North and South, he instilled in one man's mind an image of himself as brash and arrogant. This misunderstanding, although minor in the short term, would end up having a significant long-term influence, overriding many of the positive aspects of Charles Pinckney's political career.

Colonel Pinckney left a fairly sizable estate to his family when he died in the fall of 1782. In his will, written twelve years earlier, he reserved property valued at £53,000, including land near the Coosawhatchie and Pee Dee Rivers, to be sold to pay his debts. He also instructed that sixty of "the worst of my plantation slaves" should be sold for the same reason. He left his mansion on Queen Street in Charlestown to Charles, as well as other lots in the city. He stipulated that the remainder of his estate, including his three plantations of Fee Farm and Drainfield in St. Bartholomew's Parish and Snee Farm in Christ Church, be distributed equally among his wife and children. He appointed Frances executrix and Charles, brother-in-law Miles Brewton, cousin Charles Cotesworth, and friend Peter Manigault as executors. Brewton, of course, had perished at sea in 1775.[1]

Despite his attempt to leave his family financially secure at his death, the act of taking protection during the Revolution had cost him dearly with the twelve percent amercement levied by the Jacksonborough Assembly. Frances petitioned the South Carolina House of Representatives for a reduction in the amercement in February of 1783. By this time, Charles had probably not arrived back in Charlestown, as her petition was made alone. The house referred it to a committee, which refused to recommend the reduction.[2]

On 30 March, Frances wrote her half brother Robert in Philadelphia. She had previously agreed to care for Robert's son Billy during an extended visit to South Carolina. Now, however, since the death of the colonel, she was reluctant to do so. Because she would be spending much of her time at Snee Farm, she feared such a country estate would allow a young boy too many opportunities to get into trouble or hurt himself. She did not inquire regarding Charles, which probably indicates he had already returned home earlier in the month.[3]

In April of 1783, however, Charles had pressing personal and local issues to handle before turning to national politics. One of the most important concerned not only the estate of his father, but also that of his uncle, Miles Brewton. The colonel had been a legatee of Brewton's and, as such, became responsible for his debts, the legal consequences of which continued to rise over several years and constantly plagued Charles' own financial situation. In addition, he watched as the city of his birth tried to come to grips with the turmoil resulting from the war and British occupation. The major concern of the planter and merchant elite was regaining the economic stability they held prior to the war. They wanted to come to terms with British merchants to whom were owed great debts—both those in London and those who had remained in Charlestown—and to be reimbursed for slaves who had sought refuge with the British. They also concerned themselves with class differences that seemed to be springing up in the city. Some of the city's artisans and mechanics who operated in competition with British merchants resented the ease with which their competition continued to operate. But the planter elite needed the British merchants and, despite the debt they had already incurred, continued to amass the bill. Artisans and mechanics held rallies in the Charlestown streets and attempted to create a coalition with backcountry farmers, bringing the old geographic division into the growing turmoil.[4]

In order to deal with the chaos, a group of the area's legislators created an act of incorporation for the city. On 13 August 1783, Charlestown officially became Charleston, an incorporated entity. One of the first issues facing the young municipality concerned the disorder. The city enacted moral codes, fire codes, and new slave codes in attempts to squelch both the licentiousness and physical threats to the town. Even those who opposed the planter elite recognized the need for stability, and their apprehensions were assuaged somewhat when several artisans were elected to the city council.[5]

While Charleston struggled with restoring stability, the backcountry continued to have problems of its own. During the war, neither loyalist nor patriot had hesitated to burn and loot each other's property. The resultant hostilities and tensions did not cease simply because the war did. Additionally, an influx of immigrants arrived in the area, coming down the great wagon trail from Pennsylvania, Virginia, and North Carolina. According to David Ramsay, conditions across the entire state created "such an amount of civil distress as diminished with some their respect for liberty and independence."[6]

With the state in flux, Charles divided his time between the St. Bartholomew's Parish plantations left him by his father and his house in Charleston. In January of 1784, he petitioned the House regarding the amercement of the colonel's estate, repeating his mother's bid of nearly a year earlier. Once again the house referred the petition to a committee, and once again the Pinckney estate remained amerced at 12 percent. It would be three years, in January of 1787, before the matter of amercement was finally settled. The new assembly reconsidered some of the amercements, treating some more leniently and removing others from the list altogether. But the body never removed the colonel's estate from the roster of amerced properties, although they did allow several years for payment.[7]

Shortly after petitioning the South Carolina House, Charles became a member. In a special election held to replace Edmund Hyrne, who had died in December 1783, voters chose Charles to represent St. Bartholomew's Parish. On 2 March, after entering the house chamber, speaker Hugh Rutledge inquired whether Charles was ready to qualify. When he responded in the affirmative, he took his seat and joined the Fifth South Carolina General Assembly for the remaining days of its last month in session. During his short tenure, he sat on only one committee, charged with the responsibility of determining how a certain judge was to be paid for his services to the state.[8]

One of the last issues facing the legislature before it adjourned on 26 March concerned the election of representatives to the United States Confederation Congress meeting in the fall. During the previous year, Charles had written and published in pamphlet form *Three Letters Addressed to the Public.* Therein he argued for a means to provide a continuous sum of money for the operation of the Congress. Such an argument illustrated his belief that a strong central government would be essential to the survival of the new nation. His eloquence in those pamphlets, along with the reputation he had gained by his efforts in the Revolution and from speaking on behalf of his fellow prisoners on the *Pack Horse* and *Torbay,* coalesced with the family and social ties he had maintained in Charleston and Philadelphia with his cousins and the Middletons. As a result, on 23 March, the assembly elected him along with Henry Laurens, Jacob Read, John Bull, and Alexander Gillon to serve in the Confederation Congress. Alexander Gillon was a major supporter of the anti-British forces within the state, advocating strict measures against loyalists. He also pushed to move the state capital from Charleston to the banks of the Congaree River. His anti-British stance and support for moving the capital endeared him to artisans, mechanics, and the backcountry. When elected to the Congress, he refused to serve as a form of protest, as he had done less than a year earlier when elected lieutenant governor. But this protest cost his supporters in the long run, as they lost what could have been a valuable and important voice on their behalf. Shortly after the election, John Lewis Gervais, one of Charles' fellow assembly members, wrote to Henry Laurens, who had just returned from Paris helping negotiate the treaty formally ending the war with Great Britain. Laurens himself did not serve in the Congress, probably because of ill health. He also declined to serve in the Sixth South Carolina Assembly or the national Constitutional Convention in 1787, where he would again have had the chance to work with his future son-in-law. Gervais expressed his confidence in Charles to Laurens and indicated the state had been blessed to have such a capable yet young representative on the national level. Charles Pinckney's star was beginning to rise.[9]

He probably spent the first part of the summer overseeing his plantations, practicing law, and preparing for his trip. He left South Carolina sometime in July, escaping the state's summer heat and humidity for the cooler climes to the north. By early August he was in Rhode Island, suffering from "slow fever" and "constant headaches" for which he had tried "a thousand remedies" to no avail. He apologized to friends he wrote for being a poor correspondent, explaining that he had been advised to do little reading or writing until well. By the first of November, he had made a recovery and hurried to Trenton, New Jersey, where Congress was then sitting. Despite his ill health and the delay it caused, he arrived earlier than most of the other delegates and before any of his fellow representatives from South Carolina. Taking his place in the small French Arms Tavern, recently renovated for use by Congress, he must have remembered the spaciousness of the accommodations for the South Carolina General Assembly and contrasted them with those of the federal Congress. The large, two-story brick structure at the northwest corner of Broad and Meeting Streets in Charleston was much more opulent than the somewhat cramped quarters of the tavern.[10]

The following day, Jacob Read joined his fellow South Carolinian, who promptly corresponded with South Carolina governor Benjamin Guerard. Pinckney informed the governor of Read's arrival and told him that, once a quorum of the states had arrived, members of Congress would determine whether to remain in Trenton or move to "some more convenient place." As the month wore on, a quorum had yet to arrive, no decision had been made, and Pinckney and his fellow delegates waited impatiently for business to begin. Henry Laurens, who had been elected but had not been back to Charleston since returning to the country from Europe, stopped by and presented his credentials before heading home on 17 November. He would not return. On the twenty-ninth, Congress finally convened with a quorum. On the next day, delegates from eight states elected Virginian Richard Henry Lee president. Pinckney, again writing Governor Guerard, expressed his optimism that the coming session would be conducted "with Unanimity and Decision." The two men had formed a close bond when they were confined on the *Pack Horse* together and coauthored the letter to Balfour. He added that, while he and his fellow South Carolinians would protect the interests of their state, he hoped all the delegates from all the states would "do everything in their power to promote the general Welfare, convinced that the Commerce and Consequences of the several States must eventually depend on the dignity and Stability of the federal Government." Already he was declaring his conviction concerning the importance of a strong central federal government in order to assure the integrity of the new nation.[11]

Pinckney regularly informed Governor Guerard of the Congress' progress. Towards the middle of December, three subjects weighed heavily on his mind. The first centered around a treaty of commerce with England. The second dealt with the right of Americans to navigate the Mississippi River contrary to the wishes of the Spanish government. The third concerned the importance of negotiating treaties of peace with Indians to the south and west. Pinckney again emphasized to the governor the importance of unanimous and decisive action on the part of the Congress in order to stave off unrest, especially in the West. It is clear he held both strong opinions about the role of the central government in helping alleviate potential economic and physical problems and staunch concern for the plight of inhabitants in the Southwest. He also expressed his desire to continue public service, not only at a national level, but back home in the South Carolina Assembly, affirming his willingness to serve again if reelected.[12]

One of Charles' first major assignments as a member of the Congress involved serving on a committee to determine whether the United States should appoint a minister to Spain. Pinckney, along with William Houston of Georgia, John Jay of New York, Gunning Bedford of Delaware, Elbridge Gerry of Massachusetts, and Samuel Hardy and James Monroe of Virginia reported to the full Congress on 17 December that such an appointment was necessary. The resolution passed and Congress charged the committee with the additional task of drawing up a draft of instructions for the prospective minister.[13]

Charles Pinckney and James Monroe first became friends while serving on this committee. Monroe was equally young, born within only a few months of Pinckney. He had been elected to Congress the previous year and had lived with Thomas Jefferson while the assembly met in Annapolis, Maryland. During the earlier part of the year, he had supported Jefferson's 1784 Ordinance regarding western lands and statehood, which originally included a prohibition of slavery in the Northwest Territory. This ordinance became the first of three major land ordinances to come out of the Confederation Congress, culminating in the Northwest Ordinance of 1787. Monroe also served on a committee to seek land for a permanent seat for the federal government, but due to sectionalism, his committee's suggestion for a site near Georgetown on the Potomac was squelched. He also advocated using permanent troops under Congress' authority to man posts in the Northwest. His adversaries in Congress, fearing what they saw as a standing army, prevented passage of his plan.[14]

During the summer recess, Monroe had toured the West, partly of his own interest in the territory and partly at the behest of Jefferson, who had originally planned to accompany him but instead traveled to Paris to serve as United States minister to France. Monroe arrived in Trenton on 16 October and, like Charles Pinckney and others who arrived early, tried to relieve his boredom while he waited for other delegates to arrive. Also like Pinckney, by December, he too was of such an optimistic attitude that he wrote Jefferson in agreement that the general concern of most of the delegates centered around the welfare of the Union. From the two delegates' independent statements and mutual concerns, it is certain they had much to discuss and became not only nationalist political allies, but friends as well. The friendship would prove to be a useful one to both men years later as each came to the other's defense after their reputations and abilities had been questioned.[15]

In 1784, Charles Pinckney's principal concern rested in the young nation's new mission to Spain. He, Monroe, and their colleagues prepared instructions and presented them to Congress two days before Christmas. The orders, drawn up in Monroe's hand, set the stage for all further dealings with Spain during the period of the Confederation. It called for setting the boundaries of Florida at the thirty-first parallel and, even more importantly, establishing a permanent right to navigation of the Mississippi by the United States. It also reflected the commitment of all the members of the committee, including Charles, to adopt a hard line towards Spain regarding the subject of navigation of the indispensable waterway. Although Congress originally planned to give the instructions to a new minister to Spain, election of a diplomat never took place. Instead, Spanish envoy Don Diego de Gardoqui arrived in the United States in the summer of 1785 and began direct negotiations with the secretary of foreign affairs, John Jay.[16]

On the same day the committee presented its instructions, Congress adjourned. After wrangling over where to reconvene, the body decided that New York City offered the most appropriate and convenient seat until a more permanent location could be decided upon by yet another committee established for that purpose. Over the holiday break, Charles headed south to Philadelphia to visit friends and family. The weather turned brutally cold, with ice in the Delaware River preventing ships from entering or leaving port. Pinckney busied himself reviewing the previous session's proceedings as well as the committee's reports regarding establishment of a permanent seat for the government.[17]

In early January, he wrote a long letter to Governor Guerard detailing many of Congress' activities and intimating to him his desire that the central government be strengthened in regards to trade and commerce abroad. Recognizing major defects in the Articles of Confederation under which the government operated, he suggested that the power to act should exist on a national level and not be hamstrung by the actions of independent states:

> It is so clear that the states can only derive consequence and power from an attention to agriculture and commerce that the necessity of a regulating power somewhere must be obvious to every one who has considered the subject—it is plain also that this power can be placed only in Congress, and I should suppose that after being invested with it, their regulations will be so constructed, as not only to rescue our Commerce from its present oppression, but by a tonnage on foreign Shipping, exporting our produce, or by preventing the Vessels of one nation importing the product or manufactures of another, and regulations of this kind, encourage the American Merchant to import and export in their own Vessels. If we should not favour our Citizens more than Strangers, our Commerce must be destroyed for want of giving proper encouragement to their Industry, and the State instead of traders will only have Commissioners.

As he had in his *Three Letters,* Pinckney once again affirmed his support for a stronger central government by suggesting that the Articles of Confederation be revised to eliminate shortcomings. They allowed for no unifying measures to protect exports that were often excluded from British markets. Artisans and merchants who suffered most at the hands of such British exclusionary practices called on the states to enact tariffs to protect them from imported goods. Most states did manage some type of protection via tariff measures, but the inconsistencies were such that intrastate rivalries often developed. By siding with merchants and artisans, Pinckney showed remarkable insight into the unifying ability of a Congress empowered to assist export trade. Monroe professed the same type of concern for merchants and artisans, despite—like Charles Pinckney—being a planter himself. The two men and other nationalists in Congress would soon go beyond simply calling for revision of the Articles. A convention to completely revamp the government was slowly starting to gain support.[18]

As January passed, the weather prevented a quorum of states' delegates from traveling to New York in time to reconvene on the eleventh as originally scheduled, so Congress did not meet until the twenty-fifth. Once again Charles Pinckney and James Monroe found themselves working side by side in an important assignment. Prior to Charles' arrival in Trenton the year before, Congress had passed the Land Ordinance of 1784, dealing with the admission of states in the Northwest Territory. Thomas Jefferson had originally envisioned admittance of a territory to statehood at the point when its population reached that of the smallest state already in the Union. The plan anticipated that approximately ten states would be carved from the territory. According to Jefferson and republican philosophy in general, the smaller the state, the better. But after his travels in the region, James Monroe had come to the conclusion that the inhabitants of the area needed experience with governing before earning the status of citizens of a new state. This concern gave rise to the assignment in which Charles Pinckney assisted Monroe.[19]

The Ordinance of 1785 called for a colonial form of government within a territory for a period prior to its admission to statehood. The authors did not insert a clause excluding slavery, as Jefferson had originally planned, probably due to the sectional characteristic of the committee, which consisted of three southerners—Monroe, Pinckney, and fellow South Carolinian John Kean—and only two northerners—Rufus King of New York and William Samuel Johnson of Connecticut. They also reduced the number of states anticipated for the area from ten to five. Jefferson, although disappointed in this part of the plan, acquiesced to Monroe's judgment, largely because of the latter's sojourn in the territory.[20]

Monroe's term in Congress ended in 1786, and William Samuel Johnson became chairman of the committee. At the urging of Rufus King, the committee reinserted the slavery exclusion, despite objection by all of the southern delegates, including Pinckney. Additionally, it added more stringent conditions before a territory could enter the Union as a state, including a population requirement of sixty thousand. The Northwest Ordinance, which finally passed in 1787, became one of the few and perhaps most important acts of legislation to come out of the Confederation Congress. It cemented the reputations of two of Congress' youngest members, Pinckney and Monroe, although neither was still involved when the final version was passed on 13 July 1787.[21]

Despite this youth, or perhaps because of it, Charles Pinckney was determined to be a key player in the Confederation Congress. He served on a substantial number of committees during his three years as a representative from

South Carolina and involved himself in numerous other matters, including diplomacy and the compensation for damages to indigents caused by the Revolution. On Monday, 31 January 1785, he seconded a motion on a resolution calling for the establishment of a minister plenipotentiary to Great Britain. He then made a motion, seconded by Monroe, that the vote be set for the following week and wasted no time nominating John Rutledge—former South Carolina governor, delegate to the Continental Congress, and family friend—to the post. Rutledge declined the nomination, probably because of political obligations in South Carolina. Pinckney then placed into nomination Robert R. Livingston, who had previously been secretary of foreign affairs. Livingston's name, however, was withdrawn, and Congress next considered John Adams for the post. Southerners, including Pinckney, worried that Adams, a New Englander renowned for his "acerbic nature" and "vain countenance," would not endeavor diligently enough to assure the British government reimbursed southern states for slaves who had escaped during the Revolution. Despite the concerns, on 24 February, Congress chose Adams as the minister to the court at London.[22]

Towards the middle of February, Pinckney and his fellow delegates received a treaty of peace signed by the commissioners and the western Indians. The ratification of such a treaty and peace with the western tribes were of prime importance to Pinckney. Hostilities in the western part of South Carolina had caused a great deal of concern. Backcountry citizens not only feared the natives, they resented the lowcountry power base, which they believed did not do enough to safeguard the upstate. Pinckney believed it imperative that the assembly in South Carolina act to ratify the treaty and promised Governor Guerard that he would forward a copy of the treaty to the state as soon as it became available.[23]

The state of South Carolina obviously approved the work of its three delegates to the Confederation Congress. It reelected them about the same time Pinckney was corresponding regarding the Indian treaty and also chose David Ramsay and John Kean to join them. Ramsay had served in the Congress in 1782 and 1783. Kean, who would be serving his first term, shared one past experience with Pinckney. He too had been one of those captured by the British after the fall of Charlestown and held prisoner aboard the *Pack Horse* in the harbor. He eventually served with Pinckney on the committee partly responsible for the Northwest Ordinance. In early March, Pinckney was also reelected to the South Carolina Assembly, this time from Christ Church Parish. His duties in New York at the Confederation Congress, however, kept him from qualifying for that seat.[24]

One of those duties involved a trip back to Trenton in the spring of 1786 to address the New Jersey Assembly. The assembly had passed a resolution refusing to comply with a Congressional requisition of September 1785 for federal supplies. Congress chose Pinckney, along with Nathaniel Gorham of Massachusetts and William Grayson of Virginia, to travel to Trenton and attempt to persuade the assembly that the resolution should be rescinded. Gorham was nearly fifty years old and had served in the Continental Congress in 1782 and 1783. Grayson, also nearing fifty, had served as regimental commander with George Washington during the Revolution and had been appointed to Congress by the Virginia Assembly in 1784. Despite the maturity and experience of Gorham and Grayson, they allowed the junior member of their committee to deliver the major address to the New Jersey legislature, attempting to persuade it to comply with the Congressional requisition. Although Grayson followed him, Charles Pinckney carried the major burden of persuading the assembly.[25]

The three informed New Jersey governor William Livingston of their arrival at Trenton on Sunday, 12 March. The following day, Pinckney, speaking on behalf of his fellow committee members and his fellow delegates in the Confederation Congress, addressed the assembly. He first called attention to New Jersey's ratification of the mode of assessing the amount of requisition among the various states, as well as the assessment itself. More importantly, in the very first moments of the speech, he made the following suggestion: "Nay more, if she [New Jersey] conceives herself oppressed under the present confederation, let her, through her delegates in Congress, state to them the oppressions she complains of, and urge the calling of a general convention of the states for the purpose of increasing the powers of the federal government, and rendering it more adequate to the ends for which it was instituted. In this constitutional mode of application there can be no doubt of her meeting with all the support and attentions she can wish." With such advice, Charles Pinckney became one of the first delegates in Congress to espouse publicly the idea of calling a constitutional convention. A little over a year later, in July of 1787, during the Constitutional Convention, Pinckney submitted a revised version of these remarks to Matthew Carey, editor of the *American Museum.* The subsequent version concentrated less on New Jersey's failure to comply with the requisition and more on the need for a change in government. Pinckney also placed a greater emphasis on his own opinion regarding the need for a change, adding to the above quote, "I have long been of opinion, that it was the only true and radical remedy for our public defects; and shall with pleasure assent to and support, any measure of that kind, which may be introduced, while I continue a member of that body."[26]

The judgment of the two senior members of the committee in allowing their young colleague to be their primary spokesman proved astute. On the following day, the New Jersey Assembly considered a resolution containing the language, "that this house, anxiously desirous of promoting among all the states a lasting union, established upon principles of justice and equality, are ready to accede to any measures founded on such a basis." Some members thought, however, that such language admitted to too much power on the part of the central government and substituted a new motion, which acquiesced to the requisition but omitted the language above.[27]

Aside from struggling with the issue of commerce within the Confederation, Congress also dealt with the lack of power over the matter internationally. The inability of Congress to negotiate treaties of trade has been termed by preeminent Constitutional scholar Andrew McLaughlin "one of the cardinal defects of the system." In April of 1784, an amendment to the Articles of Confederation had been submitted to the states giving Congress broader powers. It won the ratification of only two states. One of the first letters Charles Pinckney wrote to Governor Guerard expressed his own reservations about the issue of commerce. The fears expressed in that letter were realized later in the year when Great Britain refused to negotiate trade agreements with the impotent Confederation Congress. John Adams, who had been so excited about his ministry to Great Britain only a few months earlier, felt frustrated and defeated because he was unable to enter into a commercial treaty at the Court of London. According to still another historian, the British response to America regarding commerce after the war and the straits in which the young nation found itself as a result, probably fostered ideas of a constitutional convention more than the individual ideology of "many who sat in that August body."[28]

Like Adams in England, New Yorker John Jay, who had recently been named secretary of foreign affairs, felt frustrated at home in the United States. Difficulties in dealing with Spanish ambassador Don Diego de Gardoqui plagued Jay, and negotiations between the two regarding the cession of navigation rights on the Mississippi would eventually lead to another well-received speech by Charles Pinckney. The South Carolinian was beginning to gain a reputation for his eloquence. But the aftermath of the issue would also prove to be the beginning of a decline in that same reputation.[29]

John Jay had been chosen secretary of foreign relations in May of 1784 and began acting in that capacity in late December. One of the most important tasks for Jay involved negotiating a treaty with Spain regarding commerce and the right of navigation on the Mississippi. Although the Treaty of Peace between the United States and Great Britain conferred that right in the infant nation, there was no equal agreement between Spain and Great Britain. Thus, the question remained unanswered between Spain and the United States. Congress considered the right to navigation a subject on which there could be no compromise and instructed Jay as such. Conversely, Spanish minister Gardoqui had been instructed that he could not compromise on Spain's determination to restrict that same right.[30]

Because of the stalemate, Jay began seeking alternatives. He had come to the conclusion that any damage done to United States commerce by a temporary restriction of thirty years on the right of navigation would be outweighed by benefits and opportunities arising from a treaty with Spain. When Jay expressed his opinion to Congress, it appointed James Monroe head of a committee to consider his proposal. The committee also contained two northern delegates, Rufus King and Pennsylvanian Charles Petit. Both believed that there should be leeway regarding the United States position. Monroe was incensed. Residents in western Virginia and North Carolina, far from Atlantic ports, depended on sending products west to the Mississippi. In contrast, New Englanders and even some southerners tended to agree with Jay that the amount of goods going west was not as important as the amount of goods traded via the Atlantic if a treaty with Spain could be settled. A deadlock eventually occurred within the committee, and finally, at King's urging, the three referred the matter to the entire Congress for its consideration.[31]

Monroe wasted no time assembling a united southern faction to oppose Jay's request, enlisting Pinckney in the endeavor. On 2 August, Jay addressed Congress, making his arguments. Over the next two weeks, the delegates spent most of their time dealing with the subject. Tempers flared and talk of a break-up of the Union ensued. Jay's opponents feared that westerners who needed the Mississippi trade route would ally themselves with Spain. Some members from New England talked of creating a federation of their own in the North.[32]

On Thursday, 10 August, Charles Pinckney took the floor. Not yet thirty, he understood both the gravity of the situation and the importance of the speech he was about to make. Standing at his desk, he began by reviewing the argument made by Jay and his supporters. "I will agree," he concluded in his introductory remarks, "that an equal commercial treaty would be of more advantage to this country with Spain, than with any other in Europe, except Portugal." However, he cautioned, "I am not convinced that the relative situation of Spain and the United States is such as ought to render us, at this time, particularly anxious to conclude a treaty upon the principles proposed." By prefacing his comments with the statement, he cleverly laid the groundwork for both his opposition to Jay's request for modified instructions and his own contention that Congress should be given more power to regulate trade and commerce. Such power, in Pinckney's view, was absolutely necessary in order to assure the stability of the nation.

The two themes most prominent throughout the lengthy speech were the integrity of the Confederation and the inadequacy of Congress. Towards the end, after detailing specific reasons why the treaty Jay proposed was undesirable, especially to those in the South and West, he averred, "It is confessed our government is so feeble and unoperative, that unless a new portion of strength is infused, it must in all probability soon dissolve." His conclusion neatly summed up not only his opposition to the treaty but his desire for unity among the states and a more powerful Congress to ensure that unity:

> Upon the whole, as the present treaty proposes no real advantage that we do not at present enjoy, and it will always be the interest and policy of Spain to allow; as our situation by no means presses us to the formation of new connections; and as the suspension demanded, may involve us in uneasiness with each other at a time when harmony is so essential to our true interests—as it may be the means of souring the states, and indispose them to grant us those additional powers of government, without which we cannot exist as a nation, and without which all the treaties you may form must be ineffectual; let me hope that upon this occasion the general welfare of the United States will be suffered to prevail, and that the house will on no account consent to alter Mr. Jay's instructions or permit him to treat upon any other terms than those he has already proposed.

Despite Pinckney's eloquence, he could not overcome the sectionalism that he so feared. At the end of the month, on 29 August, Congress voted to rescind Jay's instructions by a margin of seven to five. New Hampshire, Massachusetts, Rhode Island, Connecticut, New York, New Jersey, and Pennsylvania voted for the resolution. Maryland, Virginia, the Carolinas, and Georgia opposed it.[33]

Although Pinckney, Monroe, and the rest of the southern delegates had been defeated on the resolution allowing Jay to give up rights to the Mississippi in his negotiations, they knew they had not lost in the larger picture. Any treaty negotiated, according to the ninth article, needed the assent of nine states for ratification. Thus the northern bloc lacked the crucial two states needed if in fact Jay was successful in negotiating with his new instructions. Pinckney and Monroe teamed together for one further effort to derail Jay's plan. Pinckney wrote and the two men laid before Congress a resolution questioning the validity of the change in instructions based on a vote of seven to five when a vote of nine to three was needed for ratification. The resolution failed—by a vote of seven to five.[34]

Pinckney remained unsatisfied. Despite his calls for unity and harmony, on 16 August he fired off a blistering letter to John Jay and minced no words informing him that, as far as the southern delegates were concerned, the original instructions remained in effect. "It is our duty to . . . say to you that if you proceed we shall consider you as proceeding upon the powers incompetent and unconstitutional and that we shall not hold the states we represent, bound to ratify or attend any treaty you may form." When he completed the letter, he gave a copy to his friend and ally James Monroe for his approval. Monroe took one look at it and urged Pinckney not to send it. Monroe, describing it as having an "intemperate and factious appearance," mailed a copy of the draft to his friend James Madison, who had been holed up all summer at Montpelier reading everything he could get his hands on regarding political philosophy. One of the biggest threats to a nation's stability, Madison had come to believe, was the development of factions. Based on his opinions and his reading of Pinckney's draft letter to Jay along with Monroe's comments, Madison came to the erroneous conclusion that someone so "intemperate and factious" as Charles Pinckney could spell nothing but trouble for stability in the Union. Little did Monroe know when he portrayed his friend in such a manner, his description painted a lasting picture in Madison's eyes of Pinckney as an arrogant and less than effective delegate. Madison took this opinion with him when the two met less than a year later in Philadelphia, and he would subscribe to it the remainder of his life.[35]

It had been a busy year for the young delegate from South Carolina. Perhaps nothing showed more foresight and intellectual acumen than his call for a convention to amend the Articles of Confederation. On 3 May, emboldened by the reception of his speech to the New Jersey Assembly less than two months earlier, Pinckney made a motion that Congress assign a committee "to take into consideration the state of public affairs." A few days later, his friend and fellow South Carolina delegate David Ramsay informed John Adams that "a plan will shortly be brought into Congress to recommend a continental convention for the purpose of enlarging the power of Congress." The recommendation, had it been introduced, would have occurred almost simultaneously with the call by the Virginia legislature earlier in the year for a convention in Annapolis on 4 September to address the issue of commerce.[36]

There is no clear evidence other than Ramsay's statement to Adams that Pinckney himself was toying with the idea of introducing a motion in Congress calling for a convention. Over the next three months, he decided to make one last attempt to revise the Articles of Confederation in order to rectify the Union's problems. More than two months passed before Congress finally assigned a grand committee consisting of Pinckney and eleven other delegates to deal with the issue. On 7 August, the committee presented seven new articles, all but one of which dealt with commerce, either at the international level or between Congress and the states. The first proposed article, which would have become number fourteen, gave Congress greater authority to regulate international trade and interstate commerce. Numbers fifteen through seventeen concerned requisitions of Congress to the various states and penalties and assessments for those states that fell into arrears or refused to pay their assessed amounts. Article 18 provided that any change in the Union's system of revenue required eleven states' approval. Finally, the last article set up a court system for hearing cases arising from disagreements over commerce or between federal officials.[37]

Despite the recommendations made by the grand committee, Congress never considered the report. The Jay-Gardoqui negotiations and the sectionalism produced by that event overshadowed them. However, more important than the neglect by Congress of the matter was the communication out of Annapolis in October. The report of representatives in attendance called for a convention in Philadelphia during May of the following year in order to consider defects in the Union. Congress delayed responding to the call until spurred into action by Shays' Rebellion in Massachusetts in January. Pinckney, serving on a committee to consider the disturbance, spoke to his fellow delegates on 19 February and urged that troops requested by Massachusetts for the purpose of quelling the insurrection be withheld as he "suppose[d] the insurrection . . . to be already crushed." Two days later, Congress finally replied to the Annapolis request, at which time it endorsed the convention.[38]

On a cool Thursday evening during the early spring, a joint session of the South Carolina General Assembly met. The session first elected three new delegates to the United States Congress to serve for the coming year. Then it elected five delegates to the coming constitutional convention to be held in Philadelphia: John Rutledge, Charles Cotesworth Pinckney, Pierce Butler, the elderly Henry Laurens, and the young Charles Pinckney. Pinckney had not attended Congress since 21 February, the day on which it agreed to endorse the convention, and he would not do so again. He had returned to Charleston where he had begun courting Henry Laurens' daughter, Polly. He also began pulling together ideas into a plan of government for the fledgling republic. A little less than three months later, he would attend the gathering of delegates in Philadelphia that would place him firmly in the echelons of American founding fathers —and in the midst of a controversy that continues even today.

Three

Forging the Republic

When Charles Pinckney walked into the Pennsylvania State House on 25 May 1787, he was completely unaware that he was also walking into a controversy that would eventually call into question his contributions to the United States Constitution about to be drafted there. At twenty-nine years old, he was not quite the youngest member of the delegation. The only known portrait of him depicts him at around this age. He is immaculately dressed in a yellow coat, probably broadcloth. Underneath, he wears a similarly colored vest into which he has tucked his left hand. His right hand lies across the arm of the chair in which he is sitting. Just beyond him, behind a slightly parted curtain, stand rows of green-spined volumes on several tiers of shelves, indicating his voracious appetite for knowledge as well as his love of books. Because he is sitting, it is hard to determine his height, but his face is round and his forehead high below a powdered wig pulled back and slightly above his earlobes. He has intense eyes and a broad, fine nose above slightly feminine lips. Maj. William Pierce, a delegate to the Constitutional Convention from Georgia, described him as "a young man of the most promising talents" and "in possession of a very great variety of knowledge. Government, Law, History and Phylosophy are his favorite studies, but he is intimately acquainted with every species of polite learning, and has a spirit of application and industry beyond most men. He speaks with great neatness and perspicuity, and treats every subject as fully, without running into proxility, as it requires. He has been a member of Congress, and served in that Body with ability and eclat." Pierce also attributed to Pinckney the incorrect distinction of being the most youthful member at the Convention, reporting that he was twenty-four years old. Later, the mistake would serve as fodder for Pinckney's critics, who accused him of falsifying his age in order to appear more experienced and knowledgeable than his years might have warranted. And although Pinckney himself was probably not responsible for Pierce's mistake, years later he did not clear up the misconception. According to South Carolina biographer J. B. O'Neall, he "frequently spoke of the deep diffidence and solemnity which he felt, being the youngest member of the body."[1]

Pinckney attended the Convention in the company of many friends, acquaintances, and a cousin, Charles Cotesworth Pinckney. Pierce Butler, with whom he had formed a friendship during their previous time together in Philadelphia towards the end of the Revolution, also attended. John Rutledge, patriot, South Carolina governor, and family friend rounded out the delegation from the Palmetto State. The fifth delegate, Henry Laurens, was too sick to attend. Many of the other delegates had been in the Confederation Congress and, as most were nationalists in their political alignment, they were, in all likelihood, on good terms with Pinckney.

He arrived on 17 May and stayed at the home of Mrs. Mary House on the corner of Fifth and Market Streets. James Madison and two other Virginia delegates, Edmund Randolph and James McClurg, also boarded there. In a repeat of Pinckney's experience at the Confederation Congress in Trenton, the remaining delegates were slow to arrive, and Mrs. House's tenants grew increasingly impatient. They spent their time discussing various ideas regarding government and the shortcomings of the Articles of Confederation, all the while awaiting the arrival of enough of their fellow delegates to begin the task at hand.[2]

On a rainy Friday morning, enough delegates had arrived for the Convention to begin. The date was 25 May. Although some states were without full representation, the entire South Carolina delegation, except Henry Laurens, had arrived. On a motion by Robert Morris of Pennsylvania, the assembled body quickly chose as president George Washington, who then made a few brief, self-deprecating comments, thanking his peers for the honor and decrying his lack of experience on such a novel occasion. Next, the members appointed a secretary who read the credentials of each of the assembled delegates. Afterwards, Charles Pinckney made his first contribution to the Convention. He moved that a committee "to prepare standing rules and orders" be formed. His fellow delegates appointed him, Virginian George Wythe, and Alexander Hamilton of New York to the Committee of the Rule. Almost as quickly as they had convened, the delegates adjourned, ending the first day of the Constitutional Convention.[3]

Most members took Saturday and Sunday off. Pinckney, as a member of the rules committee, did not. Instead, he spent the weekend meeting with Wythe and Hamilton, forming the parameters within which the Convention would operate. When the delegates reconvened on Monday, Wythe presented the rules the three had established. After two motions, including one from Pierce Butler calling for secrecy in the proceedings, the Convention adjourned until

Tuesday morning at ten o'clock, so that Pinckney's committee might incorporate the additional rules suggested by fellow delegates.[4]

On Tuesday, the committee presented the revised rules and, following Butler's suggestion, required that the proceedings be kept secret. As a result of this rule, years passed before anyone knew with any degree of accuracy what occurred within the closed, hot, stuffy chamber. Several delegates eventually published their notes, including Madison, who made the most detailed description of the proceedings. Important questions, however, would remain unanswered. One of them centered on Charles Pinckney and his actions on that Tuesday morning.[5]

After the rules passed, Edmund Randolph of Virginia introduced fifteen resolutions for establishing a new form of government. This list of resolutions became the basis for the Virginia Plan. In Madison's notes on the convention, he details a thorough description of Randolph's presentation. Then he adds, almost as an afterthought, "Mr Charles Pinkney [*sic*] laid before the house the draught of a federal Government which he had prepared to be agreed upon between the free and independent States of America. Mr. P.['s] plan ordered that the same be referred to the Committee of the whole appointed to consider the State of the American Union." Another delegate, Robert Yates of New York, also recorded the event, writing, "Mr. C. Pinkney [*sic*], a member from South-Carolina, then added, that he had reduced his ideas of a new government to a system, which he read, and confessed that it was grounded on the same principle as of the above resolutions."[6]

Although Pinckney did more than just "lay before the house" his plan, as Madison indicated, neither did he read it in its entirety, as Yates reported. Instead, he summarized deficiencies he perceived in the Confederation and remedies he believed could be found in a new government:

> In a government, where the liberties of the people are to be preserved, and the laws well administered, the executive, legislative, and judicial, should ever be separate and distinct, and consist of parts, mutually forming a check upon each other. The Confederation seems to have lost sight of this wise distribution of the powers of government, and to have concentered the whole in a single un-operative body, where none of them can be used with advantage or effect. The inequality of the principle of Representation, where the largest and most inconsiderable states have an equal vote in the affairs of the Union; the want of commercial powers; of a compelling clause to oblige a due and punctual obedience to the Confederation; a provision for the admission of new states; for an alteration of the system, by a less than unanimous vote; of a general guarantee, and in short of numerous other reforms and establishments,

> convince me, that, upon the present occasion, it would be politic in the Convention to determine that they will consider the subject de novo.

Many of his fellow delegates did not come to the Convention with the idea that a government should be formed "de novo." Roger Sherman of Connecticut, for example, believed that only amendments to the Articles of Confederation would be necessary. Even Edmund Randolph, in his presentation of the Virginia Plan did not call for the Convention to form an entirely new government. Instead, he proposed "that the articles of Confederation ought to be so corrected and enlarged as to accomplish the objects proposed by their institution." But Pinckney spoke very plainly that the articles no longer sufficed in the governance of the young nation.

Pinckney reminded his fellow delegates that the citizenry of the republic watched and waited for the Convention's outcome. "From your deliberation much is expected," he told them, "the eyes, as well as hopes of your constituents are turned upon the Convention; let their expectations be gratified. Be assured, that, however unfashionable for the moment your sentiments may be, yet, if your system is accommodated to the situation of the Union, and founded in wise and liberal principles, it will, in time, be consented to. An energetic government is our true policy, and it will at last be discovered and prevail." He concluded by informing his fellow delegates of his own plan for the new government. The style in which he did so belies his critics—both contemporaries and historians—who accused him of arrogance and vanity:

> Presuming that the question will be taken up de novo, I do not conceive it necessary to go into a minute detail of the defects of the present Confederation, but request permission to submit, with deference to the House, the draught of a Government which I have formed for the Union. The defects of the present will appear in the course of the examination I have given each article that either materially varies or is new. I well know the Science of Government is at once a delicate and difficult one, and none more so than that of Republics. I confess my situation or experience have not been such as to enable me to form the clearest and justest opinions. The sentiments I offer, are the result of not so much reflection as I could have wished. The Plan will admit of important amendments. I do not mean at once to offer it for the consideration of the House, but have taken the liberty of mentioning it, because it was my duty to do so.

This plan that Pinckney "mentioned" soon became embroiled in controversy. He gave it to the Committee of Detail for their consultation on 24 July, and none of the reports of the proceedings mention it again.[7]

Over forty years passed. In 1818, John Quincy Adams, preparing publication of the official journal of the Convention, contacted Pinckney and requested a copy of his plan. Pinckney responded that he did not have the actual plan. He would send a facsimile, he replied, "differing only in form and unessentials." Accordingly, Adams included the document in the published journal. Twelve years later, in 1830, James Madison informed historian Jared Sparks that the published Pinckney draft did not appear to be the same one originally submitted at the Convention. He explained that, according to his notes of the proceedings, which he would only allow to be published after he died, the ideas and articles for which Pinckney now claimed credit actually originated with the Virginia delegation and its plan. He also stated that he had planned to ask Pinckney about the discrepancies but had not had the opportunity to do so before the South Carolinian died.[8]

The exact language of the Pinckney draft is not known. Historians have been able to piece it together from a myriad of sources, including Pinckney's own broadside of the plan, titled *Observations on the Plan of Government Submitted to the Federal Government,* and notes found in Pennsylvania delegate James Wilson's papers. That parts of the plan were found in Wilson's papers supports Pinckney's statement to Matthew Carey in 1788 that he placed the original plan before the convention and gave his only copy to "a gentleman at the northward." Although the reconstructed draft is not as similar to the Constitution as that sent to Adams, it did contain many concepts and provisions that made their way into that document.[9]

Nonetheless, some historians have been critical of Pinckney's claims regarding his contributions. One of Madison's biographers called the South Carolina delegate a "sponger and plagiarist." Madison himself, shortly after the convention, expressed his disdain for Pinckney to none other than George Washington. In an October 1787 letter, Madison wrote criticizing Pinckney's lack of discretion in publishing his *Observations on the Plan of Government,* as well as a pamphlet of the Jay Treaty speech he made in Congress. Madison informed Washington he was sending "a pamphlet which Mr. Pinckney has submitted to the public, or rather as he professes, to the perusal of his friends; and a printed sheet containing his ideas on a very delicate subject [the Jay Treaty]; too delicate in my opinion to have been properly confided to the press. He conceives that his precautions against any farther circulation of the piece than he himself authorizes [*sic*], are so effectual as to justify the step." In conclusion, Madison stated he hoped that Pinckney would not be "disappointed" and that in sending a copy to Washington, "I fulfil his wishes only."[10]

In his reply, George Washington appears to have concurred with Madison's sentiments. He stated that "Mr. C. Pinckney is unwilling (I perceive by the enclosures contained in your favor of the 13th [*sic*]) to lose any fame that can be acquired by the publication of his sentiments." From that point forward, Pinckney began being depicted as vain and arrogant. Thus, forty years later, when the draft he provided Adams overstated his original contributions, Madison and others quickly asserted that he had falsified the document to enhance his own reputation, not recognizing that by 1818 Charles Pinckney could have been genuinely confused over what he had submitted to the Convention in 1787.[11]

Another seventy-five years passed before historians began to unravel *The Mystery of the Pinckney Draft.* Just after the turn of the century, James Franklin Jameson and Andrew C. McLaughlin began examining the papers of James Wilson. Independently of each other, they made illuminating finds. Jameson discovered a group of excerpts indicating they had been drawn from the plan Pinckney had submitted. McLaughlin actually discovered Wilson's sketch of a draft "submitted to the Federal Convention by Charles Pinckney." Accordingly, he reconstructed Pinckney's plan showing that, although not terribly original—many of the provisions could be found within state constitutions, especially New York's, and the Articles of Confederation themselves—much of it became incorporated into the final version of the United States Constitution.[12]

The plan provided for a strong central government consisting of three "separate and distinct branches" (Article 1). Pinckney had seen firsthand the effects of the weak Articles of Confederation and the manner in which the republic was hamstrung in its dealing with foreign nations. The legislative branch would consist of a Senate and a House of Delegates. The House would be elected proportionate to the white population, with blacks being counted as three-fifths for the purpose of representation. The provision stemmed from a similar proportion for representation of slaves used in a revenue bill in the Confederation Congress in 1783. The Virginia Plan did not fully address the issue. To fill the Senate, states would be divided into districts according to population and given representatives according to their respective district. The larger the population of the state, the more senators it would have (Article 2). The legislature would be responsible for "raising a military" (Article 6); "regulating trade with the several States as well with Foreign Nations as with each other" (Article 7); forming a post office, "regulating Indian Affairs," and "coining Money" (Article 8); "ordering the Militia of any State to any Place within the U.S." (Article 13); choosing the president (Article 3); and "instituting a federal judicial Court" (Article 10).

The president would serve for a term of seven years, responsible for "[informing] the Legislature at every session of the condition of the United States."

In other words, the president would deliver what has come to be known as the State of the Union address. The president would also be the commander in chief of the military and responsible for inspecting the various departments within the government. He would have the power to call the legislature into session in time of an emergency and dismiss them "when they cannot agree as to the time of their adjournment" (Article 3). The House of Delegates would have the power of impeachment and the senators and federal judges the power to try the executive (Article 12).

The judicial, appointed by the legislative branch, would hear cases brought against United States officers and settle matters between states and between a state and the federal government. There would also be a court of admiralty. Judges would be appointed for a term of "good behavior," although the manner of appointment was not specified (Article 10). Pinckney even attached a small bill of rights (Article 18) providing for "the privilege of the writ of habeas corpus—the trial by jury in all cases, criminal as well as civil—the freedom of the press and prevention of religious tests as qualifications to offices of trust or emolument." On the issue of religious tests and separation of church and state, Pinckney proved himself to be a champion. Although his complete bill of rights did not become incorporated into the final version of the Constitution, his restriction on religious qualifications did. On 20 August he submitted to the Committee of Detail a long list of proposals, including this: "No religious test or qualification shall ever be annexed to any oath of officer under the authority of the U.S." Article 6 of the final draft of the Constitution states, "No religious test shall ever be required as a qualification to any office or public trust under the United States."[13]

The issue of separation of church and state was important in another submission to the Convention by Pinckney, in which he was joined by James Madison. Indicating the importance to both men of an educated electorate, on 14 September they proposed that Congress be empowered "to establish a University, in which no preferences or distinctions should be allowed on account of religion." The Convention ultimately rejected the proposition, and the matter was left to the various states. Pinckney would take the issue back home with him to South Carolina where he would advocate a similar measure as well as the importance of public education in general to the survival of a republic.[14]

The joint proposal with Madison could indicate that Pinckney probably obtained some of his ideas for a plan of government from conversations and discussion at Mrs. House's boarding house before the Convention began. He picked up others during his term in the Confederation Congress. And he was also adding to his library with such volumes as French finance minister Jacques Necker's *A Treatise on the Administration of the Finances of France,* which he bought in New York only a few days before arriving in Philadelphia. But regardless of their origins, his offerings at the Convention were substantial and important and, as illustrated in the matter of religious qualifications, utilized by his fellow delegates as they decided on the final document. While no one will probably ever be able to determine how many of his ideas were solely his own, the act of putting together a cohesive and cogent plan of government by himself illustrates the astuteness with which he came to the Convention and the effectiveness of his presence there.[15]

After Pinckney presented his plan, the delegates adjourned for the day. Because so few of his personal papers are extant, ascertaining how he spent his evenings is difficult. He probably had a light dinner at one of the taverns in the city or at the house where he roomed with other delegates. He could have also visited friends he had made during his previous time spent in Philadelphia. But most likely, he stayed in his room, poring over notes and books, educating himself on government, trying to buttress his already impressive knowledge on the subject in order to be well-informed and, as a result, well-spoken during the daily sessions of the Convention.

The next day, Wednesday, 30 May, the Convention formed a Committee of the Whole for the purpose of debating the various issues. George Washington stepped down from his seat as president and turned the committee over to Nathaniel Gorham, who presided over the delegates while they maintained that procedural distinction. The Convention also passed resolutions put forward by Edmund Randolph that stated, in part, "that a union of the states merely federal will not accomplish the objects proposed by the Articles of Confederation, namely the common defense, security of liberty, and general welfare" and "that a national government ought to be established consisting of a supreme legislative, executive, and judiciary." Showing that he was concerned that the new government be given too much power, Pinckney questioned Randolph regarding whether the resolution might completely disestablish state governments. After Randolph assured him such was not the case, the South Carolina delegation joined five others in voting in favor of the resolutions. With their passage, the delegates established once and for all that the Convention would not be about a mere revision of the Articles as Randolph had suggested the day before, but about the establishment of a completely new government.[16]

Although Pinckney made numerous statements and contributions while the delegates in the Convention deliberated, aside from the draft he submitted on the third day perhaps his most important contribution was a speech he made on Monday, 25 June. It was prompted by Alexander Hamilton's assertion that solutions to certain issues facing the body could be found by looking at the British system of government. Pinckney rose quickly to his feet and disagreed.

He stated his conviction that America's uniqueness required that she need look only to herself for the answer to her problems. The speech that ensued had such an effect that even Madison, who had almost completely ignored the Pinckney draft in his notes, printed a detailed account.[17]

Pinckney began by extolling widespread suffrage and equality, assured of indefinite continuance because of the vast expanse of land:

> The people of the United States are perhaps the most singular of any we are acquainted with. Among them there are fewer distinctions of fortune and less of rank than among the inhabitants of any other nation. Every freeman has a right to the same protection and security. And a very moderate share of property entitles them to the possession of all the honors and privileges the public can bestow. Hence arises greater equality than is to be found among the people of any other country and an equality which is more likely to continue—I say THIS EQUALITY IS LIKELY TO CONTINUE!—because in a new country possessing immense tracts of uncultivated lands, where every temptation is offered to emigration and where industry must be rewarded with competency, there will be few poor and few dependant! Every member of the society—almost—will enjoy the equal power of arriving at the supreme offices and, consequently, of directing the strength and sentiments of the whole community. None will be excluded by birth and few by fortune from voting for proper persons to fill the offices of government. The whole community will enjoy in the fullest sense that kind of political liberty which consists in the power the members of the State reserve to themselves, of arriving at the public offices, or at least, of having votes in the nomination of those who fill them.

Pinckney argued that such an incomparable society would most certainly be unable to use a constitution based on a British model of proper balance between the Crown and the people. He chronicled the derivation of British nobility, stating that an American constitution based on a British model would not work in a country where there existed almost ubiquitous equality among white males and where no one had wealth enough that "they may have a dangerous influence."

He continued, describing the "true situation" of his young nation as "a new extensive country containing within itself the materials for forming a government capable of extending to its citizens all the blessings of civil and religious liberty capable of making them happy at home! This is the great end of republican establishments! We mistake the object of our government if we hope or wish that it is to make us respectable abroad. Conquest or superiority among other powers is not or ought not EVER to be the object of republican systems. If they are sufficiently active and energetic to rescue us from contempt and preserve our domestic happiness and security, it is all we can expect from them. It is more than almost any other government ensures to its citizens!" He divided these citizens into three classes, based not on wealth but on profession: "professional men" or politicians; "commercial men" or those dealing with commerce and ill-suited for government; and "landed interests" or cultivators of the soil from which the "professional men" should be drawn. The three classes depended on one another, making each one's own self-interest dependent on protecting the interests of the other two.[18]

Pinckney may have been overly optimistic and overstated the equality of his classes, but from almost the beginning of his public life he expressed an interest and concern for those members of the South Carolina backcountry that his own socioeconomic strata had seemed to disdain. The reason Pinckney reached out to this group is complex and both draws from and provides insight into Pinckney's character and personality on several different levels. It might be expected that someone as vain and arrogant as Pinckney was at times perceived to be would have found it unseemly to appeal to those the lowcountry elite thought of as rabble and who attracted backcountry advocate Rev. Charles Woodmason. But if these descriptions of Pinckney are not given the weight they have been given in the past, it becomes easier to assess his motives. The vanity and arrogance seen by others can also be interpreted as a mask Pinckney adopted to conceal a self-consciousness or feeling of inferiority that developed when his father took protection from the British after the fall of Charlestown. "Taking protection" was a polite term. It is certain that some of the more radical revolutionaries in South Carolina, like Christopher Gadsden, deemed the Colonel's act as outright treason. Such negative opinions were bound to have had some ill effect on young Charles, who was only in his early twenties at the time and seeking to establish himself in South Carolina society.

Despite any inferiority Pinckney may have had, his reasons for being concerned with the plight of the inhabitants of the backcountry were more likely a mix of two compelling motives. First, he had very real concern for these yeoman farmers and small planters in the upstate. He constantly sought to better their position with admonitions to the South Carolina legislature when he served as governor in the coming years. He was especially concerned for law and order in the area as well as public education, as shown in the proposal he introduced with James Madison. Pinckney was republican enough in his outlook to realize that by improving the lot of yeomen in the state, he also improved the lot of the entire state and put it on a more sound footing in the developing nation. By doing all that he could to instill virtue in the backcountry residents, he attempted to ensure that they would embrace his idea of government. He was prescient enough to foresee a type of Jacksonian democracy that would arrive long after he had passed from the scene. But in this trend, he saw a role for himself. And therein lies another motive for his concern with the lower economic classes.

From the time of his very first wrangle in the Confederation Congress over John Jay's treaty attempting to deny navigation on the Mississippi, Pinckney was ardent in his passion that such restriction of a major water route would be detrimental for those trying to gain a footing for themselves in the struggling young nation. He was convinced that if the United State government turned its back on the westerners, they would have no alternative but to look towards other nations for protection, especially Spain. The letter that Pinckney wrote in September 1786 but never sent to John Jay speaks of the inherent danger in terminating navigation on the Mississippi by the western settlers. But even prior to the time that this issue came to a head, Pinckney expressed concerns to South Carolina governor Guerard. As early as December 1784, very soon into his first term in the Confederation Congress, he wrote of fear that the settlers in the West "may proceed with hostilities toward each other and that it may not be in our power to restrain them." He also expressed his desire that treaties be concluded as quickly as possible, ending hostilities between Indians and the interior's inhabitants and building a "permanent confidence between them."[19]

Protecting and enabling the common class of man in the interior of the country became a preeminent goal in Pinckney's mind early in his public career, perhaps because he recognized the importance this geographic area and its economic interests could eventually play in the growth of the nation. For instance, in 1790, while serving his first term as governor, he wrote to a Virginia acquaintance requesting any and all information he could send regarding the cultivation of tobacco. He explained that the inhabitants of the area had taken to growing the crop, but "in general they do not seem to understand the planting and curing of it . . . and some of our industrious poor lose a considerable portion of their product." In such a request Pinckney indicated his idea that the "industrious poor" might eventually become a force with which to be reckoned.[20]

Pinckney saw this rise in the status of the common man more than a quarter of a century before it actually happened. He also saw therein the chance for political power he could probably never attain in competition with his cousins and acquaintances in the lowcountry. He would always be in their shadow. His father, despite being an early supporter of the Revolution, had take protection from the British, thereby permanently tainting the family name. And although he was wealthy, the Colonel never amassed the kind of fortune held by his cousins or the Manigaults or the Alstons. In addition, what he did have was amerced 12 percent and was further burdened by the estate of Miles Brewton.

The younger Charles would prove himself to be far more adept at politics than managing plantations and making money. For his own political power he chose a path linking him to the lower echelons of the upstate inhabitants, as opposed to the wealthy neighbors amongst whom he lived. If he could not enjoy power by extending his economic status, he would do so by doing what he did best: serving in the political arena, thereby alienating and infuriating many of those most like him economically, but building a unique power base in South Carolina.

Pinckney's detractors in South Carolina may have called him vain, arrogant, or a traitor to his class—the latter no doubt reminding him of a similar description of his father—but his efforts at unifying the state across class lines would contribute overwhelmingly to Thomas Jefferson's eventual election in 1800. Although the republicanism Jefferson envisioned by the turn of the century would not encompass the same sorts of people as Jacksonian democracy twenty-five years later, Pinckney's efforts in reaching out to upcountry planters in South Carolina laid the groundwork for the type of thinking that would result in universal white manhood suffrage. The growth of the cotton economy also greatly contributed to this shift of the power base when it finally occurred towards the end of the century. And those benefiting from that shift did not necessarily come from the traditional economic and political power within the state. On the contrary, many rose to power in the upcountry who had started as yeoman farmers. Even by 1815, equality of condition for white men did not exist, but equality of opportunity had come a long way towards being a reality, in no small measure because of the type of optimism and vision espoused by Pinckney in his speech to the Convention and his eventual efforts to unite his home state.[21]

In that speech, he also held fast to the idea that he had been advocating over the past few years that only a strong central government could cure the ills now facing the young nation. But just as he expressed fear of too much power over the states when Edmund Randolph presented his plan, he now voiced apprehension concerning government at the expense of the people. Even the bill of rights he attached to his plan showed that he recognized that the government could become too powerful. Such concern as early as the 1787 Convention disproved critics who later accused him of being an ambitious political traitor to his class and family when he broke from them and supported Jefferson in 1800. This break did not occur, as some alleged, because he felt insulted when President Washington bestowed an ambassadorship on his cousin and not him. His ideas were much more deeply rooted and prescient, proving in the long run to be more influential in South Carolina and the nation than those of his conservative political enemies.

In 1787 those ideas had yet to mature. While his speech was remarkably visionary in terms of the coming democracy in the United States, some of his actions in the Convention belied the faith in the common man that eventually arose from such ideology. He constantly opposed any plan making either of the two houses electable by popular vote. On 6 June, he moved "that the first branch of the national legislature be elected by the state legislatures and not by the people." Two days later he stated that the second branch "ought to be permanent and independent and that the members of it would be rendered more so by receiving their appointments from the state legislatures." He concluded that such elections would "avoid rivalships and discontents incident to election by district." Clearly, at this stage Pinckney distrusted the citizenry at large. Individual white male landholders could aspire to his professional class and govern effectively and with virtue. En masse, however, the people could not be trusted.[22]

Pinckney also hesitated to completely trust the northern states. This distrust led to a break between him and fellow South Carolina delegates, which foreshadowed the break that would come towards the end of the century and led to his staunchest defense of slavery at the Convention. If his earlier speech proved to be prescient, one he made nearly a month later did not prove to be accurate. It arose out of the debates over how navigation acts would be passed and, thereby, whether the North would control commerce. During the discussion the delegates eventually approached the question of slave importation. On 22 August, Pinckney addressed his fellow delegates regarding the slave trade and its treatment in the document being created. "If slavery be wrong, it is justified by the example of all the world!" he asserted. He supported his statement with a brief history of ancient Greece and Rome. "In all ages one half of mankind have been slaves," he continued, warning that any attempt by delegates in the Convention at halting the slave trade would meet with vehement resistance by southern delegates and possibly derail the entire Convention. Even if a document containing such a provision made it beyond the walls of the Pennsylvania State House he believed it could never be ratified by the South. Give us time, he assured the hall, and his state, including himself, would vote to suspend the practice.[23]

Like all eighteenth-century American southerners, Charles Pinckney grew up, grew old, and died in the grips of a human chattel slavery system. He defined himself and his white peers in many ways by the "other" that surrounded them, constant reminders of what he and all white men could become if they lost their independence. Independence was a key element of republicanism, and without it a republic could not exist. In the South, the existence of African slaves constantly reminded whites that they, too, could lose their independence and become slaves to an overpowering federal government.[24]

Pinckney appears to have been the type of paternalistic slave owner often seen among the gentry class in the South. There is no indication he mistreated his slaves, but the fact that he held them at all says much about the manner in which he either closed his eyes to their plight or created excuses for what many of his northern friends and contemporaries saw as the obvious immorality of one man owning another. Considering the extent to which Pinckney educated himself, read and collected books from around the world, and corresponded with anti-slavery forces in the North like Rufus King, it is evident that he probably exposed himself to quite a bit of anti-slavery writing and rhetoric. This exposure did not cause him to question slavery, at least not in public. In fact, as time passed and the institution became threatened, his stance regarding slavery hardened and provided ammunition for succeeding generations until the Civil War.

There are only a few real indicators of Pinckney's attitudes towards African Americans. He respected the role they played supporting the patriot cause during the Revolution. While many slaves supported the British and fled to His Majesty's troops for freedom, others remained loyal to the colonists. Pinckney spoke of these black patriots in a speech on the Missouri Compromise in 1820. He stated that blacks in general were "as valuable a part of our population to the Union as any other equal number of inhabitants." He described how slaves helped in building fortifications, specifically mentioning the role they played in constructing the palmetto barriers at Fort Moultrie. He also described almost glowingly the manner in which blacks took up arms against the British in the North and fought alongside whites.

But while he may have complimented the service of blacks during the Revolution, he remained unwilling to bestow upon them the very equality that inspired it. A few moments later in the same speech, he decried the efforts of the North to depict the South as violating either God's or man's laws in the maintenance of its peculiar institution. He averred that blacks were happier in a state of slavery because they were uneducated and incapable of caring for themselves. He illustrated what he perceived as typical southern slaveholding paternalism by pointing out "that every slave has a comfortable house, is well fed, clothed, and taken care of." He went on to describe how they were surrounded by family, omitting that they could be and often were sold away from loved ones. He stated that their medical care was equal to that of whites and that in their old age they continued to be cared for even after they were no longer productive. He concluded, "The great body of slaves are happier in their present situation than they could be in any other and the man or men who would attempt to give them freedom would be their greatest enemies!" By detailing his own personal experiences with slavery, he sought to illustrate that the institution was not necessarily the evil some northerners portrayed it as being. In South Carolina, at least to Charles Pinckney, slavery was a very real benefit to both whites and blacks.[25]

That a person of color could ever attain equality or the status of citizen within the new nation seemed ludicrous to Pinckney. He stated during another speech on the Missouri question that he could never "have conceived it possible such a thing could ever have existed" within the confines of the republic. Enslaved blacks existed to provide the South a specially constituted labor force. They also provided an escape hatch of sorts for poor whites—many of whom made up the backcountry about which Pinckney would become so concerned—who could always point to black slaves as being in worse condition than themselves.

But he did seem to try to be fair in his public treatment of slaves. One indicator of his attitude occurred while he was governor in 1791. A slave named Moses had been sentenced to death. Although the death penalty for slaves was not uncommon, juries hesitated to hand down the sentence because of the cost involved in destroying such "property." As governor, Pinckney routinely delayed executions for two weeks until he could review the case in its entirety and determine if the sentence should be reduced. He delayed Moses' execution as well, stating to those who would urge him not to do so, "It is always done in the conviction of a white man and it is my duty to require it in the case of slaves." His hesitancy could have been based more on his concern over the irretrievable loss of pecuniary interests for the master than for the life of Moses. But in referring to the man, he used the pronoun "fellow" and not a more impersonal term such as "slave" or "property." It was not necessary that Pinckney express such concern for the life of Moses had he not genuinely felt compassion for him and desired that he be subject to as fair treatment as possible, considering the circumstances.[26]

During the debates on the slave trade and the navigation acts, Pinckney showed that he would not be cowed by either northern delegates or older and perhaps more experienced members of his own delegation. All of the South Carolina delegates except him favored acquiescing to northern demands that passage of navigation acts be by a simple majority in exchange for extending the slave trade. This simple majority would assure that the North controlled issues of commerce. Pinckney, in an argument reminiscent of the debate on the Jay Treaty, stated that it would be in the South's best interest to require a two-thirds majority in passing navigation bills. A simple majority giving the North such control could be disastrous for the South's economy. When the delegates voted, South Carolina, despite Pinckney's urging to the contrary, broke with the other southern states and voted with the North. Then, at Pierce Butler's urging, the

Convention voted to incorporate a fugitive slave clause as a quid pro quo for giving up the demand for the two-thirds majority.[27]

Pinckney's defiance of his peers on the navigation and slavery issues, in light of what Butler did as soon as the simple majority measure passed, suggests that the young South Carolinian might not have been well connected with the other members of his state's delegation. Had he known about the plan for gaining a fugitive slave provision, it is possible he would not have remained so adamant. The other members of his delegation probably glanced apprehensively at one another. And Pinckney may have felt betrayed afterward if he had been kept in the dark on the matter. Or he may have believed that even a fugitive slave provision was not worth the damage that could be done to the South by giving the North the simple majority on issues of navigation. This episode illustrates that Pinckney appears to have been his own man at the Convention, either by design or because of some bitterness towards him from his fellow delegates. Perhaps they resented his youth. Perhaps he seemed vain or arrogant, just as his detractors would maintain through the years. Perhaps they held the actions of his father during the Revolution against him. Regardless, Pinckney probably smarted for a long time at being ignored over what he saw as such an important issue, especially by his fellow South Carolinians. This resentment, in combination with his evolving political views, sowed the seeds for the break he eventually made with his family and economic peers, choosing his own way against the Federalists in his home state.

Despite the disagreements that occurred between Pinckney and northern delegates, his collaboration with them on other issues indicated his strong desire that individual rights be protected by the document being created. On 20 August, he and Gouverneur Morris of Pennsylvania presented a bill of rights of sorts in the form of thirteen proposals, which was referred to the Committee of Detail. The proposals called for the writ of habeas corpus, freedom of the press, restrictions on the military, and prohibitions from religious tests or qualifications for federal office seekers. The proposals never emerged from the committee.[28]

As the Convention drew to a close, Pinckney attempted a couple of last-ditch efforts to exert his influence. On 10 September, he expressed concern over the Senate's power to convict the president in instances of impeachment. Although he offered no alternative, he feared that the president could become too dependent on and influenced by the Congress if such power over him rested in both houses of the legislative branch. "If he opposes a favorite law," he stated, "the two houses will combine against him and under the influence of heat and faction throw him out of office!" Most of the delegates ignored Pinckney's suggestion. They were more fearful of an executive that would be too powerful than a legislature suffering from the same defect.[29]

Pinckney was also worried about trial by jury in civil cases. Most delegates generally accepted that such a right would be protected in a criminal matter. But not all agreed to such a right in civil proceedings. On the last full day of the proceedings, Sunday, 16 September, Pinckney and Elbridge Gerry of Massachusetts attempted to insert the clause, "And a trial by jury shall be preserved as usual in civil cases." The addition met with opposition from others, including Pinckney's cousin Charles Cotesworth, who averred that such a clause would be "pregnant with embarrassment." The proposal lost by a unanimous vote, but the Seventh Amendment in the Bill of Rights eventually protected the right.[30]

Later on the same day, Pinckney rose in the Convention one last time. Many of the delegates, including some from his own state, believed he had overstepped his bounds on occasion and presumptuously made recommendations beyond what would be seemly for a member only twenty-nine years old. He had even been so arrogant as to submit his own plan of government. In reality he had been a driving force and had even provided an overarching ideology regarding the unique nature of the document being created as well as the system of government that would emerge from it—in many ways far ahead of its time. In his final address to his fellow delegates, he continued to relate his optimism for the fate of the Constitution and the United States government. He expressed his aversion to submitting only individual portions of the document to the various states for their consideration, maintaining that "nothing but confusion and contrariety could spring from the experiment." He believed that submitting the document in anything but its entirety would eventually require the delegates to reconvene and consider each state's concerns. He strongly objected to any such reconvening stating, "Conventions are serious things and ought not be repeated." He admitted to not being completely satisfied with specific areas of the document, returning once again to the simple majority for navigation acts and his perception of the weakness of the executive. Despite such reservations, however, and "apprehending the danger of a general confusion and an ultimate decision by the sword," he believed the document should be signed and sent to the states in its entirety for ratification.[31]

After the majority concurred that there should be no second convention, some dissatisfied delegates walked out, including such important contributors as George Mason, Edmund Randolph, and Elbridge Gerry. But the remaining thirty-eight members passed the new Constitution unanimously and adjourned for the day. On Monday, the secretary read the freshly copied document aloud as the delegates listened. Benjamin Franklin, old and infirm, addressed the delegates, stating that the document probably could not be improved upon and came close to perfection. Despite Franklin's opinion, there was one final revision concerning the ratio for representatives in the House. Then the Constitution was ready to be signed.[32]

As Charles Pinckney made his way to the front of the room and stood looking at the document he had so long advocated and desired, he realized that the battle had only just begun. Ahead lay the long and difficult road to ratification. He would do all in his power to see that his state—inhabitants from both the lowcountry and the backcountry—would support the document. Taking the quill pen from his cousin Charles Cotesworth, he leaned over the table and signed his name. In doing so he became one of an elite group of men whom posterity would come to call Founding Fathers. He handed the quill to Pierce Butler and returned to his seat, ready to set out on a long-delayed voyage and then back home to South Carolina and the young woman whom he would eventually marry.

Charles Pinckney, *attributed to Gilbert Stuart. Courtesy of Philipse Manor Hall State Historic Site, New York State Office of Parks, Recreation, and Historic Preservation.*

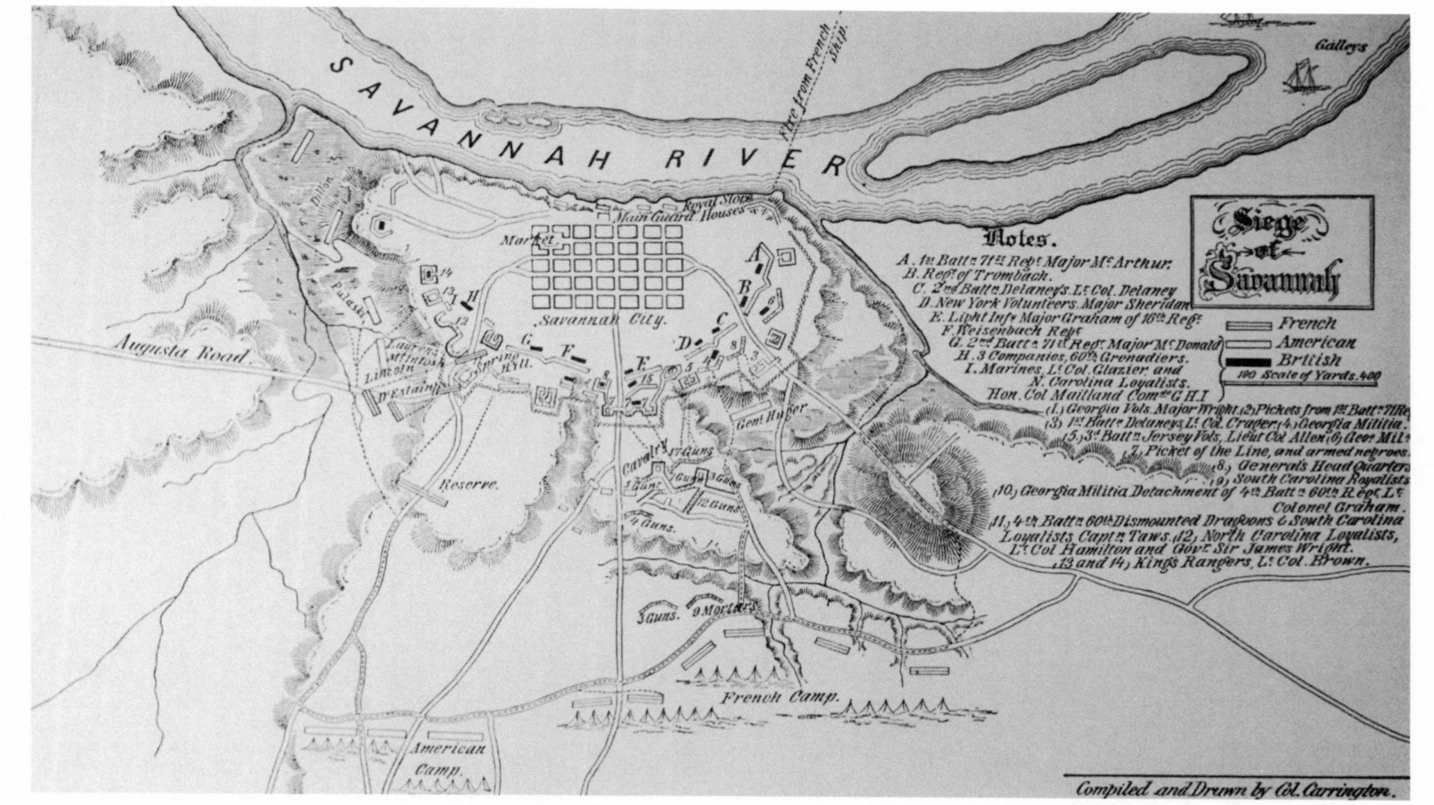

Siege of Savannah, *compiled and drawn by Col. Edward Carrington. Reprinted, by permission, from Henry Carrington,* Battles of the American Revolution, 1775–1781 *(New York: A. S. Barnes & Co., 1876).*

Charleston, The Capital of South Carolina, *by Samuel Smith after Thomas Leitch, 1774, hand colored engraving on paper. Courtesy of Gibbes Museum of Art/Carolina Art Association, 58.22, Charleston, S.C.*

Scene at the Signing of the Constitution, *by Howard Chandler Christy. Courtesy of the Architect of the Capitol, copyright 1985, United States Historical Society. This painting is located in the east stairway of the House of Representatives wing of the U.S. Capitol.*

A View of the Capitol of Washington before It Was Burnt down by the British, *by William Russell Birch, circa 1800. Courtesy of the Library of Congress. This painting depicts the U.S. Capitol as it appeared around the time of Jefferson's first inauguration.*

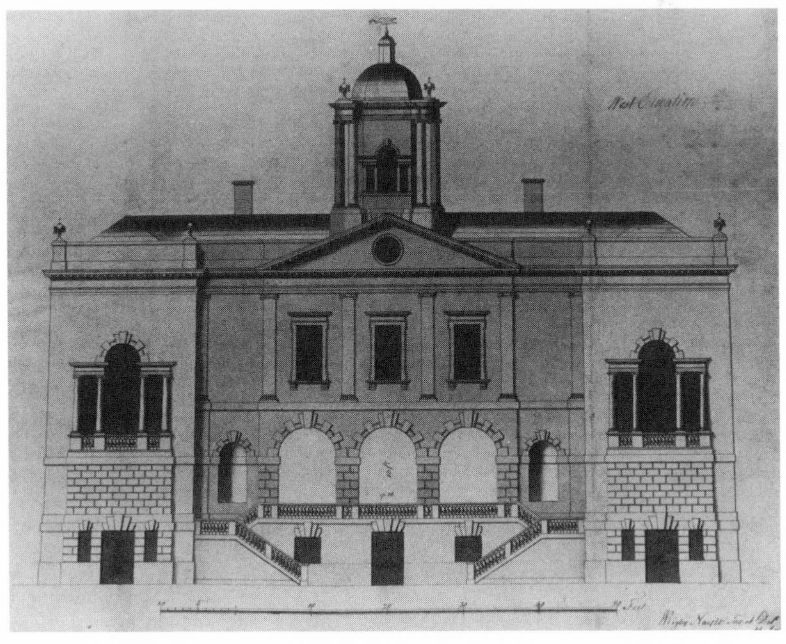

Charleston Exchange, *by William Rigby Naylor. Courtesy of South Carolina Department of Archives and History.*

Thomas Jefferson, President of the United States, *engraving by Cornelius Tiebouth, circa 1801. Courtesy of the Library of Congress.*

James Madison, President of the United States, *engraving by David Edwin, circa 1809–17. Courtesy of the Library of Congress.*

James Monroe, President of the United States, *engraving by Goodman and Piggot, 1817. Courtesy of the Library of Congress.*

Four

Founding a Family and a New State Government

At the close of the Constitutional Convention, Charles Pinckney set out, once again, to fulfill a lifelong dream. Before returning to South Carolina, he made arrangements to take his much-delayed trip to Europe. The Revolution interfered with his education in London, and the death of his father prevented him from traveling abroad after the war. But on the day after the convention ended, George Washington wrote a letter of introduction for him to the Marquis de Lafayette. In mid October, he paid a visit to his new friend Benjamin Franklin who, despite his age and infirmity, penned several letters of introduction for his young colleague. Like most letters of introduction, those written by Washington and Franklin spoke very highly of Pinckney, recommending to the addressees "a gentleman of fortune, family, and character" in whose conversation they would "be much pleased . . . as he is perfectly acquainted with our public affairs." Even though the letters were standard in their form and style, that Franklin and Washington agreed to write letters indicate the admiration they must have had for him, even though Washington may have had his reservations. Franklin, on the other hand, wrote privately to one of the addressees, banker Ferdinand Grand in Paris, praising Pinckney once more as "a man of fortune and an excellent character."[1]

Despite Pinckney's intentions to travel abroad, fate once again interfered to prevent him from doing so, this time in the form of the South Carolina constitutional ratifying convention. Over the next few years, he capitalized on the name he had made for himself in the national arena. He presided over the South Carolina ratification of the United States Constitution. He played a key role in the creation of a new South Carolina constitution. Finally, his fellow South Carolinians elected him to the highest office in the state. He used that position to further his own influence and solidify a political base that, by the turn of the century, would play an essential role in the nation's political transformation.

At the same time, he married into one of the most prominent families in South Carolina, pursued his agricultural interests, and began a family.

He returned to South Carolina from Philadelphia and wasted no time beginning his endeavors. He served in the close of the Seventh General Assembly in early 1788 and started pushing conventions to ratify the national Constitution and create a new constitution for the state. On 14 January, at the close of the state ratifying convention, he moved that the delegates should stay on to "frame a new constitution or form of government for this state upon such principles as shall appear to them best calculated to preserve the happiness of the people and insure the strict administration of the laws." Although his motion failed, it indicated that Pinckney had once again been considering the plight of those disaffected residents of the backcountry who lamented their lack of proper representation in the assembly. The South Carolina Constitution of 1778 had required that reapportionment occur in 1785. But the legislature, controlled by lowcountry representatives, had failed to do so. Pinckney probably believed that linking the ratifying convention with a state constitutional convention would assuage the fears of the delegates from the backcountry, many of whom were against ratification of the United States Constitution.[2]

For three days in January, the assembly addressed the issues surrounding a possible ratifying convention. On the sixteenth, Pinckney rose before the house and delivered a lengthy speech, laying out the history of the federal convention and defects in the Confederation. He emphasized not so much the need for a strong central government as he did protection of the states in regards to commerce: "Hence arose the necessity of some general and permanent system which should at once embrace all interests and, by placing states upon firm and united ground, enable them effectually to assert their commercial rights." He stated a mere revision of the Articles of Confederation would not have been effective because they were "founded in paternal and persuasive principles with nothing permanent and coercive in [their] construction." He discussed arguments over representation in the two houses and the Great Compromise that settled that debate. He averred that of the three branches created by the Constitution, the judicial was most important, and as such, the delegates conferred upon it more power than some would have liked. He lamented, however, that the executive did not receive as much authority as he had hoped, fearing in particular the role of the Senate in impeachment and removal.

He also expressed his acceptance of the document without an attached protection of certain rights, because in the federal government "no powers could be executed or assumed but such as were expressly delegated," while at the state level "the indefinite power was given to the government except on points that were by express compact reserved to the people." He finished his speech by addressing the benefits of a federal republic to the maintenance of a republican form of government in general, especially in a land as vast as the United States, concluding that the "experiment" that emerged from Philadelphia was one worth making: "We are now about to make it upon an extensive scale and under circumstances so promising that [I] consider it the fairest experiment that [has] ever been made in the favor of human nature."[3]

Following Pinckney's speech, Rawlins Lowndes rose to voice his opposition to a convention. Acting as a mouthpiece for the backcountry representatives who agreed with him, Lowndes had often run against the opinions of his fellow lowcountry inhabitants. He expressed reservations about the proposed Constitution, indicating he did not think it adequately protected the interests of the southern states. He thought the president had too much power and was concerned there would probably never be a president from South Carolina or Georgia. He also resented interference in the importation of slaves, even though the restriction as agreed upon in convention and codified in the Constitution lay twenty years down the road. Edward Rutledge ended the day's debate by maintaining his position that the articles were too unwieldy to allow the new nation to succeed.[4]

Over the following two days, the debate continued on general terms. Pinckney only spoke once more. The floor was occupied for the most part by Lowndes, a few backcountry representatives who dared to support him publicly, and those like Rutledge and Charles Cotesworth Pinckney who used their experience at and insight into the Convention in attempts to assuage the fears of opponents. At the end of Friday, 18 January, the assembly voted and agreed to call a ratifying convention. The next question related to its location. On Saturday morning, the delegates began debating the issue of whether it would take place in Charleston or somewhere in the interior of the state. The future capital of Columbia had been laid out the previous year, and many of the backcountry representatives hoped the convention could be held there. They believed that having the convention in Charleston virtually assured ratification because of the influence of the lowcountry elite, the majority of whom supported the Constitution. Eventually, however, the coastal inhabitants prevailed, selecting Charleston as the location by a margin of only one vote—seventy-six to seventy-five—and setting the date for Monday, 12 May 1788.[5]

Pinckney did not postpone his trip abroad solely because of the business in the South Carolina House. He had also fallen in love. Henry Laurens' younger daughter, seventeen-year-old Mary Eleanor, or Polly as she was called, had smitten Pinckney with her looks, European manners, and in all likelihood, wealth. When the elderly Henry Laurens gave his consent to the marriage, the stage was set for the unification of two of South Carolina's most prominent families.

Polly had been born in Charleston on 26 April 1770 to Henry and Eleanor Ball Laurens. The event proved to be a mixed blessing. On the day following the birth, Laurens wrote to a friend of his distress over the health of his wife who had experienced a trying delivery. Several days later her condition had worsened, and he had not even had the occasion "to take any notice" of his infant daughter.[6]

Eleanor's death on 22 May left Henry Laurens the widowed father of five children. Overwhelmed by the responsibilities of raising a family alone, Laurens eventually turned to his brother and sister-in-law, James and Mary Laurens, for assistance in the care of his new daughter and her older sister, Martha. Henry and his three sons sailed to England, where the boys were to be educated. His daughters remained in Charleston under the care of their aunt and uncle, but by 1775 they too had set sail for England. Henry Laurens, meanwhile, had returned to Charleston.[7]

Within two years, in 1777, James' ill health, along with events occurring in America, where the family patriarch now found himself in rebellion against the English Crown, prompted the group to move to Vignon in the south of France. Polly grew up in the pleasant French village, far removed from her homeland and the political and cultural climate that made such an impression on her future husband. Along with her aunt and uncle, her older sister, Martha, raised her into a young woman. Martha routinely received letters from her father in South Carolina urging her to "take care of my Polly, too." Her brother John described his younger sister as somewhat spoiled by her Aunt Mary but still "the admiration of every body." She also seemed to be quite a tomboy: "Polly thinks the restraint incident to her Sex, very mortifying—and asked one day with as much Gravity and Innocence, if they would not let her wear Breeches and become a Boy. She envied Harry his freedom very much and would wish to be upon the same footing with him. When she was told that this Change would not be effectual she proposed what she thought would infallibly answer the purpose—to be re-christen'd and have a male Name." Polly remained in skirts for the rest of her life and in France until her uncle died in 1785. After the funeral, she and her aunt joined Martha, who had already gone to England, to await passage back home to South Carolina.[8]

Polly arrived back in South Carolina at the age of fifteen more French than American. Over the next three years she tried to adjust to life in and around Charleston and at her father's three-thousand-acre plantation, Mepkin, on the Cooper River. It is not known when she and Charles Pinckney first met, but it is likely the two became acquainted sometime during Pinckney's return home between his duties in Congress and those at the Constitutional Convention in 1787. Perhaps Pinckney and the other delegates paid visits to the Laurens home to discuss the upcoming meeting in Philadelphia and he fell in love with her there. He could have also met her at the home of his friend Dr. David Ramsay, who married Polly's sister, Martha. The insular Charleston society provided numerous opportunities for the two to meet. Over the next year a courtship ensued, and upon his return from Philadelphia in the fall he made plans to marry his "little French girl" the following spring.[9]

On 27 April 1788, in the descriptive phrase of his friend John Sanford Dart, Pinckney "enter[ed] Hymen's shackles with Miss Laurens." The wedding took place at Mepkin. Eighteen-year-old Polly was quite a catch for thirty-year-old Charles. If there had been any doubts in his own mind or in the minds of others about his standing in the lowcountry of South Carolina, the marriage went a long way towards finally laying them to rest. Despite the actions of the colonel, Charles had proven himself in the Revolution, had helped to produce the new Constitution pending ratification, and had married into one of the wealthiest and most highly respected families in the state. The dowry accompanying his new bride would assist in paying debts haunting him from the estate of Miles Brewton as well as the Jacksonborough Assembly's amercement. Other young suitors in the Charleston area probably vied for the hand of Polly Laurens. That she chose Charles Pinckney, with her father's blessing, tells much about Pinckney's reputation in the Charleston lowcountry.[10]

Pinckney could not enjoy his new marriage for too long before having to return to work. The South Carolina ratifying convention was due to meet in a few days, and Pinckney, obviously a vocal supporter of the new Constitution, had been elected a delegate. The division within the state over ratification persisted, mostly along geographic lines. Those residing in the backcountry opposed it, while, with few exceptions, those in the lowcountry supported it. Supporters cited two main reasons for ratification. The first and most important centered around the desire for an effective means of regulating trade abroad and conducting affairs with foreign countries. The second dealt with issues of economy and commerce arising between the states themselves. American merchants tended to agree with both, but their British counterparts were most concerned with the second. They had much to lose as a result of the economic impact of the Constitution regulating commerce abroad. However, the ability of the federal government to regulate and control currency issues and to enforce contractual obligations between the states clearly benefited them. Many still had interests in the lowcountry and were owed debts by its inhabitants.[11]

Opposition to ratification centered around two concerns as well. Many opponents feared the power of the executive. Others worried about the lack of a bill of rights. During January's debates in the house, Abbeville County resident James Lincoln joined a handful of backcountry residents who dared speak out against the formidable united forces of the lowcountry. But the most vocal critic of the proposed Constitution was the lowcountry anomaly Rawlins Lowndes. Unlike many representatives from the backcountry, he felt quite comfortable speaking out against his fellow lowcountry elite and often took stands in opposition to his friends and neighbors. But his failure to be intimidated did not pay off in the long run. As a result of his outspoken demeanor, Charleston did not elect him to attend the ratifying convention. St. Bartholomew's Parish did elect him, but he refused to accept the election, feeling chagrined that he had been passed over by his neighbors in town. Thus the upcountry opponents of ratification went to the convention without one of their most effective voices.[12]

On 12 May delegates began assembling in Charleston. Even prior to the convention, the slate of those elected assured the Constitution would be accepted by South Carolina. The only dissent came from the backcountry, but representation was weighted so heavily in favor of the lowcountry by the Constitution of 1778, the delegates from the upstate could not hope to block ratification. The convention began on the thirteenth in the Exchange Building, just down Broad Street from the State House, which had been destroyed by fire in February. Charles Pinckney's cousin Thomas served as president.[13]

Pinckney himself made the opening statement. He began by repeating the ideas of American uniqueness he had voiced nearly a year earlier at the Convention in Philadelphia. He revisited issues of government and civil liberties as they related to ancient civilizations and Great Britain. He wasted little time in appealing directly to his opponents in the backcountry. Not only did they fear the power of the president and the lack of a bill of rights, but they chafed at being outnumbered by the Charleston elite. So Pinckney addressed an issue many of them resented: the rule of primogeniture. Common in English law, but rapidly becoming a thing of the past in early America, the rule said that the estate of someone who died intestate would go to the firstborn son. Although wills could be made to overcome the rule, the general practice of passing one's real property to one's firstborn son had persisted. But Pinckney pointed out that such a rule was anathema to the American way of life and "no less consonant to the principles of a republican government than it is to those of general equity and parental affection." He continued, "To endeavor to raise a name by accumulating property in one branch of a family at the expense of the others equally related and deserving is a vanity no less unjust and cruel than dangerous to the interests of liberty. It is a practice no wise state will ever encourage or tolerate." Such a statement surely stung many of the lowcountry delegates, considering that South Carolina had still not done away with the rule. Although some people continued to bestow greater amounts of property to eldest sons—especially the plantation recognized as the family seat—the practice was becoming rarer. Pinckney concluded on the subject: "We may suppose that in future an equal division of property among children will, in general, take place in all the states and one means of amassing inordinate wealth in the hands of individuals be, as it ought, forever removed!" Pinckney once again proved prescient: South Carolina abolished the rule in 1791.[14]

He then moved to a discussion of the three classes of men he had also detailed in Philadelphia. But he amended his definition of landed interests by including the mechanical, seeking to calm the fears of both the backcountry farmers and mechanics and artisans near the coast. It is one of the first instances where Pinckney recognized that such an alliance might eventually play a more prominent political role in the state's development. He also addressed the concerns of those who believed that the only honest means of gaining wealth was through agriculture. Although Pinckney agreed in general with such an idea, he did not agree that all commerce was "essentially cheating," as "a very celebrated author" had once supposed. Pinckney believed that honest commerce not only existed but should be sanctioned by the government. Honest commerce, he stated, was that which best served the agricultural means of acquiring wealth. He supported his point by tying his three classes together: "The merchant is dependent upon the planter as the purchaser of his imports and as furnishing him with the means of remittances. The professional men depend upon both for employment in their respective pursuits and are, in their turn, useful to both. The landholder, though the most independent of the three, is still in some measure obliged to the merchant for furnishing him at home with a ready sale for his productions." He concluded his discussion of class along the same lines as he had done in Philadelphia, addressing the equality available to all America's citizens. The new government created by the Constitution would recognize "no distinctions but those of merits or talents" and would embrace "virtue and worth for her own, wheresoever she can find them."[15]

Pinckney's ideas concerning the equality of opportunities available to all citizens probably once again raised a few eyebrows among his lowcountry brethren. His comments reflected classical republican ideology that would come to be associated with Jefferson and Madison over the next few years. By the end of the 1790s this ideology led to a split in which Pinckney played a major role in South Carolina and, by extension, at the national level. But in 1788, no one—except perhaps Pinckney himself—could foresee that this address to his upcountry neighbors and their lowcountry socioeconomic peers would lay the foundation for further steps he would soon take to unite South Carolina across economic, geographical, and political lines.[16]

Continuing his address, Pinckney next discussed the differences between the various states in terms of "territory, manners, population, and products." He asserted that, despite the differences and contrary to popular belief, republics could actually function better in a larger territory than a smaller one because communication between and assembly of those who would seek to overthrow the government would be more difficult. He contrasted republics with monarchies and aristocracies, addressing the fears of those who believed the Constitution gave the executive too much power. He assured them that the delegates in Philadelphia, while giving the president enough power to "execute the laws with energy and dispatch," had also "defined his powers and bound them to such limits as will effectually prevent his usurping authorities dangerous to the general welfare." He discussed restrictions on the Senate, assuring the backcountry that the nation could never dissolve into an aristocracy. Finally, he lauded the House of Representatives as "the moving-spring of the system," answerable most directly to its constituents.[17]

In his closing remarks, Pinckney returned to the theme of American originality, attempting to appeal to both the opponents of the Constitution from the backcountry and his allies from the coast:

> How grateful then should we be that at this important period—a period important not to us alone but to the general rights of mankind—so much harmony and concession should prevail throughout the states; that the public opinion should be so much actuated by candor and an attention to their general interests; that, disdaining to be governed by the narrow motives of state policy, they have liberally determined to dedicate a part of their advantage to the support of that government from which they received them! To fraud, to force or accident, all the governments we know have owed their births. To the philosophic mind how new and awful an instance do the United States at present exhibit in the political world! They exhibit, sir, the first instance of a people who, being dissatisfied with their government—unattacked by foreign force and undisturbed by domestic uneasiness—coolly and deliberately resort to the virtue and good sense of their country for a correction of their public errors.

Some delegates probably viewed Pinckney's assertion that "harmony and concession" predominated the political scene as a bit disingenuous in light of those like Rawlin Lowndes in the lowcountry, who was absent, and his equally vehement counterparts from the backcountry, who were present. But Pinckney could be sure for at least the majority of delegates at the ratification convention that harmony existed.[18]

Nearly a week later, on 20 May, the delegates began going through the Constitution paragraph by paragraph. When the convention reached the tenth section of Article 1 regarding restrictions on states in the matter of commerce, Pinckney spoke again regarding concern over a measure that would restrict the states. Calling the provision the "soul of the Constitution," he spoke of the vast amount of exports produced agriculturally by South Carolina—at that time second only to Virginia. Regulation of commerce would preserve honesty within the republic. "Henceforth," he said, "the citizens of the states may trade with each other without fear of tender laws or laws impairing the nature of contracts." Even more important would be the impact the provision would have on foreign creditors. "No more shall paper money, no more shall tender laws drive their commerce from our shores and darken the American name in every country where it is known," he declared. He concluded: "Your government shall now indeed be a government of laws. The arm of justice shall be lifted on high and the poor and the rich, the strong and the weak, shall be equally protected in their rights. Public as well as private confidence shall again be established, industry shall return among us, and the blessings of our government shall verify that old but useful maxim that with states, as well as individuals, honesty is the best policy!" By turning restrictions on the state of South Carolina into future benefits for the poor and infirm, Pinckney played to those who were least trusting of a stronger federal government and most likely to fall victim to the volatility of the marketplace.[19]

On the next day, in an attempt to delay what by now had become inevitable, Revolutionary War hero and antifederalist Gen. Thomas Sumter moved that a vote on the issue be delayed until October. But his motion failed, and on 23 May 1788, South Carolina ratified the Constitution. The ratification occurred not because the majority of the state's inhabitants supported it but because the power base in the lowcountry did. The state's 1778 constitution had skewed representation in favor of the lowcountry elite to such an extent that the backcountry dissidents never stood a chance despite nearly 80 percent of the state's white population being located there. The final vote was 149 to 73. Only 16 out of 137 delegates voting from the coast opposed it. Of those attending from the backcountry, 27 favored ratification while 57 voted against it.[20]

Over the summer, Pinckney probably remained in Charleston. But by October, he had left the city for one of his plantations in the country. There he tended to and managed his agricultural pursuits and interests. He was also enjoying being a newlywed and the lengthy amount of time he could finally spend with Polly. They wasted no time trying to start a family. Charles preferred a son, believing one to be "worth a dozen daughters."[21]

He was also enjoying his role as one of the most prominent politicians in the state. He was reelected to the assembly and served for the remainder of the year. In early January of 1789, supporters mentioned his name as a possible candidate for the United States Senate. When he refused the position, the assembly elected him governor on 21 January by a margin of 108 votes. On Monday, 26 January, he stood before a joint session of the house and senate in the Exchange Building and took the oath of office of governor of South Carolina from Jacob Read, the Speaker of the House of Representatives, who administered it. He made a short speech expressing his appreciation for being elected to the office and his intention to carry out the law with "justice and mercy." The following Saturday at noon, the state feted its new governor with an official proclamation and ceremonies at the Exchange Building and Granville's Bastion.[22]

Despite his experience and prestige on the national level, becoming governor of his state was the culmination of Pinckney's political life so far. Although he exercised little real power—he had no veto and was limited to two two-year terms after which he could not be reelected for four more years—the office "was regarded as being, in addition to a position for public service, a sort of civic crown with which to honor exceptional public men." Appropriately, the South Carolina capital would remain only one year longer in Charleston before moving to Columbia in accordance with a 1789 act of the legislature. Pinckney had demonstrated throughout 1788 his concerns for the entire state and not just the wealthy inhabitants of the lowcountry who had held power for so long. From the time of his motion in January regarding a state constitutional convention linked to the federal ratifying convention to his various speeches within the latter, Pinckney had reached out to constituents and supporters for whom many in his own geopolitical world felt disdain. In a very real sense he was simply pursuing his own vision first expressed in his 25 June speech at the Philadelphia Convention. And if his vision meant more political power for himself within the state and perhaps even on a national scale, so much the better.[23]

During the first year of his governorship, the legislature finally took steps to replace the Constitution of 1778. The South Carolina Constitutional Convention met in Columbia during May of 1790. The legislature had finally agreed to move to the new capital overlooking the Congaree River after a tactic of stall and delay by opponents of relocation. On 13 March 1789, Governor Pinckney issued a proclamation calling on all public officers "to remove on the first day of December Next to Columbia" and on the legislature "to Convene at the said Town of Columbia on the first Monday in January next." On 4 January 1790, writing from Greenwich, his Congaree plantation just south of Columbia, Governor Pinckney sent a message officially affirming the move of the state capital from Charleston to Columbia.[24]

Pinckney's personal life was also in a state of flux. Sometime in early 1789 his wish was realized when Polly bore him a son whom they in all probability christened Charles. In a March letter to James Madison, Pinckney boasted of his legacies, both public and personal. "I have done a great deal of business," he wrote, "sometimes in public and more frequently of a private nature. But what is more than all, I have become a husband and father." Despite his happiness, he wrote that "a wife and son are although pleasing, yet serious concerns." He was soon to find out just how serious child rearing could be. Within months the boy was dead.[25]

To deal with the grief of losing his son, Pinckney threw himself into politics and the management of his plantations. Greenwich had originally been in possession of his uncle, Miles Brewton. After Brewton disappeared at sea, it passed to Brewton's sisters Rebecca and Frances. After Rebecca renounced her interest in the property, Frances gave it to her son in 1783. Over the next ten years, he established a home as well as a major political base on the property. He built a brick building on the grounds that served as an office during his terms as governor and a hub from which he could make his influence felt throughout the state.[26]

In May of 1790, the state constitutional convention finally convened in Columbia with Charles Pinckney presiding. The location proved beneficial to the backcountry delegates only to the extent that more of them could attend. The new constitution did not go as far as most of them would have liked in alleviating their concerns. The lowcountry, despite having a smaller white population, remained a more powerful influence in the form of wealth and apportionment. The convention confirmed that the capital would remain in Columbia, but even that did not take place without a fight—although the move had already been made! To assuage the powerful lowcountry representatives, the delegates divided the state into two districts, upper and lower, with a treasurer for each district. Both the secretary of state and surveyor general had to maintain offices in both Columbia and Charleston. In addition, the Court of Appeals, the highest court in the state, was required to meet in both divisions.

On the question of representation, the lowcountry allowed very few concessions. The constitution provided for one member of the senate for each county or parish. Charleston, comprised of Saint Michael's and Saint Philip's parishes, therefore received two senators. And although the house was reapportioned so that the backcountry received more representation, the increase was only slight. The delegates also reduced the overall power of the house, cutting its membership from 208 to 124 representatives. Thus, despite the desire of backcountry delegates and because of the power of their lowcountry counterparts, especially men like Edward Rutledge, the convention did not produce equal representation to the white population of the state. And there was no provision for reapportionment in the new constitution, unlike the existing one. Finally, the delegates increased property qualifications to such an extent that most yeoman farmers, many of whom lived in the backcountry, could never have served in the legislature.

The new constitution also ended once and for all religious qualifications for holding office. It insured freedom of religion, trial by jury, and freedom of the press, much like the United States Bill of Rights, which had been passed by the state in January. Although Pinckney may have been disappointed in parts of the new constitution, he must have been proud to see both his state and nation finally adopt protections of individual rights he had championed during the Constitutional Convention in Philadelphia. And although the constitution did not give the backcountry much of what it desired, the fact that the inland farmers could force such a convention on their coastal counterparts indicated that their influence and power was growing, albeit slowly and subtly.[27]

As the influence of the backcountry increased, Charles Pinckney continued to combine his established credibility and influence with that growing base in order to rally the state around his emerging political ideology. The combination of the inland white voting population and Pinckney's coastal prestige would soon serve to defeat the Federalist lowcountry elite and bring to power the Jeffersonian Republicans in the coming "Revolution of 1800."

Five

First Terms as Governor

When Charles Pinckney left the South Carolina Constitutional Convention in 1790, he did so with mixed emotions. The lowcountry elite of which he was a member had not sacrificed the power it so jealously guarded. Entrenched power does not divest itself easily or quickly. Pinckney had real concerns about the dissatisfaction that remained among inhabitants of the backcountry. All of his life he had seen those residents who resided far from Charleston slighted and ignored by the lowcountry power base. He had defended his western neighbors on several occasions. In Congress, when John Jay was willing to offer the rights to the Mississippi as a bargaining tool, Pinckney vociferously championed the cause of the backcountry yeomen, fearing a dissolution of the state if that important means of transportation became closed to them. In the Constitutional Convention in Philadelphia, he spoke indirectly regarding the future of those western pioneers. In the South Carolina legislature and constitutional convention, he had addressed them more pointedly, attempting to assuage their apprehensions and champion their causes, all the while assuring ratification of a constitution they feared.

During the 1790s, South Carolina began to undergo a major shift, which occurred over the next thirty years. Beginning in 1794, a cotton boom transformed the state and the region. With the invention of the cotton gin in 1793, the crop began to flourish in the backcountry. The rise of the cotton planter transformed the area from a subsistence-farming region into one of the leading producers and exporters in the state, dependent upon a cotton-based economy for its introduction into the prosperous world markets so long enjoyed by rice and indigo planters in the lowcountry. Because cotton did not involve as great an initial expenditure of capital as did rice, it was easier for backcountry yeomen to make an investment that resulted in prosperity. Simultaneously, changes occurred in the lowcountry. For instance, indigo lost its appeal as a cash crop due to international competition and loss of British subsidies after the Revolution. Pinckney himself felt the impact of such developments. From 1792 to

1794, the price he received for his indigo crop fell from seventy-six to thirty-six pounds sterling per cask.[1]

Furthermore, although the cultivation of rice had shifted from inland to tidal during the second half of the eighteenth century, the golden age of the lowcountry was in decline by 1820, as a surplus on world markets caused the price of Carolina rice to fall. The economic future of the state began to shift towards the West and cotton. By 1799, inland planters like Wade Hampton sent the first large crops of cotton from their plantations near Columbia to markets and wharves in Charleston. Riverboats began plying the waters as far inland as they could. Canals were dug to connect waterways. Entrepreneurs began to operate ferries and build new wagon roads. By 1825 such changes had rendered the state nearly unrecognizable from what it had been in 1790.[2]

Charles Pinckney contributed to this transformation in a major way. In 1790, South Carolinians elected him governor of their state for the first of the four terms he eventually served. He spent much time dealing with a slave revolt in the Caribbean that had a direct bearing on South Carolina. As a result, he sought to strengthen the state's defenses by seeing to it that new militia acts passed in the legislature. He also continued building his political base. He entertained George Washington at Snee Farm and at his house in Charleston during the president's visit to the state in 1791, attempting to enhance his political prestige at home and nationally. But his overeagerness for an ambassadorship from Washington added to the stains that had begun to blemish his reputation on the national level. Maintaining his solicitude for the inhabitants of the western part of the state, he encouraged them in legislative matters and urged the state assembly to enact measures to prevent internal and external threats to the backcountry.

In 1790, unlike almost any other politician in South Carolina, Pinckney foresaw what the next few years would bring in the state and on the national scene. Unlike his lowcountry family and friends, he recognized the economic and political potential that existed in the backcountry. At the beginning of the decade, for instance, he requested agricultural information from Col. Edward Carrington of Virginia, with whom he had become acquainted during their terms together in the Continental Congress. "The upper settlement of the interior and frontier parts of this state," Pinckney wrote, "has introduced into our upper country the culture of tobacco in a very extensive manner." He then lamented that his fellow South Carolinians were not enjoying the same sort of success with the crops as planters in Virginia. "Some of our industrious poor," he continued, "lose a considerable portion of their products."[3]

Although his concern for the growers of tobacco illustrates his vision for the development of the backcountry, Pinckney probably could not foresee the technological innovation that ensured the realization of his vision. When Eli Whitney invented the cotton gin in 1793, very little time passed before the entire state began to change. By the end of the decade, Pinckney himself began sending bales of cotton to Charleston from Greenwich, as well as property he owned further down and on of the opposite side of the Congaree River in the Orangeburg District. In the state's first census in 1790, he listed forty-five slaves on his Orangeburg land. And although rice continued to be the main agricultural product Pinckney grew at his plantations on the Ashepoo and Black Rivers in the lowcountry, he supplemented it with lumber, corn, and, from "the Congarees," cotton. He also contributed to improved transportation within the state by operating a ferry over the Santee River at his plantation Mount Tacitus in 1795.[4]

Just as he wrote to Edward Carrington regarding the economic and agricultural concerns of his state, Pinckney also expressed his concerns regarding political stability in a letter to James Madison. Disappointed in the new state constitution, he lamented that "we have not gone so far as I would wish." He set himself apart from some of his lowcountry companions, referring to himself and his supporters as "we" and his opponents who would not go as far as he desired in bringing a more equitable distribution of power in the state as "they." "We" are satisfied with the judicial branch, he wrote, but "they" would not give the executive the power or the term in office that "we" desired. Such correspondence reveals insight into the development of political factions as early as 1790. He had only recently been with "them" in support of the Constitution and had sought to mollify the fears of the "we." But when debating the state constitution, he had taken positions oftentimes more in tune with inhabitants of the backcountry, including himself among them with the use of the pronoun "we." That he wrote to Madison with the details suggests that Pinckney may have perceived similar developments on a national level. He felt comfortable discussing the issues with and took a friendly tone towards James Madison, whom he believed to be an ideological companion, never suspecting that Madison had disparaged him to Washington and had already formed a less than complimentary opinion of the South Carolinian.[5]

Pinckney probably spent the remainder of the year in Charleston with intermittent visits to his plantations around the state. He also began building a political base in the backcountry, corresponding with politicians like Gen. Andrew Pickens of Ninety-Six District, to whom he wrote in July regarding such "delicate and trying" issues as the relocation of the state capital to Columbia. He expressed his optimism that the matter was concluded and "the differences it occasioned buried I hope forever in oblivion," thus ensuring "domestic harmony and prosperity." He also reminded Pickens that it was he who, as governor, had been instrumental in bringing about a settlement between the Creek Indians and the United States. "I have ever viewed the infant and exposed state of our frontiers as very essentially entitled to the attention and fostering care of the Government," he wrote and, based on his actions in the Confederation Congress, in the South Carolina ratifying conference, and as governor, he did so with an honest pen.[6]

In the fall, Polly gave birth to her second child, a daughter who was christened Frances Henrietta—after Pinckney's mother and Polly's father—at St. Philip's Church in October. The family spent Christmas together in Charleston but headed inland shortly thereafter for the beginning of the legislative session. Pinckney once again took up the cause of backcountry residents.[7]

Although as governor he had little real power, he used his addresses and letters to the assembly to urge that the body take action on various issues. He spoke optimistically regarding the recent assumption of state debts by the federal Congress, envisioning the extra monies as instrumental in "extend[ing] to every part of the state those benefits of inland navigation under the want of which they have so long and inconveniently labored." Again, Pinckney was setting himself apart from coastal representatives who had opposed state funding of inland navigation less than two years earlier.[8]

Another problem continuing to confront inland inhabitants of the state centered around courts and jails or, more precisely, the absence of those institutions. The problem had plagued the state throughout the period of the Regulators and continued to exist. Jails and courthouses were in disrepair and spread haphazardly across the state, and the court schedule was unreliable. In early February, Pinckney urged the assembly to address the situation: "As there are no gaols for the District of Ninety-Six and Charles Town and as it is essential to the strict execution of the laws and that certain and regular punishment of offenses throughout every part of the state which alone ensure the continuance of the order and quietness that have for some time so happily prevailed, that there should be strong and secure gaols in every District, permit me to recommend to your honourable House a revision of the sums which have been granted for this purpose and that ample provision be made not only for erecting them where wanted but also for compleatly repairing and securing gaols and courthouses in every district." He also made recommendations for the court system, the new constitution calling for a general revamping of the system. It now became the responsibility of the legislature to add the specifics, he told them. "I can have no doubt that the Judicial which you are about to establish will not only be founded in all its parts upon those just and equal principles which should ever distinguish the system of a free government, but will be so accommodated with respect to the Division of Districts as to remove the Inconveniences under which the inhabitants of many parts of them labour in living at considerable distances from court houses and being obliged from the extent of Districts to collect too great a proportion of suits into one circuit."

Lastly he recommended that the governor be given power to call special sessions of the courts. He gave several reasons for implementing such executive authority, including the many criminals confined in one place, awaiting trial, who posed a threat to society; the risk that important testimony might be lost due to lack of speedy trials; inconvenience to those traveling if obliged to remain in one place to await testimony in a delayed trial; and "the prevalence of contagious disorders."[9]

He returned to the topic in November, urging the legislature again "that in the tax act ample provision should be made for building suitable jails in the districts where there are none." As governor, he could not take the actions necessary unless the legislature made the funds available. Despite his strong and repeated urging, the state of South Carolina's jails and court system did not show much improvement for several more years.[10]

In early March, word reached South Carolina that President Washington would be coming through the state later in the spring on his "southern tour." Pinckney had suggested the tour to Washington over a year earlier, and although Washington had replied that he would enjoy traveling through the South, his schedule would not permit it. Now, however, Washington was en route, and Pinckney eagerly invited him to stay at his own home on Meeting Street in Charleston. Washington declined the offer, stating that it was his policy not to accept such invitations, lest he cause "inconvenience" to individual households. And although Washington did stay at the homes of Joseph Manigault and William Alston prior to arriving in Charleston, he probably did so because there were not suitable public accommodations for him otherwise along the South Carolina coast. He also stayed with Thomas Heyward after leaving Charleston and stated in his diary there was a lack of "public houses on the road."[11]

Pinckney wrote again to Washington, who was traveling with Gen. William Moultrie, as they approached Snee Farm in late April. "I must apologize for asking you to call at a place so indifferently furnished where your fare will be entirely that of a farm," he stated. "It is a place I seldom go to, or things would be in better order." Pinckney had probably not been at Snee Farm of late because his duties as governor required him to spend much of his time at Greenwich near Columbia, and his duties as planter required him to visit his more prosperous plantations. On the other hand, he had probably not furnished Snee

Farm quite as "indifferently" as he indicated to Washington; otherwise he would have been reluctant to extend a special invitation to the president, especially when there were other, more well-established plantations nearby.[12]

Early Monday morning, 2 May, Washington arrived at Snee Farm. He did not stay long but did have his breakfast there. Afterwards he left for the ferry at Haddrell's Point, which carried him across the Cooper River into Charleston, where Pinckney and a group of the city's dignitaries anxiously awaited. As the president approached the Charleston peninsula, cannons sounded, welcoming him and his party to the city. Pinckney, Lt. Gov. Isaac Holmes, and senators Pierce Butler and Ralph Izard were among the officials who greeted Washington as he arrived at Prioleau's Wharf. They escorted him to the Exchange Building, where he stood on the front steps and watched a parade of dignitaries who paid their respects. Afterward Pinckney led the group to the Church Street home of Thomas Heyward. Heyward was at his plantation south of Charleston awaiting the president's visit in a few days. His house in town had been leased by the city especially for Washington's stay. Once Washington had a chance to view his lodgings, he dined at Pinckney's house at 16 Meeting Street, a few blocks away, near the battery.[13]

Over the next few days, Pinckney accompanied Washington to several of the events the town of Charleston had produced for their visiting head of state. On Thursday, Pinckney hosted another dinner for the president at his home. On Friday, he held a ball there in the president's honor. While guests were dancing and enjoying the finery of the Pinckney house, he and Washington walked through the garden discussing issues of the day. They also viewed Pinckney's flowering agave plant. Washington expressed interest in the unique biological specimen, also known as the century plant because it is said to bloom only once every hundred years. Pinckney promised Washington that he would send information regarding it.[14]

On Sunday, Washington attended church at St. Philip's. The Episcopal church on Church Street was the family church of the Pinckneys, and Charles, Polly, and Frances Henrietta probably all attended the services also. On Monday, the president departed, and Pinckney and a large party rode out of town, heading south to Sandy Hill, the plantation of Col. William Washington. Others in attendance included Charles Cotesworth Pinckney, General Moultrie, and senators Butler and Izard. On Tuesday morning, they all returned to Charleston, and Washington left for Savannah.[15]

Charles Pinckney viewed Washington's visit as a highlight in his own political career. The numerous visits the president made to his Meeting Street home gave Pinckney the opportunity to renew his acquaintance with the chief executive of the United States and to impress upon him his political savvy. Although he enjoyed being governor of South Carolina, Pinckney remained somewhat discontented. The numerous balls and public events whetted his appetite for a lifestyle on a grander scale than he could ever experience as governor. Despite all of his previous plans, he had yet to travel abroad. Seeking to mix public service with a personal desire to see Europe, he began formulating ideas for obtaining a position as a foreign minister. He discussed his ideas with Polly and her father, Henry Laurens. Polly was probably excited about the idea of returning to the continent, where she had spent most of her youth. Laurens also thought such an appointment would benefit his son-in-law and agreed to write a letter to President Washington on his behalf.[16]

Pinckney himself soon embarked on a plan that would increase the stain on his reputation. The circumstances arose from his personal ambition as well as his mistaken notion that James Madison was his friend and confidant. On 6 August, he sat at his desk on Meeting Street and wrote a letter to Madison. He began it by appealing to "our former intimacy" during both the Confederation Congress and the Constitutional Convention. "I am induced to make you the following communication," he wrote, "in the confidence of a friendship assured that you will only mention it to the person and in the manner I wish—as it is upon a subject of some delicacy." He went on to explain that he had heard that there would be several foreign ministerial appointments made by the end of the year. Other men might be better qualified than himself for such an appointment, he admitted, but many of those already had duties that would necessitate their refusal if named. He hoped Madison could speak on his behalf to the president and went on to explain why he was qualified.

Although he wrote the letter purely for political purposes, it illustrates how Pinckney viewed himself or at least wished others to view him. "You know me and how far I am qualified for public business," he continued. "I can only add that having a fondness for public life I have unremittingly applied myself to the studies necessary to form a public man, since I had the pleasure to see you. The situation I hold has given me a full scope, and I can assure you that I have as much industry as when you knew me and that by becoming a married man I have only added steadiness and I hope solidity to it. It is true I am not an old man, but I think I have lived long enough to have at least acquired the knowledge necessary to this situation. Besides, it is the age of young men."

He lamented that he would have to sacrifice benefits from his present position as governor but indicated that his wife's connections with France and her knowledge of the French language could aid in any position in that country. He also mentioned his father-in-law's numerous business acquaintances in Europe, which he believed would make his own situation abroad "agreeable and respectable."

He concluded by listing the various public offices he had held, including his term in the Congress and his role at the Constitutional Convention, "in both of which you well know I used every exertion to bring about the present constitution." He expressed a preference for London and then asked Madison to be a bit disingenuous: "I hope at the time you mention it to the President, you will do it as from yourself and use all or any of the arguments I have stated which you think proper." In a postscript, he also asked Madison to talk with Thomas Jefferson, the secretary of state, regarding the appointment, "if you think proper."[17]

One can only imagine how Madison reacted when he received and read the letter. There is no record of a response, but the request probably surprised the Virginian, and he may have even been offended by the manner in which Pinckney had asked him to approach Washington. It is clear from his correspondence to Washington after the Convention that Madison had never felt particularly close to Pinckney. He probably viewed the South Carolinian in an unfavorable light before the two had ever met, as a result of Monroe's description of him as "intemperate and factious." Whether Madison actually spoke to Washington regarding the appointment is unknown. But in all likelihood he did speak to Thomas Jefferson on the subject. The animosity Madison felt towards Pinckney, sowed in the Confederation Congress and sprouted in the Constitutional Convention, received a heavy dose of fertilizer as a result of Pinckney's letter.

A few days after writing to Madison, Henry Laurens wrote to the president extolling his son-in-law's "honor and integrity." But despite the recommendation, when Washington made an appointment to the Court of St. James in London early in 1792, he did not choose Charles Pinckney. Instead, he chose another Pinckney, cousin Thomas. Some historians have emphasized Charles' resentment at being passed over for the appointment. It has even been alleged that the appointment of Thomas led to the eventual break between the two cousins and their respective branches of the family. This break, according to the supposition, would become a key factor in Charles' defection from his Federalist family and support of Thomas Jefferson in 1800.[18]

But such a theory seems quite unfounded. On the contrary, Charles Pinckney had been a consistent proponent of republican ideology and a persistent spokesperson for the backcountry inhabitants who also supported Jefferson in 1800. He had aligned himself ideologically—although erroneously on a personal level—with Jefferson's protégé James Madison. Had Pinckney truly been upset because he believed he had been unfairly treated, he would have directed his anger towards secretary of state Thomas Jefferson, whom he had never met, rather than the esteemed Washington, whom he considered a friend. To assert that Pinckney turned against a family member who received the appointment he wanted and aligned himself with someone who, for all he knew, made that appointment, is simply not credible.

Despite not receiving the foreign appointment, Pinckney soon found himself embroiled in foreign affairs as governor of South Carolina. As the summer of 1791 drew to a close, events taking place in the Caribbean alarmed the state. In August, slaves on Haiti—then the French colony of Saint-Dominque—staged a successful revolt. The insurrection occurred in part because enslaved blacks sensed the spirit of revolution in the air as a result of events taking place in France. Since the beginning of the French Revolution in 1787, most South Carolinians had supported it. They also hoped that a constitutional monarchy might develop on Saint-Dominque, incorporating ideas of republicanism that had fueled the revolution in the United States. For instance, when Washington arrived in Georgetown during his visit to the state over the summer, toasts had been raised to both Louis XVI and the National Assembly. In fact, most Americans supported the early stages of the French Revolution, hoping it would parallel the successful one in America, which had relied so strongly on French assistance.[19]

When news of events in Saint-Dominque began trickling into the port of Charleston from the various trading ships, apprehension quickly developed. Pinckney himself received one of the first official notifications of events at sugar plantations on the island. Towards the end of August, Deputy Polony arrived in Charleston and presented Pinckney with a communication containing resolutions from the Saint-Dominque General Assembly. They contained descriptions of horrors calculated to incite South Carolinians to send aid. The letter from the president of the assembly accompanying the resolutions began, "The miseries of St. Domingo are at their highest pitch." It continued, "This rich country will soon be nothing more than a heap of ashes. The planters have already bathed with their blood the ground that their hard labor had rendered fertile." He requested "troops and ammunition and provisions, for famine will soon be over the country and we should only be able to save our inhabitants from the sword to see them fall by famine." One resolution stated that "the slaves have risen, . . . the whites who had the government of them are murdered, [and] . . . the assembling of the Negroes increases every day." It concluded with a chilling warning, especially for South Carolina and its minority white population: "The scourge which is now laying waste the most valuable French possession in America threatens all the neighboring colonies if they do not unite to destroy the source of it."[20]

Pinckney wasted little time in responding to the beleaguered white planters. He could sympathize with their plight, conditions in the lowcountry of South Carolina being somewhat comparable to those in Saint-Dominque. Along most of the coast blacks outnumbered whites by four to one, and the possibility of a similar insurrection always lurked in the back of white minds—especially since a similar event had occurred along the Stono River south of Charleston earlier in the century. In early September, Pinckney wrote to the president of the Saint-Dominque General Assembly, assuring him that he felt very close to the French, especially in light of their assistance to the colonies during the Revolution. However, he informed the president that Article 1, section 9, of the United States Constitution prevented the state of South Carolina from sending troops on its own to assist the island planters. "By the Constitution of the United States all foreign affairs were transferred to the General Government who shall have the authority to direct the national force," he explained. "The individual states are expressly constrained from any interference without the consent of Congress." He also sent copies of the correspondence to George Washington and expressed his opinion that events in Saint-Dominque could develop into a "flame which will extend to all the neighboring islands, and may eventually prove not a very pleasing or agreeable example to the Southern States."[21]

Over the next few weeks, refugees from Saint-Dominque began arriving in Charleston. Their presence and the stories they brought with them acted as living proof of the precarious situation in which the white elite existed in and around Charleston. In December, when the legislature reconvened, Pinckney sent a message that "while we sympathize with our friends and lament their suffering, they very strongly prove the policy of having our militia always in a situation to act with the promptness and effect as circumstances may require." A few days later, on 12 December, Deputy Polony addressed the legislature in Columbia, and the assembly passed an act that strengthened the militia in the state.[22]

In his address, Polony described horrible crimes taking place in Saint-Dominque, holding not just the slaves but all people of color on the island responsible for the massacres occurring there, including those who were free or mulattoes. The legislature also agreed to supply up to three thousand pounds sterling worth of provisions to the French government. Over the next year, the continued arrival of refugees—white, black, and mulattoes—intensified fears, and the legislature eventually prohibited further admission of "Slaves, Negroes, Mulattoes, Indians, Moors or Mestizoes" for a period of two years. Despite all the fear, support for the Revolution in France remained fairly strong until 1793, when events occurring in France caused similar revulsion in America. The fall of the capital of Saint-Dominque in the same year and the complete takeover of the island by the forces of Toussaint L'Ouverture reinforced the disillusionment.[23]

While South Carolinians in general worried that black immigrants to their state might sow seeds of insurrection in their own midst, slave owners became concerned with an even more pressing situation: slaves who were seeking refuge in Florida. In January 1792, Pinckney wrote again to Washington, expressing his concern that runaway slaves were being harbored in the Spanish possession. Washington referred the matter to secretary of state Jefferson, who wrote to Pinckney in April. By the time the legislature met later in the year, Pinckney could deliver a newly enacted treaty between the United States and Spain for the return of fugitive slaves. By its terms, the Spanish authorities in Florida agreed to send any slaves escaping into the territory to Amelia Island near the border with Georgia until a representative from the United States could collect them. Spain was to be reimbursed for the expense involved in apprehension and maintenance of the runaways.[24]

It was within this climate of worry, concern, and, at times, fear that Charles Pinckney held his own slaves. At one time or the other, he owned as many as two to three hundred. He probably left most of the day-to-day contact with his field workers to his overseers. He was too involved in his political career to do otherwise most of the time. And depending on where a slave lived and worked on Pinckney's plantations, his or her conditions differed markedly. In the lowcountry, on rice plantations near Georgetown or the Ashley-Combahee-Edisto River Basin, slaves probably had a great deal more autonomy than their inland counterparts. Along the coast, most slaves worked in the task system. Slaves in the lowcountry brought many of the rice-producing methods with them from West Africa, which were then adopted by their owners. As a result, they tended to be more skilled at particular tasks, and planters often trusted them with more independence in their work places. This trust also made for more autonomy in a slave's personal life. Once a slave completed an assigned task, he or she could spend the remainder of the day fishing, hunting, or growing crops for his or her own family's consumption. Additionally, owners often left lowcountry plantations for long periods of time, leaving the slaves with little white influence and allowing them the opportunity to create their own distinct culture. Although lowcountry slaves remained in every sense the property of their white masters, the abilities brought from Africa and passed down to succeeding generations may have increased a sense of personal empowerment. The long periods of isolation away from whites may have given them the chance to establish personal lives, spaces, and communities to a much greater extent than slaves in other geographic locations and agricultural pursuits.[25]

In contrast, at Pinckney's land along the Congaree River near Columbia and in the Orangeburg District, slaves grew cotton as the major agricultural product.

Most cotton planters and overseers used the gang system in its production. In the gang system, slaves worked for long hours alongside each other doing whatever was necessary depending on the season of the year. In the spring they all planted, in the summer and fall they chopped, and in the late fall they harvested. Few specialized skills were needed. Implementation of a task system was therefore not necessary or economically efficient. The gang system resulted in some of the harshest conditions, as slaves toiled from sunup to sundown, doing repetitive tasks requiring little skill or specialized talent. Few slaves in such a setting could find distinguishing tasks to set them apart from their peers.[26]

In addition to those slaves engaged in agricultural endeavors, Pinckney also used "boat Negroes" on his ferry at the Santee River. Many slaves became boatmen during the late seventeenth and early eighteenth centuries. Pinckney's father-in-law used slaves to man small schooners that plied the rivers of the lowcountry hauling agricultural products to the ports and bringing provisions back to the plantations. A major problem concerning slave owners who used slaves in this manner involved constant avenues available for the slaves' escape. Boatmen spent long periods of time unsupervised by their masters or any other white. They enjoyed a greater amount of autonomy than other groups of slaves, including those working in the task system, and had numerous opportunities to flee. And because they were alone so often, escape could go undetected for quite some time. One of Laurens' slaves attempted to escape so often that Laurens threatened to sell him. As a result of the number of escapes, owners eventually began using free blacks to man their crafts. There was no labor shortage. Slaves who had been employed as boatmen had the opportunity to make and save money. They sometimes smuggled goods to fellow slaves or poor whites. With money made from smuggling, many were able to purchase their own freedom. Once free, they naturally sought employment in a position with which they were familiar. Whites, tiring of slave escapes, became quite willing to hire them.[27]

The men who ran Pinckney's boats may very well have been free blacks. If not, he treated them quite well. Every two to three months he bought ten to twelve gallons of rum for them. Most slaves only had the opportunity to drink legitimately during special occasions, such as at Christmastime. Pinckney's willingness to keep his boatmen supplied with alcohol indicates they may have been free. Perhaps he had seen the problems his father-in-law had encountered with slave boatmen. Perhaps he had experienced similar problems himself and therefore chose to use free blacks on his boats. It is also possible, of course, that the rum he supplied could have been an attempt to placate slave boatmen and reduce their desire to escape. Whether a cask of rum in trade as a trade-off for freedom appealed to those whose position afforded them so many chances to escape seems doubtful.[28]

Most of the personal interaction between slaves and their masters took place in a domestic context. House slaves, especially in the Charleston lowcountry, developed a high regard for themselves compared to those who labored in the fields. They looked down on slaves who did not work in the "big house" and even felt a sense of superiority over poor whites. Masters encouraged this class system as a means whereby those slaves closest to them felt pride in their status. Such pride, whites hoped, would instill in house slaves more affection for their owners, thereby precluding clandestine acts of rebellion such as poison or arson.[29]

Little is known of Charles Pinckney's domestic slaves. His will indicates a few who enjoyed higher status than others. In it, he granted freedom to several: Primus, Cate, and Betty and Dinah, both of whom were "washerwomen." Dinah seems to have been somewhat special to him. He not only gave her freedom, but he also freed her children, Anthony, John, Peneta, and Carlos. Pinckney also directs that the four be "suitably maintained and bound out for trades." Why would Pinckney mention these four slaves by name and seek to establish their future? One answer is that they were perhaps more than just the children of a house slave. Pinckney never remarried after the death of his wife. It is also interesting to note that two of the children had Spanish names and one, Carlos, had the Spanish name of his master. Pinckney's will also expressed his desire to have a namesake, and in it he tried to persuade either of his grandsons to take his name by increasing their bequest if one should do so. There is no direct proof that Pinckney fathered children with Dinah or any of his slaves, but the freeing of this small group is evidence. It is possible that Dinah simply accompanied him to Spain when Jefferson appointed him minister there in 1801. She could have had a relationship with a Spanish man with whom she had the children. It is also possible that the father was from South Carolina and because of Pinckney's affection for Spain he gave two of his slave's children Spanish names.[30]

To shed more light on the question, it may be helpful to look at it in context of recent evidence that lends support to oral histories that Thomas Jefferson may have fathered at least one child with his slave Sally Hemings. There are many parallels between Pinckney and Jefferson in both their private and public lives. Politically, both were ardent Republicans and champions of rural agrarianism. Privately, both overextended themselves financially and failed at their own agricultural pursuits. Both men's wives died fairly young, and neither ever remarried. Both suffered rumor and innuendo that they were engaged in relationships with women of color. The allegations concerning Jefferson first came to light during the election of 1800. Those surrounding Pinckney surfaced towards the end of his life. Most advocates of the Jefferson-Hemings relationship suggest it was of lengthy duration and affectionate, not at all like the even-more-common slave quarters rape that characterized much of southern miscegenation. The liaisons supposedly began when Jefferson was minister to France. Jefferson freed Sally and her children in his will. Did Charles Pinckney have a lengthy relationship with Dinah that began in Spain, lasted the rest of his life, and caused him to free her and the children in his will? The answer may never be known, but it is indeed a fascinating supposition.[31]

During the last few months of 1792, Pinckney was still happily married to Polly. He probably spent his time tending to his various plantations and family life. His rice crops had proved profitable, a beneficiary of the efficient task-slave system. But unfavorable weather—floods in the spring and a drought in the summer—and the beginning of a collapse in the market spoiled any chance that his indigo would bring him much of a profit. In April of 1792, he had sold seventeen casks of the blue dye for just over £1,293. In 1793 he would sell only ten casks for £757. Meanwhile, Polly gave birth to a second daughter, whom they named Mary Eleanor for her mother.[32]

In October he wrote to his cousin Thomas, who had just arrived in London, apprising him of crop and weather conditions in the state and issues surrounding Indians on the frontier of the state. The letter was congenial and informative, but he omitted any mention of the slave insurrections or the revolution in Saint-Dominque. Thomas Pinckney's position as minister in London and the danger that the correspondence could be intercepted probably made him think twice before writing anything negative concerning the French Revolution and its effect on slavery.[33]

Although Pinckney's letter to his cousin abroad revealed no indication of any envy at the position, his actions a few days later showed that the possibility of gaining a position on the national level remained on his mind. Finding the courage to write the president personally, he wrote to Washington and listed the reasons he believed he would be a suitable prospect for an appointment. He stated that his term of governor would be over at the beginning of 1793. He reminded Washington that his "education and pursuits have been entirely adapted to public life." He closed by revealing his awareness of the letter Henry Laurens had written on his behalf, as well as the possibility that "some others have likewise done so." There is no record of the president's reply, but Charles Pinckney never received an appointment from Washington.[34]

While Pinckney waited for Washington's response, and just before the legislature met in November, he wrote Benjamin Waring, the town commissioner and treasurer of the upper division of the state. Pinckney urged Waring to take steps to facilitate the timely arrival of delegates from the interior regions of the state to Columbia for the opening of the General Assembly. Because they arrived late, Pinckney wrote, they missed important votes. He had received letters during the recess that he believed would be considered in the upcoming session, and he instructed Waring to forward the letters within the interior so the backcountry delegates would be prepared when they arrived in Columbia. One important issue was the presidential election that would take place in the fall. The legislature would choose the electors, and Pinckney wanted to make sure the representatives from the backcountry had a voice in the process.[35]

On 26 November he sent a message to the legislature informing them of duties he believed to be most urgent. Appointment of the electors topped his list. He also informed the assembly that they should examine the state's militia and its conformity with the recently passed federal Militia Act of 1792. He delighted in informing them that the state militia had been much improved as a result of an act they had passed in December of the previous year. But, quoting the United States Constitution, he urged that additional steps be taken: "A well regulated militia being the most natural and safe defense of a free people, permit me earnestly to recommend to you the adoption of such measures as are calculated not only to accommodate them to the act of Congress but to encourage and confirm the spirit which prevails at present among our citizens and which must ever be favourable to order and good government." Finally, he advised them on the state of the state as he evaluated it at the end of his term in office and urged them to continue their efforts "to strengthen and confirm those measures which can never fail to secure respect and obedience to our laws and happiness to our citizens." With this optimistic challenge, Governor Pinckney greeted the last session of the South Carolina legislature during his term in office.[36]

In early December distressing news reached Pinckney's family in Columbia. Polly's father, Henry Laurens, died on 8 December. Whether Charles or Polly were at Mepkin plantation for Laurens' cremation is not known. But if they were in attendance, Pinckney returned in a short time to Columbia for the remainder of his term, which ended in early 1793. Over the next few years the record is scarce regarding his life. He did not return to the public arena until May of 1795. But in between, important events occurred politically and personally.[37]

In his personal life, Pinckney returned to the practice of law, managed his plantations, and attended to the ongoing settlements of the estates of his father and his uncle, Miles Brewton. He spent a few weeks at Snee Farm in February of 1794 before returning to Charleston later in the month. Polly soon informed him she was pregnant again, but as the year and her pregnancy progressed, her health began to decline. On 24 September she gave birth to the son Pinckney had long desired. The two named him for his recently deceased grandfather,

Henry Laurens. But their happiness and excitement was short-lived. Within a month, Charles Pinckney's "little French girl" was dead, suffering a fate similar to her mother's.[38]

Little is known of Pinckney's personal relationship with Polly or with women in general. He married into the wealthy and prominent Laurens family because he had obviously become smitten with Mary Eleanor, but there were also practical effects. In doing so, he hoped to secure both his fortune and status within the state. In his 1791 letter to Madison enumerating his qualifications for a post abroad, he wrote that his marriage had given him both steadiness and solidity. He also mentioned his wife's upbringing and knowledge of the French language as reasons to be considered for a post in France. He obviously believed that, despite a proscribed role for women within the domestic arena, his own political position could be strengthened by his wife's assets.

White women played an indispensable role in the stability and endurance of Pinckney's beloved republic. To him, their place in southern society was important and secure, and although he wrote little on the subject, we can place him with his republican contemporaries by examining what historians have discovered about the general role of women in the early days of the republic, before and after the Revolution. He probably agreed with those contemporaries in his own attitudes towards women and the gendered tenets of western civilization upon which they were based. Furthermore, ideas and attitudes based on gender linked together behavior and attitudes of men like Charles Pinckney towards all groups of "others" within the South. Ideas of "manliness" pervaded all southern social situations.[39]

In Lockean ideology, women were considered dependent upon men because they were weaker biologically. Both sexes were accorded certain natural rights and liberties, but women were dependent to a great extent on the biologically dominant male. A later philosophy, the Scottish Commonsense Enlightenment, de-emphasized personal liberties in favor of personal duties to the state. In the early American republic, both of these played major, yet somewhat competing, roles. Men became the beneficiaries of Lockean liberties while women were subjugated by Scottish duties. In that manner women became more responsible for instilling virtue in children and insuring the survival of the republic. Thus, two distinctly gendered spheres arose: public for men and domestic for women. In the public sphere, men exercised their rights and liberties, creating documents like the Declaration of Independence and the Constitution and serving their country in the political arena. Women, on the other hand, worked within the confines of the domestic arena, raising children and instilling within them the attributes of virtue so necessary for the survival of republican society.[40]

For Charles Pinckney and others of his generation in South Carolina, issues of gender were intimately connected to those of class identity and relationships. The gender constructs that Pinckney and other early republican founders held melded with the common yeoman's perspective to create southern society. By acting as a link between geopolitical and economic sections of society, Pinckney became an integral part of this creation. Yeomen extended gendered ideas about their own households into attitudes about society at large. Hierarchical notions present within yeoman homes and domestic settings became the basis for what they expected the public arena to epitomize. Order and stability in their own households justified the same within the larger community. By embracing such ideas, these "masters of small worlds" succeeded in legitimizing the power of their more wealthy counterparts who operated on a much larger scale. Without the impetus of yeoman households and the empowerment given them by such republican elites as Pinckney, southern society may have taken on a very different flavor. Pinckney courted the residents of the backcountry for his own personal political gains as well as the Jeffersonian republicans. He also knew the important contributions these members of the state could make to the perpetuation of South Carolina slaveholding society. All through the 1790s, by attempting to assuage their concerns that they were being overwhelmed by their elite neighbors to the east, Pinckney helped them extend their own gender constructs about mobility within their domestic situation to the statewide community. Had they not believed that they, too, could have made the climb from yeoman to planter, as Pinckney constantly reinforced with his optimism and reform for their region and situation, they might not have held so tenaciously to those ideas.[41]

Such gender-based attitudes towards slaves, women, and South Carolina society helped create the larger world of southern honor, which Charles Pinckney would defend so ardently in his 1820 speech before Congress on the Missouri question. When the North criticized slavery for making the South "less manly and republican, and less worthy," he responded with a list of heroic deeds done by southerners to show "valor, wisdom, and patriotism" within the region. To Charles Pinckney and many of his contemporaries, the South was the epitome of republicanism. By denying yeomen all the rights of planters, the South protected itself from an uneducated and non-virtuous rabble. By holding forth the chance that they could advance to the ranks of the landholding elite, they could strive for education and virtue that would ensure such advancement. By giving women the responsibility of instilling virtue and instructing the South's progeny, the region created an essential place in its republican society for females. As the institution of slavery moved from being seen as a necessary evil to a positive good, white southerners saw themselves exercising a paternalistic and generous attitude towards a black population they alleged were unable to fend for themselves. At the same time, they could use that population for economic expansion and white individual independence, reminding white men of the plight that awaited them should they lose their independence.[42]

Like most white Jeffersonian men of his day, Pinckney related philosophies about life in a republic to his personal domestic management as well as his public career. He used certain aspects of his personal domestic situation, especially regarding his wife and her family connections as well as his own familiarity with French culture, to pursue his own public political career. In doing so, he melded his own domesticity with a public persona that helped him achieve success at political levels, confounding his opponents. The social, cultural, and political aspects of the society in which he lived had great influence on Pinckney. By examining those aspects, we can tell a great deal about him and those with whom he dealt. His prominent role in South Carolina assured that he, too, influenced society, founding and forging it to suit his optimistic vision, first of a republican nation and then of a Republican nation. By the end of his life, that vision would be of a restrictive nation, preventing a large part of its population from enjoying its fruits. And in trying to attain the third, his rhetoric would supplant his contributions to the first two.

Upon the death of Mary Eleanor, Pinckney dropped out of public view for nearly a year. Less than six months after her passing, his mother, Frances, the other prominent adult woman in his life, died. He then assumed her debts, which, according to the numerous claims made against him later for her obligations, were quite extensive. He also became responsible for raising his three children, one of whom was a newborn infant. He sought out a suitable replacement for their mother in order that they could receive the instruction and instillation of civic and republican virtue he considered essential in their upbringing. Martha Laurens Ramsay, his sister-in-law, became his choice to raise Henrietta, Mary Eleanor, and the infant Henry Laurens. Pinckney, on the other hand, did the only thing he knew to do to occupy his time and get his mind off of the tragedies: he turned once more to politics.

Six

Fathering a Political Party

Within a period of six months Charles Pinckney sustained the loss of both his wife and his mother. With his children in the care of their aunt, he dealt with his grief by returning to the political arena. For close to a year, he had been out of public view, and conditions in South Carolina continued to be volatile. Over the next few years, Pinckney would try to deal with that volatility by serving another term as governor and building a political organization that would transform both his state and nation. By 1800, the interests with whom he had repeatedly aligned himself over the past ten years came into their own, creating a party that won major victories in South Carolina and a "revolution" at the national level when its standard-bearer, Thomas Jefferson, became president. The years leading to that apex proved to be among the most exciting, dynamic, and ultimately defining moments in American political history. Pinckney played an indispensable role in those events—but at great personal expense.

It is necessary to look at a few political events leading up to 1800 to understand the culminating events of that year, beginning in 1793 in Charleston. Early in the year, the French ambassador, Citizen Genet, began his tour of the United States, arriving first in Pinckney's hometown, where Charlestonians greeted him with great fanfare. Such a reception helped give Genet a false impression of American support for the French. The confidence created by that impression led him into direct conflict with President Washington's neutrality policy regarding the French and the British. During his ten-day stay, conservatives and future Federalists, such as Pinckney's cousins Thomas and Charles Cotesworth Pinckney, feted the Frenchman, with the latter providing the horses for his trip north. John Rutledge and Ralph Izard dined with him. Only William Loughton Smith expressed reservations about all of the hoopla, calling it "foolish." South Carolina's governor, Revolutionary War hero William Moultrie, did everything in his own power to assist Genet, viewing his support as a return of that shown by France towards America during the Revolution. He allowed Genet to outfit four ships for the French cause that eventually began bringing British plunder into the port at Charleston. Genet also made arrangements for an expedition into Spanish Florida.[1]

Support for France reached its zenith in South Carolina when Genet left on his trip north. Republican societies flourished all across the state, including Charleston, where there had long been a distaste for British merchants but where the conservative elements of the city were divided over support for the French Revolution. Mechanics and artisans, sympathetic to their French counterparts, made up over half of Charleston's Republican Society of South Carolina. But it was the inhabitants of the backcountry who most supported the French cause. Over the next few years, events at several levels would cause many of the lowcountry elite to rethink their advocacy of the French. The disastrous results of the Genet mission marked one of the first indicators of future political turmoil. As Genet overestimated American support for his country and acted contrary to Washington's policies, the admiration and respect for the president trumped whatever good wishes existed for either Genet or France.[2]

On a local level, Charlestonians came face-to-face with what the white population saw as the horror of too much republicanism. Refugees from Saint-Dominque began pouring into the state only months after Genet's visit. From July to November they came, bringing with them confirmation of the nightmarish rumors white South Carolinians had been hearing and fearing. The lowcountry political faction, desperate to moderate a radical republican ideology they held responsible for the Haitian Revolution and feared could result in a similar fate for South Carolina, became even more resentful of the backcountry. They now saw the inhabitants in the western part of the state as not just poor, uneducated simpletons but actual threats to the stability of the state itself.

On the national scene, a rift began to open between Washington's secretary of state, Thomas Jefferson, and his treasury secretary, Alexander Hamilton. This split allowed United States citizens to attach two important faces and personalities holding radically different views to growing factions, which would lead to the formation of the first political parties. Charles Pinckney sided with Thomas Jefferson and played a large role in this development.

The rift centered around three main issues. The first dealt with the role of the federal government. Hamilton proposed a national bank, believing the central government should be active in supporting the moneyed interests of the young nation. Jefferson argued that the Constitution did not give the federal government the authority to create such a bank. He remained wary of too much centralized power and feared that the alliance of power and money could lead to a monarchy. The second issue arose from foreign policy considerations brought on by war between France and England. Identifying England as both the enemy during the Revolution and the epitome of a monarchical form of government, Jefferson sided with France in the war. He had been minister there during much of the previous decade and admired the French Revolution up to that time, seeing in it the advancement of enlightened republicanism fostered by the American Revolution. Some events in France shocked Hamilton, who feared such radicalism could lead to something far worse than a monarchy —anarchy. Finally, Jefferson aligned himself with the South and farming interests. Hamilton supported the commercial interests in the Northeast. The lowcountry merchants and planters of South Carolina formed an important exception to this regional generalization.[3]

Until the latter half of the decade, division hounded the Federalists within the state and also the nation. But domestic and international events soon transpired to unite them. The Jay Treaty, negotiated in 1794 and 1795, illustrates one division among South Carolinians. John Jay, Pinckney's old nemesis from the Confederation Congress, had replaced Thomas Pinckney as ambassador to Great Britain. In negotiating a treaty to settle matters left unresolved from the Revolution, Jay capitulated on nearly every issue with the exception of the withdrawal of British forces from the American northwest. In return, the United States granted England most-favored-nation status. Jay, a New Yorker like Hamilton, failed to address many of the concerns with which he had been charged by Congress. One of these directly impacted the South. After Lord Dunmore's Proclamation in 1775, thousands of slaves fled to the British lines seeking freedom. Southerners had never been reimbursed for those losses, and the Jay Treaty remained silent on the issue. In the Northeast, home of commercial interests, trade with England would prove beneficial and help support Hamilton's programs. Most New Englanders, therefore, supported the treaty. In the South, however, support was minimal.[4]

On 16 July 1795, Charlestonians gathered at Saint Michael's Church to discuss the matter. The crowd consisted of both the lowly and elite, the city's politicians and planters sitting in the pews beside its artisans and mechanics. Former governor John Mathews presided, and John Rutledge first addressed the gathering in an oration described as "radiating more heat than light." A few days later, on the twenty-second, Charles Pinckney traveled into town from the upstate to give his opinion on the treaty. It was one of his first public appearances since his wife's death. Making his way past a gallows strung with effigies of Jay, John Adams, King George, and South Carolinians Jacob Read and William Loughton Smith, both of whom supported the treaty, he entered the church. In contrast to Rutledge's vitriol a few days earlier, Pinckney assured those in attendance that his speech would be more rational, "moderation," he asserted, "being essential to the discovery of the truth." In this moderation one can see the developing ideology that led to his eventual support of Thomas Jefferson and the Republicans.[5]

He began by examining both the authority for making the treaty and the person who negotiated it. Nowhere in the Constitution did President Washington have the authority to appoint a minister to negotiate a treaty without first explaining the specifics of the proposed negotiations to the Senate. "The words 'by and with the advice of the Senate' [in Article 2, section 2] admit no other explanation," he stated. "He cannot be said to advise with them upon a measure, if he forms a treaty without their knowledge, and merely leaves to them the power of determining whether they will ratify it or not, after it has been solemnly concluded by the minister." He criticized Jay, recalling his treaty with Spain years earlier and the manner in which he had negotiated the right to navigation of the Mississippi. Being careful not to criticize Washington regarding either issue, he concluded the first part of this speech by stating he could not understand why the president had acted as he did, "considering [his] character, general good sense, and unshaken integrity." Although he never mentioned his name, he seemed to indicate that his cousin Thomas, whom Jay replaced, would have been a much better person to serve as negotiator.[6]

In this first segment of the speech, Pinckney indicated his view—at least in circumstances surrounding the Jay Treaty—that the Constitution should be interpreted narrowly. The theory of implied powers greatly offended anyone who construed the Constitution so narrowly as to assert that the president had to submit his intentions for treaty making to the Senate prior to the beginnings of those efforts. In such a strict interpretation Pinckney fell in line with Jefferson and others who used the same logic arguing against Hamilton's bank.

Pinckney next addressed the specifics of the treaty, and several themes emerged. He reiterated his devotion to France. In several places he complained about Jay's attitudes towards the American allies: "The negotiator has endeavored to render this country as unfriendly as he could to the French. . . . He has displayed all his resentment to the only truly useful and valuable ally we have ever had!" He also lamented the effect the treaty would have on American trade and commerce in general and on South Carolina in particular:

> We are entirely agricultural and while our commerce is unfettered and the present competition for our productions encouraged and protected by law, while we are sure of having American shipping in sufficient numbers to support our commercial rights, our planters will grow rich, the trade of our merchants become every day more extensive and respectable, and our country will be happy. But let it be once known that foundation is laid for the diminution of our shipping, that we are not to enjoy the rights of neutrality or an

> independent commerce, that our vessels are to be liable to seizure, and we are again to look to other nations for the means of transportation, it will at once dampen the hopes of our planters and merchants and injure the value of their estates, check their enterprising views, and lessen the general happiness.

He blasted Great Britain, maintaining that "They are therefore more dependent on us than we are upon them and our situation will soon force from them a much more advantageous trade than the treaty proposes."[7]

He closed by warning that, if ratified, the treaty would become a law from which there could be no recourse unless all the parties involved consented. He urged Washington to maintain his standing with the American people by rejecting it. Otherwise, he averred, "they will always lament that a name which has hitherto been so distinguished should, at the close of its career, be voluntarily fixed to so injurious and degrading a measure." Finishing on an optimistic note, he assured those listening that he believed Washington would make the right decision. "We know we can trust him," he said and, taking one final jab at his nemesis Jay, added he "wished the event had proved we could have trusted Mr. Jay as well." Those assembled greeted the speech enthusiastically. One observer described it as "a most tremendous burst of indignant eloquence."[8]

The first portion of this eloquence is much more informative of Charles Pinckney's political ideology than his specific oppositions to the treaty itself. His loyalty to France and his disdain for John Jay became evident. In three areas—his strict interpretation of the Constitution, his distaste for Great Britain and devotion to France, and his personal animosity for the Federalist Jay—he clearly aligned himself with the Jeffersonians. And in his statements regarding South Carolina, he purposely included mechanics with the planters as parties whose interests he championed. One high Federalist, Ralph Izard, resenting Pinckney's support for the mechanics, artisans, and backcountry yeomen, wrote Jacob Read that "nothing from [him] could produce much effect" because there existed "universal abhorrence and contempt" for the former governor. However, two days after the speech, Pinckney's neighbors in Christ Church Parish sent a resolution to John Mathews supporting their "fellow citizens in Charleston" and "opposing the impending treaty." And over the next few months, newspapers published resolutions from across the state opposing it. Although Pinckney's speech did not produce such a response on its own, he was certainly not "universally abhorred." In fact, in a little over a year, South Carolinians elected him to his third term as governor. The abhorrence, in all likelihood, proved universal only among certain lowcountry Federalists.[9]

When the United States eventually ratified the Jay Treaty, anti-British sentiment increased in the state, especially in the backcountry. Lowcountry residents had mixed feelings. William Loughton Smith and Jacob Read both voted to ratify it. In fact, Read cast the deciding vote—then delayed his trip home for nearly six months, fearing for his safety. But if the Federalists had split over the treaty, what they saw in the backcountry united them. The violence towards Read, the agitation against Great Britain, the example of Saint-Dominique, and the threat to stability in the state as a result of the backcountry's rabble-rousing all contributed to unifying the Charleston elite. By the election of 1796, although unified, they could not sway the state for John Adams, even though native son Charles Cotesworth Pinckney shared the Federalist ticket.[10]

As the state became increasingly Republican and despite Jacob Read's assessment, Charles Pinckney had no problem winning his third term as governor in 1796. Continuing to use both his office and Greenwich plantation as his means for building a political base, he spent the next four years involved in politics and experimenting with the growth of cotton. Recognizing the economic potential in transportation endeavors in the upstate, he also reestablished a ferry at his Mount Tacitus plantation on the Santee River.

In 1798, the threat of a French-instigated invasion of the state by black troops from the West Indies confronted him. Seeing the ratification of the Jay Treaty as an alliance between the United States and Great Britain, the French government began making plans for a possible invasion of the American continent. The tension increased when Adams won the presidency in 1796 instead of the more sympathetic Jefferson. France expelled the American ambassador and began harassing American shipping. Adams, seeking to protect United States commerce, sent a delegation including Charles Cotesworth Pinckney to France. The French government made matters worse when it rebuffed the group after not so subtly suggesting a payment from the United States as a means to avert a crisis, resulting in the sensational XYZ affair. By April and May of 1798, rumors of war between France and her old ally ran rampant up and down the eastern seaboard, especially in the South, where the proximity to the French West Indies caused even greater concern.[11]

Governor Pinckney wasted little time in acting as the rumors increased. In the early part of the summer of 1798, he urged fortification of defenses throughout the state. In May, he ordered troops on the coast to their highest state of urgency. He visited Col. Christian Senf at his home and discussed the situation with him. Senf, a Hessian captured at the Battle of Saratoga, had been sent south by Henry Laurens to be the state's engineer. Pinckney also rode up to Columbia to meet with the major generals and brigadiers of the state's upper division, advising them to be ready at a minute's notice to move towards the coast, if necessary. The state, meanwhile, constructed gunboats and a new fort on Sullivan's Island.[12]

After entering into agreements with the governors of North Carolina and Georgia to assist each other in case of invasion, Pinckney called nearly forty members of the legislature from the lowcountry to meet at his home on Meeting Street and discuss the situation. At the meeting, the representatives agreed to allocate £7,000 for defense and £2,000 additional for powder, if needed. Pinckney justified the meeting prior to the formal convening of the legislature scheduled for November as an attempt to deal with an emergency situation. According to Pinckney, all assembled decided "to take upon themselves to agree to such measures of defense as might immediately be gone into." He cited the example of Gov. William Moultrie, who called a similar meeting in 1793 in response to rumors of a slave insurrection in Virginia, as precedent. In short, the group prepared for what most feared would be imminent war. On 24 July, a few days afterwards, the *City Gazette and Daily Advertiser* applauded Pinckney for his efforts, writing that South Carolina's citizens believed Pinckney was doing everything in his power "to meet, or avert" the "prospect and approach of evil."[13]

When the legislature finally met in November, one of Pinckney's first messages included an explanation of the above steps he had taken to meet the threat. He also informed them of a wide variety of his views on different issues. Because he would finalize his political break with his family a few months later, this message is perhaps the best indicator of his ideology at that crucial period. It illuminates his views on social issues like slavery, education, and civil liberties and is one of only a few documents that reveal so much about his opinions on such a broad range of issues.

Despite the urgency of the situation brought on by the possible war with France, he did not begin his message with the explanation of his activities with lowcountry legislators over the summer. Instead, he returned to a favorite subject: the situation of the judiciary within the state. Just as he had done several years previously, he reiterated the importance to the entire state of having an effective and available system, "neither the Rich, the Honoured, or the Humble being without its influence or above its control." Pinckney was convinced that the extent of judicial power must be limited for it to be "consistent with the principles of Republican Government." Only in instances of contempt of court should a judge have a right to usurp a trial by jury. Judges should have very little discretion regarding punishment of crimes, he asserted, challenging the legislature to be as specific as possible when enacting statutes pertaining to criminal law. He believed that the caprice of judges should be limited because so few administered justice to so many, concluding, "It is to guard the privileges of our citizens and the great Palladium of our Liberty the Freedom of the Press against injuries that may arise from the passions and prejudices of any individual that I have made these remarks."

The seeming disjointed allusion to freedom of the press actually reflects Pinckney's opinion of the reaction of the Adams administration and others to the French threat. Over the next two years, with the enactment of the Alien and Sedition Acts, Pinckney became more convinced than ever that Hamilton and the Federalists posed a threat to fundamental liberties in the young republic. He continued: "Considering as I have always done the Freedom of the press as among the greatest of our public blessings, while I almost adore its good qualities, I am content to throw a veil over its abuses. I know it is impossible to touch without destroying it and as I believe it to be the only true means of preserving our national Liberty in the world, I trust that our country which has received such important benefits from its operations will never cease to cherish and protect it. I hope it will be our boast as I know it is our interest while other Nations are endeavoring to fetter and destroy, to guard it as a sacred trust received from our ancestors and to deliver it with its rights undiminished to those who are to succeed us." Within a few years, Pinckney saw the rights he so cherished threatened by political opponents under the guise of a wartime national emergency.

He next discussed his opposition to judicial review. He did so by posing a question: whether it would be better for citizens of the state to have their laws determined by the regularly elected houses in the legislature or by judges appointed for a term of good behavior and accountable to no one. Obviously he preferred the first and advised the legislature to amend the state constitution to prevent judicial usurpation of their power. He spoke of the importance of juries, stating that "no Government can too highly praise their rights." He emphasized the importance of a defendant being judged by his or her peers and offered suggestions to improve upon the system in South Carolina, including his belief that only three-fourths of a jury need agree in order to reach a verdict in civil cases. Although he preferred arbitration in civil cases to actual trials, he realized its impracticality at times and thought his "three-fourths suggestion" could be an appropriate solution.

He addressed punishment of white criminals, stating he preferred confinement over any type of corporal or capital remedy except in the case of murder. "It is moderation which rules a people," he asserted, "and not excesses of severity." He continued, "Civil liberty flourishes most when the laws deduce every punishment from the peculiar nature of every crime" and concluded that certainty, not severity, was the more effective form of punishment.

Then he turned to the slave codes and treatment of blacks. He advised the legislature to review the codes and enact stricter measures regarding slave passes. He also encouraged more effective slave patrols. Then he contradicted himself on the matter of punishment, suggesting that the introduction of a "free person of color or slave" from the West Indies be deemed a capital offense.

He concluded emphatically: "As most of you are planters and deeply concerned in giving all the security and protection in your power to this species of property, I am sure you will excuse the anxiety I feel in recommending the subject to your early and earnest attention as they are the instrument of our cultivation and of the first importance to our wealth and commercial consequence, in the present uncertain and eventful state of things there can be no subject which calls more powerfully on you for attention nor none which I think you will more promptly apply." The horrors relayed by white refugees from Saint-Dominque obviously weighed heavily on his mind, just as it did on most of the representatives in the legislature.

From slavery, he moved to education. He recommended that the legislature take steps to establish public schools, and in his comments are found his recipe for a successful republican government—although much of what he said probably did not impress the lowcountry elite. He reminded the legislature of the importance of an informed and educated electorate, necessary to the selection of the best representatives who in turn would enact the best laws. "Be assured that *General Education* is the only solid foundation upon which true Republicanism can ever rest," he wrote.

> It is always the characteristic of a free people while a deplorable ignorance too frequently prevails in the Dominions of the Despot. In a land of Freedom like this, where no distinctions are known but those of merit and talents, where individuals are daily promoted in consequence of their own qualifications and without regard to the merit of their Ancestors, it is certainly the Duty of the State to aid in affording to all the Benefits of Education. You will not only be enabled to acquire for the public the services of its most promising citizens in whatever situations they may be found, but you will introduce generally among the People those manners which alone can preserve the Republican form.

He also urged the publication of the laws passed during each session and the distribution of them throughout the state in order to acquaint all of its inhabitants with enacted legislation.

Not until the end of his message did he finally inform the session of his activities of the previous months, preparing the state for possible war. He held out hope that the situation with France could be resolved and that an "honorable peace" could be negotiated. He stated that only a few years of true peace could enable the United States, through its trade and commerce, to become one of the major powers of the world.[14]

The republican ideology espoused by Charles Pinckney in this message obviously gave some of his Federalist opponents cause for concern. They desperately sought to regain control of the state's politics in time for the election of 1800. In early 1799, Federalists in South Carolina had received a boost in public opinion when Charles Cotesworth Pinckney returned home in February after his trip to France and the ensuing XYZ affair. But events both within the state and on the national level continued to work against them. Governor Pinckney became a major player in stopping this Federalist surge.

South Carolinians remained alert and vigilant for invasion, and most maintained a hostile attitude towards France. As the year progressed, Alexander Hamilton began using those tensions to gain power for his followers. He persuaded President Adams to enact the Alien and Sedition Acts, which trussed the right of a free press in the bindings of Hamilton's lust for power. He also persuaded Congress to fund a large standing army, of which, as inspector general, he would be in charge. His schemes caused both anger and resentment from Adams and would split the Federalist Party. By 1800, with the party in disarray and despite their strong presence in the South Carolina lowcountry, it looked as though the Federalists could lose the state again in the election of that year.

Pinckney worked hard to ensure the loss. He was incensed by the Alien and Sedition Acts, which resulted in the imprisonment of several Republican newspaper editors. Although he had advocated formation of a navy in his 1795 speech against the Jay Treaty, a large standing federal army commanded by Alexander Hamilton went far beyond anything he had ever imagined regarding the nation's forces. He had grown much closer to Jefferson and his Republican followers, fearing that the Federalists' ideas and policies would result in the central government he had helped create becoming much too strong. He had also witnessed on numerous occasions the mistreatment of the backcountry inhabitants by the lowcountry elite. It had only sharpened his resolve to promote republicanism, which he felt was best protected by the Jeffersonian Republicans. By early 1799 he had become one of the key political players in South Carolina and an ardent supporter of Thomas Jefferson.

When the federal government met in Philadelphia for the last time that winter, Pinckney had a close view of all the activity. The South Carolina legislature had elected him to the United States Senate, replacing John Hunter, who had resigned finding it "inconvenient to serve any longer." Pinckney presented his credentials on 16 February and, although far removed from his political base in Columbia, his presence in Philadelphia strengthened his contacts throughout the nation. He had not served at the national level for several years, and doing so at such an opportune time allowed him to make friends who would assist him over the coming months as he worked on behalf of a Jefferson presidential candidacy.[15]

Pinckney may not have realized at the time how his Senate seat would enable him to work much more effectively not only in South Carolina but also on a national level during the 1800 election. It gave him a forum where he could present his views on various issues and eventually publish his Senate speeches for distribution throughout the country. While he has been recognized as the father of the Jeffersonian-Republican party in South Carolina, his efforts on the national level have nearly gone unnoticed. When he arrived in Philadelphia, the election was nearly two years away. He spent that time getting to know his Republican allies and assessing the Federalist opposition that controlled the Senate. He met with Vice President Jefferson, and the two became confidants, with Pinckney providing the Virginian with copies of his own published works and promising to work hard to assure a Republican victory in the next election. He also continued refining his republican/Republican ideology in his speeches on the Senate floor.[16]

In early 1800, he addressed the Senate on the appropriateness of appointing federal judges to additional offices. Senator Pinckey averred that members of the judiciary, in order to be impartial, should be restricted from additional public trusts while on the bench. He had made similar arguments to the South Carolina legislature in his November message. He specifically addressed President Adams' plan to appoint Chief Justice Oliver Ellsworth as an envoy to France to assist with negotiations. Adams had originally chosen William Vans Murray for the job, but Hamilton and other high Federalists feared Murray would acquiesce to too many French demands. In order to placate them, Adams submitted the names of Ellsworth and North Carolina Federalist governor William Davie to assist Murray. Republicans, pleased with Adams' selection of the more moderate Murray, were disappointed when the chief justice's name was added as an accompanying minister. Pinckney even considered the introduction of an amendment to the Constitution to block the move, but decided against it because of the time involved in ratification. The bill he presented to the Senate after his address prohibited federal judges from holding any other public office. It lost by only two votes, and the Federalist-controlled body eventually confirmed Ellsworth, Murray, and Davie in one of the final acts of the spring session.[17]

Pinckney delivered another major speech on 31 January 1800, and by this time, according to friend and brother-in-law David Ramsay, he "warm[ed] for the election of Jefferson." The subject concerned a topic dear to his heart: trial by jury. No uniform method existed for choosing jurors for federal trials. Some states did not select juries by lot but allowed sheriffs or marshals to impanel them as needed from whomever they chose. To Pinckney, such ability threatened the right to a trial by a jury of one's peers. He approached the matter in the United States Senate with much the same language and logic as he did during his message to the South Carolina legislature on the same issue. "Viewing as I do impartial juries as among the most indispensable ingredients of a free government, it is my duty to declare—and I solemnly do deliver it as my opinion —that in those states in which the federal marshals have a right to summon jurors as they please, the people *are not free!*" he exclaimed. "That in those states the impartiality of your judicial tribunals and the purity of the administration of justice must depend not on the laws but the integrity and honest independence of a marshal." Such improvements, he believed, should also be advocated throughout state courts. He cited as a proper example his home state, wherein such improvements had "enlightened and . . . distinguished [its] love of liberty." Conversely, he chastised Virginia and Pennsylvania for their jury selection procedures.[18]

At first glance, opinions and orations regarding the selection of juries might not seem an integral part of the battle between Republicans and Federalists. However, the connection becomes clear upon examination of the manner in which Pinckney couched his argument:

> It is vain to think of repealing sedition laws or asserting the liberty of the press, as secured by the Constitution, until this reform takes place. This power in a marshal is a more complete and severe check on the press and the right of the people to remark on public affairs than ten thousand sedition laws, because here the power to select, and by that means govern, the opinion of juries is continual, always increasing and in a great degree subject on every trial to the wishes and directions of a President. In times of party, when opinions run high, and contending factions oppose each other with violence, it is then truly dreadful. Justice, which has been represented and ought forever to be blind to the political opinions of men, becomes on these occasions as keen-eyed as the eagle. It pounces into every recess and corner of a state, drags forth the avowed and political enemies of the accuser, and arrays them on his jury. I will hope, for the freedom of our country, this has not yet taken place—but that it may and should be guarded against, no man will deny.

Such forceful eloquence continued to uphold Pinckney's reputation as an orator and one of the most effective speakers for the Jeffersonians. His effectiveness did not confine itself to the realms of oratory, however. He also began putting together a political coalition to assure the success of the Republicans in November.[19]

This political purpose became apparent in his next major speech. In February, Federalists presented a bill before the Senate to continue a nonintercourse act with France. Pinckney and most of the Republicans were outraged.

He wasted no time attacking the matter from a partisan perspective, using constitutional, political, and regional arguments to support his position. "I consider [the bill] springing from the same source with most of the measures which have been agitated for the last two years, particularly the provisional army, and as going to establish the precedent of granting to the executive, powers, in my judgement, unwarranted by the Constitution." He asserted that as a delegate to the Constitutional Convention, he could better assess the intent of that document and its framers than many of his fellow senators. Such an assertion would become a theme for Pinckney for the remainder of his life. He believed that Congress alone had the right to regulate commerce and that the bill gave entirely too much power to Adams. He also stated that by continuing nonintercourse with France and her possessions, the greatest harm would come to the South, greater even than the harm that would come to France itself. He singled out Maryland, Virginia, North and South Carolina, and Georgia and their staples—tobacco, rice, cotton, and corn. In closing, he hurled one last arrow at the Federalists. Quoting Algernon Sydney, he compared the Adams administration to the reign of a corrupt Caesar that caused the downfall of Rome. Pinckney and his allies lost on the matter. The Federalist-controlled Senate continued the act by a margin of nine votes.[20]

In the minority, Senator Pinckney served on a committee to revise presidential election law in case of dispute. He had previous involvement with election law in South Carolina when the mode of selecting presidential electors had been changed there. As a result, Republicans in the state generally saw the election of 1798 as a triumph for their party. The state house of representatives had been able to elect a Republican speaker, and Pinckney himself had obtained his seat in the Senate partly as a result of the amendments. Looking ahead to the upcoming presidential election, Republicans sought to change the way the state chose its presidential electors. Assuming that their gains would continue for the foreseeable future, the Republican-controlled legislature took the process of choosing electors away from the public in the districts at large and placed it squarely in its own ranks. Henceforth, the party in control of the state house would also control the electors. Pinckney began urging fellow Republicans in North Carolina, Georgia, and Virginia to change their election processes as well. He wrote to James Madison in May and September, urging the Virginian to embrace the changes. "The success of the Republican Interest depends upon this act," he implored. "I am to intreat you not only to use all your own Influence, but to Write & speak to all your Friends in the republican interest in the state Legislature to have it done." Virginia did not change its mode of choosing electors precisely as Pinckney had advised, but changes occurred that produced similar results.[21]

Pinckney's committee in the Senate faced the possibility that a grand committee might be appointed by Congress to elect the president and vice president without regard to electors in the states. Such usurpation caused him a great deal of concern and gave him another opportunity to espouse his Republican ideology before the Senate. "I suppose it will hardly yet be denied that the people are the common fountain of authority to both the federal and state governments; that the Constitution reposed exclusively in the state legislatures for the formation of a part of the federal government and in the people for another part; and that in the appointment or formation of their part, the rights of the state governments are the pillars upon which the federal government must rest and that without a cordial and active performance of their duty the latter could not exist." He reminded his fellow senators that the Sedition Act had encountered much criticism and stated he found it difficult to believe that now the Federalists would contemplate such a power grab at the expense of the state governments as the appointment of a grand committee would be. Again the Federalists prevailed, and the Senate passed the bill to create the grand committee by a vote of sixteen to twelve. But the House made changes and sent it back to the Senate, which disagreed with the changes and delayed consideration of the matter until after the start of the next session. By that time the point was moot: Jefferson had been elected president, and the Federalists had lost much of their power.[22]

A tangential issue arose from Pinckney's work on the committee that caused some of his most vociferous attacks on his Federalist opponents. On 19 February, William Duane, editor of the *Philadelphia Aurora,* a Republican newspaper, published a story stating that Pinckney had not been consulted before the Senate voted on the bill even though he was a member of the committee. Connecticut Federalist senator Uriah Tracy introduced a resolution that Duane be summonsed before the Senate to account for the story. Pinckney was again outraged. He viewed such a summons as another example of Federalists trampling on individual liberties, especially two that he held most dear: the right to trial by jury and freedom of the press. On 6 March he spoke at length before the Senate, stating he felt compelled to do so, especially since Tracy's resolution mentioned him by name.[23]

He began by asking three questions: "What are the privileges of Congress and how far are they defined by the Constitution and what is the liberty of the press as it respects those privileges?" In a manner more sarcastic than sincere and taking direct aim at the Federalists who controlled the Senate, he stated that answering the questions required that he "advance doctrines extraordinary here." He argued that any power not explicitly mentioned in the Constitution was beyond the scope of Congress. He quoted from section 5 of Article 1, wherein punishment by Congress of its own members is allowed. He stated that nowhere did Congress have the right to demand someone appear before it simply because that person had offended it. He compared it to a president having the ability to physically attack someone he believed had libeled him.

Moving to the issue of freedom of the press, he observed that such a question had never been before either the Senate or the House of Representatives. In not-too-subtle a fashion, he blamed his Federalist opponents for causing it to be asked at that moment. Averring that the United States had been the best example of a government respecting freedom of the press, he stated optimistically, "However clouded or interrupted this freedom has in my opinion lately been, I entertain a hope that in a few months all its shackles will be removed." He touted the advantages of a free press to a room full of men he believed should have been quite familiar with his ideology and reasoning. The press had not only the right but the responsibility to examine public officers: "That the printing presses shall be free to every person who undertakes to examine the proceedings of the legislature or any branch of the government and no law shall ever be made to restrain the right thereof; that the free communication of thoughts and opinions is one of the most invaluable rights of man and every citizen may freely speak, write, or print on any subject, being responsible for the abuse of that liberty; that in prosecution for the publication of papers investigating the official conduct of officers or men in a public capacity or where the matter published is proper for public information, the truth thereof may be given in evidence; and in all indictments for libels, the *JURY* shall have a right to determine the law and the fact under the direction of the court as in other cases." He closed by addressing the extent to which the Congress could legitimately usurp the right of a free press and found, not surprisingly, the answer to be never. Admitting there could be possible abuses from time to time, he used the same language he had used in South Carolina, stating he was willing to "throw a veil" over those abuses. He cited Frederick the Great as being tolerant of many of his critics and then chastised certain "enlightened" Americans for being less tolerant than the European emperor. "Why should a government that means well or is confident of its uprightness and ability ever fear the press?" he asked.[24]

Despite his speech, the Federalists passed the resolution summonsing Duane. He appeared before the Senate but requested counsel. The Senate agreed but with stipulations. When Duane could not find counsel who agreed to the stipulations, he failed to return. The Federalists then directed the sergeant at arms to forcibly bring Duane back before them, but he remained elusive until they adjourned. On the last day, they passed another resolution requesting President Adams to begin legal proceedings against him. Once again, the election of Jefferson ended the matter.

Thomas Jefferson's election and the Republican victory in 1800 occurred in large part because of Pinckney's actions nationally and at home in South Carolina. He put together a coalition in his home state that held together even though another one of South Carolina's prominent native sons opposed Jefferson. He corresponded with Republicans in other states, sending them pamphlets —some of which he had written—advocating the party. He urged that they be widely distributed and requested literature from other areas of the country to be mailed to him so that he could dispense it throughout South Carolina.[25]

Pinckney was in such a hurry to come home before the first session of the Sixth Congress ended on 14 May, he dislocated his arm in an accident. Upon arriving in South Carolina, he wrote James Madison and others urging them to change their states' election laws and published a collection of his own speeches before the Senate that he believed answered the all-important question, "What do the Republican interests want by so zealously attempting a change of men?" He sent them to various states and urged allies to distribute them along with letters he had written years earlier and now also published as "Letters from a Republican Farmer." He continued to express his concern for the direction of the nation and his fear "that there is a design to change the picture of government and to take from the people and the states their right to elect their chief magistrate . . . and that no man can answer or justify it."[26]

The election of 1800 revolved around many of the issues on which Pinckney had taken such a strong and public stand, including the Alien and Sedition Acts, Hamilton's army, and the crisis with France. In May, the Federalists selected sitting president John Adams as their nominee, despite a split in the party. They also nominated Charles Pinckney's cousin, Charles Cotesworth, as Adams' running mate. Alexander Hamilton had developed major differences with Adams and preferred the election of Charles Cotesworth. He was counting on South Carolina to swing the election in favor of its native son. Republicans nominated Jefferson, along with Aaron Burr of New York. With his cousin on the Federalist ticket, Charles Pinckney's support of Jefferson placed him directly at odds with his family.[27]

In late August, he wrote a letter to Sheriff John Bynum of Orangeburg District. Although Bynum was a Republican, Pinckney hardly mentioned politics. He wrote to forestall a foreclosure on some of his property located in the district. Pinckney had been so active in politics he had been neglecting his own finances. Unwilling to be distracted from political endeavors, he appointed his cousin Daniel D'Oyley as his attorney to alleviate some of the duties involved in managing his various affairs. Slowly but surely his debts had continued to grow. Much of the debt could be traced to that of his father and his uncle, Miles Brewton, but while the shadow had lengthened he remained aloof, devoting most of his time to the coming election and not his plantations or law practice. "As to my own affairs, I never think of them," he informed Jefferson. "To secure your election has employed me, mind, body, and estate since June."[28]

He did find time to spend with his children. He read lessons to his son, Henry, and purchased a piano for his daughters and listened attentively as they practiced. Frances could often be found "playing, at ten years old, a tune and singing to it," he wrote James Madison. He confided that he often found it hard to leave his children and be away from them, "but you know I have always loved politics and I find as I grow older I become more fond of them."[29]

Otherwise, in late 1800, as he informed Jefferson, he devoted himself almost exclusively to the Republican cause. By mid October he worried that his actions might "sever and divide" him from his cousin's family. Uneasy but undeterred, he began questioning the legitimacy of those who would vote in Charleston, the Federalist power base in the state, "on the grounds that many have voted who had no rights and are not Citizens." He attacked the Hamiltonians, expressing concern that "federal Interests" were doing everything they could to shore up the "Banks and Custom Houses" in Charleston and "shake Republicanism in South Carolina to its foundations." Recognizing the more friendly interior, he wrote Jefferson, "I rejoice that our Legislature meets 130 or 40 miles from the sea."[30]

By late November he had communicated with governors of several states and distributed his pamphlets both within and without South Carolina. With only three days to go before the election, he left his home in Charleston to be on the scene in Columbia at the selection of presidential electors. Charles Cotesworth's family had already stopped speaking to him, and Federalists criticized him for remaining in the state when he should have already headed north for the beginning of the next session of Congress. "My situation here is peculiarly delicate and singular," he wrote Jefferson, "and the federalists view me with a very jealous eye." His reputation began to be attacked nationally as well. A Federalist paper in Connecticut, responding to similar allegations regarding Charles Cotesworth, accused him of sexual impropriety. Despite the criticisms and the rift with his family, he remained dedicated to the cause, "urged by those principles it is my duty never to forsake, and well convinced that the election depends on this state."[31]

When the election took place the following Tuesday, 25 November, Pinckney held his coalition together and assured the success of the party. On 2 December the electors gathered in Columbia to make the vote official the following day. Pinckney rested at Greenwich, awaiting the result he had long anticipated and for which he had worked so diligently. When word came that the Republican ticket had carried the state, he wrote to the future president, congratulating him and apologizing for remaining in South Carolina longer than he probably should have. The apology allowed him to restate all he had done for Jefferson both locally and nationally. He recounted how he had set out to see that Jefferson became president from the time he had arrived in the Senate two years earlier. He listed the publications he had distributed and the contacts he had made and with whom he had corresponded on the national level. He wrote that the Federalists in South Carolina had been doing everything in their power to combat his efforts and only his presence in Columbia had stopped them. "Most of our friends," he wrote, "believe that my exertions and influence owing to the information of federal affairs I gave them, has in great measure contributed to the decision and [been] indispensable to your success." He would remain in the state only a little longer, he concluded, "fixing the republican interest in this state like a rock from which future federal storms may beat with less probability of success."[32]

The complete details of Pinckney's activities during the pivotal election may never be known. He began his "Writings and operations for the Elections . . . throughout every part of the state" as early as June. By corresponding with South Carolina Republicans and keeping apprised of conditions around the state; by being on the scene in Columbia when the electors met; and by engaging in plain, old-fashioned hard work, Charles Pinckney had held together a coalition that succeeded at choosing Republican electors in South Carolina. He became a pariah among the lowcountry elite and his family for years to come. Some historians have asserted that had Charles Cotesworth Pinckney actively pursued either the presidency or vice presidency, his cousin's efforts may have failed. Charles Cotesworth had assured New England Federalists that he would not allow his state to cast any votes for him unless matched by votes for John Adams. At the time, however, the public viewed as dishonorable a candidate who actively pursued public office. Had Charles Cotesworth acted on his own behalf, he would have betrayed the contemporary notion that politicians should not get involved in their own campaigns, remaining disinterested statesmen. Charles Pinckney had much more leverage in his ability to see that Jefferson won the state than his cousin had in reducing that chance.[33]

Senator Pinckney finally left Columbia late in December, stopping by his property on the Santee River and near Winyah Bay at Georgetown. His children waited for him in Charleston, but "a most violent cold and sore throat" necessitated him stopping short of visiting them there. At Winyah he corresponded again with Jefferson regarding the tie that had eventually occurred in the electoral vote. Both Jefferson and Aaron Burr had received an equal number of votes, and the election had to be decided in the Federalist-controlled House of Representatives. By the end of January, Pinckney had finally arrived in Charleston, but his departure north had not occurred because he had reinjured his arm in a fall. Jefferson's election had not occurred either. Not until the middle of February, after numerous ballots in the House and a deal between Alexander Hamilton and a Delaware congressman did the election become final. Hamilton loathed Jefferson but feared Burr even more. Thus he persuaded James A. Bayard of Delaware to vote in support of the leader of the Republican Party.[34]

In early February, Pinckney left Charleston and sailed to New York en route to the new seat of the federal government in the city of Washington. He left New York, stopping by Philadelphia before arriving in the capital towards the end of the month, taking up residence in Georgetown. At his first opportunity, he visited Jefferson and gave him a packet of letters recommending several federal appointments for South Carolinians. He later regretted the act, believing it to be unseemly, and hoped that Jefferson would treat the incident as if it had never happened and ignore the recommendations.[35]

On 23 February he finally took his place in the Senate, more than three months after it had convened. On 4 March he and his fellow congressmen, along with a small group of spectators, watched as Jefferson took the oath of office and became the third president of the United States. Pinckney must have been proud that his efforts had been a major part of the event he witnessed. He probably thought of his own estranged family and kinsmen who had been like brothers to his father when Jefferson stated in his inaugural address, "We are all Republicans. We are all Federalists."[36]

Later in the month, Pinckney received his reward for his efforts on Jefferson's behalf. The president appointed him minister to Spain, bestowing upon him the political appointment he had desired for nearly a decade. In preparation for his Senate confirmation, he listed his achievements for Jefferson:

> I was elected a member of the legislature of this state within two months after I was of age. In the year 1784, when very young, I was sent to Congress and remained three years in that body which was all the time I could then constitutionally serve.
>
> In the year 1787 I was appointed a member of the General Convention at Philadelphia for having the Constitution of the United States and was the youngest member in that body. In this year Doctor Witherspoon by direction of the trustees of Princeton brought me a degree of LL.D. conferred by them on me.

> In the year 1790, I was appointed President of the Convention of this state for forming their Constitution and my name is now signed to it as such.
>
> I have been elected at three different times (each for a period of two years) governor of this state and was lately the Senator.

Within two months of his arrival in the new capital and after hearing Jefferson's conciliatory speech in the Senate chamber, Pinckney headed back home to prepare, at last, to go abroad.[37]

He spent several months attending to his affairs and worrying about his confirmation. Because of the animosity with which the Federalists viewed him, his nomination faced serious opposition. He pleaded with Jefferson to do all in his power and call upon their mutual "Republican friends" in order to assist him in the process. If, despite all their efforts, it appeared he would not be confirmed, he requested that Jefferson withdraw him from consideration so as not to impugn his honor. One of the criticisms centered around a long ago event: his conduct in the Confederation Congress over the first Jay Treaty. His continued pressuring of Jay—the same activity that had prejudiced him in the eyes of James Madison—came back to haunt him. But despite the concern, when his name came before his peers in the Senate, they confirmed him.[38]

Before leaving for Spain, Pinckney made arrangements for Daniel D'Oyley to continue handling his personal affairs. Many considered D'Oyley the most likely Republican to replace the Federalist collector at the Charleston customshouse in 1801. He also served as treasurer for the lower district of the state, having been elected in 1799. Pinckney felt comfortable with the trusted political figure, who also happened to be a cousin and friend. But his confidence was misplaced. His debts continued to mount. Over the previous two years, nearly fifty suits had been filed against him. One dealt with the mortgage on his property at Georgetown. Another dealt with the wages due an overseer at Fee Farm on the Ashepoo River. Still another involved wages due a servant who came to work for him shortly before Polly had died. Although he satisfied some of the debts before going abroad, he left others to be handled by D'Oyley. As Pinckney left Charleston in August of 1801 to fulfill a longstanding dream, his financial affairs were becoming a nightmare.[39]

Seven

Forward to Spain

Charles Pinckney's appointment to the court at Madrid finally enabled him to realize his dream of traveling abroad. But within three years of his arrival on the Iberian peninsula, he had become increasingly unhappy and grew anxious to return home. He had received word that some of his plantations lay in ruin and his financial situation had continued to decline. He wrote a long series of letters imploring secretary of state James Madison to allow him to leave, but nearly a year elapsed before he finally departed. On 12 January 1806, after two months on often stormy seas, he wrote to Thomas Jefferson, "I have the honour to inform you that I have this moment arrived and have thank God found my family well." He had served as minister to Spain for just over four years.[1]

During his term in Madrid, dissatisfaction with his performance existed at the highest levels of the Republican administration. In early 1804, Jefferson had sent a letter to James Monroe regarding Pinckney's performance. Monroe had been appointed special envoy and assigned to assist Pinckney in negotiating with Spain over the purchase of Florida. Jefferson's letter stated that some people in Washington believed Pinckney insufficient for his post in Spain. Although Jefferson did not reveal who had made the insinuations, they must have weighed heavily on his mind, for he pleaded with Monroe, "Pray, avail yourself of his vanity, his expectations, his fears, and whatever will weigh with him to induce him to ask leave to return, and obtain from him to be the bearer of the letter yourself. You will render us in this the most acceptable service possible. His enemies here are perpetually dragging his character in the dirt, and charging it on the administration. He does, or ought to know this, and to feel the necessity of coming home to vindicate himself, if he looks to anything further in the career of honor." Despite Jefferson's pleadings and even Pinckney's own desire to return home, he remained in Spain two more years.[2]

A major result of Jefferson's letter is that Charles Pinckney has been dismissed as an ineffective minister to Spain. Historians have relied on it to develop a picture of his character and reputation that is less than flattering. But the fact remains that he did not return home as both he and Jefferson desired. The postponement of his departure occurred because of the integrity and effectiveness with which he conducted his affairs and the favorable impression he made on his old friend James Monroe. Unfortunately, his extended stay in Spain also contributed to his economic problems at home and, when he returned to South Carolina, he found his finances in ruin.[3]

During his years in Spain, most of Pinckney's time was spent on three major issues. First, he attempted to negotiate settlement of spoliation claims of the United States against Spain. He succeeded in doing so, but the United States Senate delayed ratification of the treaty for so long that conditions had changed and Spain refused to ratify it. He also attempted to secure Spanish acquiescence to the Louisiana Purchase. He succeeded almost completely in this, perhaps his most important task. Finally, he attempted to obtain Florida from Spain, but even with the assistance of special envoy James Monroe, he failed. Thus he accomplished two of his three major tasks, and the third was so complex both he and James Monroe could not resolve the issue. In fact, a solution would not be found for nearly fifteen years.[4]

Pinckney arrived at the port of Den Helder in Holland on 8 September 1801 after a fifty-six-day voyage across the Atlantic, enduring strong easterly winds that slowed his progress and delayed him five days off the coast of Holland. He did not arrive in Spain until more than two months later, after visiting The Hague, Brussels, Paris, and Bordeaux. In Bordeaux, consul Isaac Coe Barret gave him a four-volume set of Neville Wyndham's *Travels through Europe.* In Paris, he contracted an inflammation in his eye that, in all probability, contributed to the delay in his arrival in Spain. He wrote Madison on 11 November indicating he was in the country, but he apparently did not reach Madrid until around 9 December, suffering from a cold and fever that incapacitated him for several weeks. Because he arrived so late, his predecessor, David Humphrey, had to delay his departure from Spain and expressed concern to Madison that he had been forced to sail during a season of abundant inclement weather.[5]

Humphrey was not the only source of dissatisfaction with Pinckney confronting James Madison. Pinckney's own secretary, John Graham, soon took the unconventional and somewhat extreme step of sending a letter to the secretary of state urging him to replace the South Carolinian with "a man of talents and address." Why would John Graham have gone above the head of his immediate superior and communicate directly with the secretary of state? The answer probably lies in the relationship between the two. Madison appears to have been Graham's mentor and wrote that he was "as among the most worthy of men and estimable of citizens." When Graham heard Pinckney had been appointed minister to Spain, he probably inquired of his mentor, asking about the future minister for whom he would be working. Madison had formed his opinion of Pinckney nearly fifteen years earlier and by this time, according to some historians, "loathed" the South Carolinian. There is no record of any previous correspondence or conversation between Madison and Graham regarding Pinckney, but it is not unreasonable to suspect that Madison probably expressed his disdain for Pinckney to his young protégé. In any event, it did not take too long before contention set in.[6]

Having seen parts of western Europe in his travels to Madrid, Pinckney next set his sights on the south, especially Italy. He began planning for a trip almost immediately, hoping to leave from Barcelona during one of the Spanish court's many sojourns there, since that city was located about half the distance from Madrid to Italy. He found himself so busy his trip did not actually occur until late 1802. John Graham was not happy. He contended that, as secretary remaining in Madrid and tending to business while Pinckney traveled, he should receive the minister's salary. Pinckney, however, maintained he would be furthering American interests in Italy since no United States minister served in that country. He wrote Madison regarding his trip and assured him that he and Graham remained on "the most intimate terms of friendship."[7]

In November, the Spanish court had been in session in Barcelona. Pinckney and Graham attended court there and on the fourteenth, Graham returned to Madrid and Pinckney left for Italy. He had originally planned to take an American frigate from the port at Barcelona to Naples, Genoa, or Livorno, Italy. Unable to secure passage, he decided instead to travel by land. He headed north to the French Riviera, stopping at Perpignan. There he probably took the Canal de la Robine north to its junction with the Canal du Languedoc. He floated east on the canal's calm waters, passing through the Malpas Tunnel and then on to Béziers. En route, he passed over a set of eight stair-step locks that facilitated his voyage and most likely fascinated him. In the late eighteenth century, South Carolinians had begun building canals between various natural waterways, helping unite the backcountry with the lowcountry. Investors in these companies usually consisted of representatives from both regions who would benefit from improved transportation within the state. Although Pinckney did not have any economic interests in such a project, he was in all likelihood interested from a geopolitical point of view, as such transportation networks could play a crucial role in his vision for the state.[8]

From Béziers, he made his way to Montpellier and Nîmes. In Nîmes, he may have marveled at the Maison-Carrée or the Temple of Diana, just as Thomas Jefferson had done fifteen years earlier. He pressed on to Marseilles, preparing to leave France and head into Italy. Whether he went by way of land or water is not known. But had he chosen the former, he would have most likely crossed the Alps and viewed the Italian rice fields around Vercelli and Novara. As a rice planter and South Carolinian, he would have been supremely interested in the cultivation of the crop in Italy, especially if he and the president had discussed the matter before he left Washington the previous year. In 1787, while traveling through the same region, Jefferson had wanted to send Edward Rutledge rice seeds from Italy, but customs prevented him from doing so. Pinckney may have decided to see the rice fields in Italy for himself after discussing the trip with Jefferson. If he traveled to Italy via water, he probably sailed from either Marseilles or Toulon, east across the Ligurian Sea to Livorno, where he arrived on 20 November.[9]

A little over a week later, on 28 November, John Graham fired off a personal letter to Madison, apologizing to the secretary of state for intruding on him in that manner. He stated that, before leaving on his trip, Pinckney had refused to give him credit for his salary, leaving him with only twenty-five dollars after expenses on which to live. He had been forced to move into Pinckney's house as a result, assuring Madison he used only the kitchen and the furniture in "the room where I sit." He continued, contradicting Pinckney's previous assertions that the two remained on good terms, "I cannot by any means admit the accuracy of the statements which he has given you. . . . His letter is certainly calculated to give an unfair impression of existing circumstances and may perhaps induce you to suppose that I have discovered a selfishness unbecoming my situation." Although he assured Madison he would agree to whatever decision the president made regarding his receipt of Pinckney's salary, Graham added that he did not believe Pinckney should have ever traveled to Italy in the first place, as amusement, not business, had been the sole purpose for the trip.[10]

In an ironic coincidence, on the same day, Pinckney, still in Livorno, also wrote Madison. He briefly described his journey through southern France and informed the secretary of state that he had been collecting information regarding commerce and would meet with consuls regarding their accounts. He also informed Madison he had heard that Rufus King, minister to France, had also been taking a tour of Switzerland, while the minister to Great Britain, Robert R. Livingston, toured Holland. He concluded, hoping that the "short tours" by the three diplomats would "be all equally useful."[11]

After leaving Livorno, he headed north to Pisa, possibly viewing the famous twelfth-century leaning tower, before heading east to Florence. By Christmas he had arrived in Rome and marveled at the ruins of the civilization from which he had learned much about creating a republic on the American continent. He took time to write his daughter, Frances Henrietta, describing all he had seen. He sent the letter, unopened, in care of Madison, suggesting that the secretary of state might be interested in reading it for himself. By the first of the year, he had reached Naples, where he wrote John Graham, informing the secretary that he hoped to be back in Spain by mid February. On 22 February, he had indeed arrived back in Madrid.[12]

On 8 March, Madison wrote Pinckney regarding the disagreement with Graham. He stated that he had discussed the matter with the president. Jefferson did not want to get involved and said he believed the matter a private one. Madison, therefore, left the settlement of the matter up to Pinckney but chided him before closing, stating that his trip to Italy resulted from "your inclination, not your duty." He also reminded Pinckney that the trip could not be funded in any manner by the United States government. There is no record of how Pinckney concluded the matter with Graham.[13]

Perhaps Madison's own distaste for Pinckney influenced John Graham before he even began working for the South Carolinian. This influence may in turn have led to the unflattering letters Graham wrote Madison soon after Pinckney arrived. In any event, one of the people in Washington to whom Jefferson referred in his letter to Monroe of early 1804 likely included his secretary of state. James Monroe, however, continued to support Pinckney. Prior to his arrival in Madrid, he wrote Pinckney expressing his happiness at being able to go to Spain "to meet an old friend with whom I have so long harmonised in political opinion, and especially on the subject committed to us." When he arrived in Madrid in early 1805 to assist in the negotiations over Florida, Pinckney implored Monroe to get a replacement for him so that he could return to South Carolina. Monroe refused, persuaded Pinckney to stay on, and acted in direct opposition to Jefferson's instructions. According to one of Monroe's biographers, he concentrated less on Pinckney's perceived inadequacies for the post and more on his honesty and "independence of foreign influence."[14]

Prior to Pinckney's trip to Italy, he had been busily engaged in United States diplomatic affairs. The manner in which he handled most of the issues indicates that while he may have been less than effective at times, his overall performance was anything but lackluster. When he arrived in November 1801 he first dealt with the matter of spoliation claims. The issue involved two types of demands: those that centered around Spanish ships that had plundered United States vessels and those against French ships that had been fitted in Spanish ports and eventually sold their United States plunder in Spain. When negotiations began in early 1802, Spanish foreign minister Pedro de Cevallos quickly acceded to demands regarding claims against Spanish vessels. However, he refused to become involved with any claims arising out of actions by the French, stating that Spain could not be expected to control everything going out of or coming into her ports. Pinckney argued that Spain should be responsible, alleging that too many French vessels had committed the acts for Spain to have been unaware of the goings-on.[15]

The convention agreed upon in August settled the claims against the Spanish ships in full. Cevallos, however, would not come to terms on those involving the French privateers. A clause was inserted whereby those issues could be settled later. Pinckney forwarded the treaty to Madison and urged its approval. Quick ratification could halt delays suffered by claimants and hasten payment of the reparations. Claims regarding the French could be handled at a more opportune time, he wrote, believing the Spanish would eventually acquiesce to those as well. He also believed allowing Spain time to pay the debts separately instead of in one large lump sum would show good faith on the part of the United States government when the all-important negotiations over Florida began.[16]

Jefferson submitted the treaty to the Senate on 11 January 1803, noting that it did not satisfy all claims but that an "express reservation of our rights" to press for those omitted had been included. The Senate did not vote until March, at which time ratification failed to carry the required two-thirds vote. A vote to reconsider the convention during the next session passed by a margin of fourteen to eight. Jefferson sent another message to the Senate on 21 December indicating that, due to the Louisiana Purchase, claims regarding French vessels could be included in negotiations with Spain over the boundaries of Louisiana. On 9 January 1804, nearly a year after it was originally submitted, the Senate finally ratified it by a vote of twenty-one to seven.[17]

By the time Pinckney and Spain received word of ratification, the Spanish government had become reluctant to affirm the treaty. Cevallos wrote Pinckney reminding him that nearly two years had elapsed since negotiations had begun and during that time new conditions had arisen. First, the United States Congress had recently passed the Mobile Act establishing a customs district in that part of western Florida that Spain claimed belonged in her possession and therefore could not have been included in the Louisiana Purchase. Second, Cevallos believed that there should be a time limit added for claims against Spain in light of the delay caused by the United States Congress. Finally, he demanded the claims regarding French vessels be dismissed altogether, maintaining that the Louisiana Purchase should have quit any spoliation claims regarding France. According to one diplomatic historian, Pinckney "must have felt the strength of the Spanish case and weakness of his own."[18]

Had the Senate followed Pinckney's advice, the claims against Spain could have been settled in 1803. There is no evidence either Madison or Jefferson urged the Senate to ratify the treaty until late 1803. Even in his January note to

Congress, Jefferson did not provide any reason why the Senate should go ahead and ratify the convention. As a result of this delay, outstanding claims would exist until the Adams-Onís Treaty of 1819, when Congress relinquished $5 million worth of the claims in exchange for Florida.[19]

Because a great deal of apprehension existed over whether Spain would actually recognize the agreement between the United States and France, the next item on Pinckney's agenda involved obtaining Spanish acquiescence to the Louisiana Purchase. In the spring of 1803 he attempted to enter into negotiations with Spain regarding purchase of the territory. "His Catholic Majesty," Charles IV, informed him that any such negotiations should take place with France, as they owned the vast expanse of land by reason of the Treaty of San Ildefonso. Despite the advice and although formal occupation of New Orleans had occurred in December, the United States continued to meet diplomatic resistance from Spain's minister, Carlos Martinez Casa de Yrujo.[20]

In January of the following year, Pinckney met with the French minister to Spain, expressing disappointment that the United States continued to have problems taking possession of the territory. At Pinckney's request, the minister met with Manuel de Godoy, the "Prince of Peace" who virtually ran the government for Charles IV. Godoy assured him the territory would be given peaceably to France. But in February, Yrujo protested not only the recently passed Mobile Act but also the Louisiana Purchase in general. Madison used Charles IV's earlier statement to Pinckney against these protestations and, within a short time, Yrujo received word that Spain would accept the transaction, with certain boundary questions in Texas and west Florida remaining unanswered.[21]

Pinckney had been instrumental in obtaining a verbal admission from the king of Spain that the Louisiana territory belonged to France. In addition, he pressured the French minister to urge Spain to relinquish her claim, even though her minister in the United States continued to protest the transaction. Although this urging took place in early January, after the actual transfer had occurred, no one in Spain knew yet that the event had taken place. Furthermore, despite the physical occupation by the United States of New Orleans, Spain could have remained a physical threat had she not accepted the turnover.

Pinckney's final major concern centered around the purchase of Florida, and as indicated above, those negotiations became entwined with those regarding spoliation claims. Jefferson and Madison sent James Monroe to Spain to assist Pinckney in the talks. Pinckney's actions prior to this time contributed not only to Jefferson and Madison's decision to have Monroe assist him, but also to the historical fallacy that his term as minister was unsuccessful.

When Congress finally ratified the convention of 1802 more than a year after Pinckney's success in negotiating it and Cevallos attached new stipulations to any ratification by Spain of that document, Pinckney saw the legitimacy of the Spanish foreign minister's arguments and could only react with "bluster and bluff." He informed Cevallos that he needed a definite answer within twenty-four hours to the question of whether Spain would ratify the convention without the conditions. Otherwise, he threatened, a critical situation would exist and he would notify Americans in Spain that they should make immediate preparations to return home. To prove he meant business, Pinckney requested his own passport from the Spanish government. He also "teased on" the issue of Florida, according to Madison, an act he had been specifically instructed not to do until Monroe arrived. When the Spanish government held firm, Pinckney backed down, withdrew his request for his passport, and waited for the arrival of Monroe.[22]

In January, Jefferson wrote the letter in which he advised Monroe to go to Spain, assist Pinckney in negotiations over the claims and the purchase of Florida, and persuade him to return home. Monroe, already in Paris, seemed unwilling to follow the instructions. A year later, he finally arrived, after a leisurely trip through France. Monroe then convinced Pinckney to remain and assist in the negotiations—a direct violation of Jefferson's orders—despite requests by Pinckney that he be allowed to return home. Pinckney even indicated to Godoy his willingness to withdraw from the meetings in order to facilitate the negotiations. However, Godoy ignored the suggestion and acted quite cordially to the minister. Monroe wrote, "On consideration of these circumstances as also of what had passed between him and the Spanish government, on the public questions depending between the two governments in which he appeared to act with *firmness and ability,* I saw no reason after the receipt of the letter of October 26 and the new commission [authorizing Monroe to act alone] why he should withdraw from the negotiation. At my request therefore he continues in it [emphasis added]." Obviously Monroe saw qualities in Pinckney that eluded Madison.[23]

Both Pinckney and Monroe seemed exasperated with the treatment they encountered from Cevallos over the next few weeks. The Spanish minister wrote numerous lengthy and noncommittal correspondence on far-ranging topics. At one point, in order to stave off the onslaught of notes, Monroe requested a face-to-face meeting. Cevallos agreed, acted cordially and agreeably, but remained just as ambiguous during the conversation.[24]

In May, Cevallos received final terms from the two Americans. They requested that Spain cede Florida in its entirety to the United States. They also sought ratification of the convention of 1802. Finally, they set the Colorado River as Louisiana's western boundary. The United States would assume the claims relating to French vessels and, in obtaining western Florida at this time, admit it had not been a part of the Louisiana Purchase. Cevallos refused, claiming that the terms harmed Spain. Monroe requested his passports and prepared to leave. According to one historian, his "five months in Madrid had accomplished nothing." When he returned to London, Monroe wrote Madison stating he was "persuaded that Mr. Pinckney will hold the ground till his successor relieves him, tho' he is most desirous of withdrawing from it." Pinckney himself wrote to Madison of the "complete and total rejection and in the highest tone by Spain of every proposition we made them."[25]

Despite the complexity of these interrelated diplomatic issues, Pinckney endured more than his share of criticism for his performance in Spain, especially his threat to leave the country and his hint at the purchase of Florida, a subject forbidden to him. Overall, however, he had gained Spanish acceptance of the Louisiana Purchase and he had succeeded in negotiating the settlement of all of the spoliation claims against Spain. Congress dragged its feet and undermined that effort, causing them to become entangled in negotiations over Florida that Monroe and Pinckney working together could not settle. Nearly fifteen years passed before the United States obtained Florida and settled the issues that confronted first Pinckney and then Monroe. John Quincy Adams finally settled the matter in 1819, when Spain had become troubled by its colonies in Latin America and could ill afford to go to war with the United States.

By July of 1805, Pinckney included the subject of his departure in almost every correspondence with Madison. On the fourteenth he wrote that he hoped to leave as soon as his replacement arrived. On the twenty-fourth he complained, "It is now near the month of August and I am still obliged to stay here contrary to my inclination and most ardent desire to return." He considered staying in Spain "most distressing and inconvenient." By July, he had still not left. He wrote Madison that he had been preparing to leave for Lisbon and passage home. But by 22 September, he had yet to leave and lamented that the mules needed to enable him to take his belongings to Lisbon had been "embargoed for the King's service" and would not be available until 2 October. On the twenty-second, he scribbled a note indicating he hoped to leave the next day or the following one.[26]

By most accounts, when Pinckney finally returned home in January, his mission had been successful. Despite his pleasant letter to Thomas Jefferson in early 1806, what he found when he arrived in South Carolina could not have been very heartening to him. A house in Charleston and properties at Georgetown had been sold and his plantation south of Columbia neglected. Creditors had filed more than forty suits against him. His cousin Daniel D'Oyley's management of his affairs had been less than efficient. On 24 June 1804, Pinckney sent a letter from Spain relieving D'Oyley of those duties. Within a year, in early

April 1805, Pinckney's new attorney, Peter Freneau, filed suit on Pinckney's behalf against D'Oyley. Although many of Pinckney's financial problems originated before he left for Spain, Daniel D'Oyley's mishandling of his affairs contributed in no small measure to Pinckney's plight. In only a short time, D'Oyley would come under fire for his conduct in the public arena as well.[27]

Had Pinckney been able to return home in 1804 he might have been able to settle his financial affairs. Instead he came home to face ruin that stayed with him until he died, bringing a shadow on his reputation to both contemporaries and historians. He served his country well during his term in Spain. He might have overstepped his bounds at one time, and he might have been less than effective in some areas. But he succeeded in at least two of the major tasks before him, and the third involved issues so sensitive and complicated they remained unsettled for many years. All the while his own financial condition in South Carolina declined. Over the next few years he would become embroiled in trying to put those finances back in order. But like so many times in the past, he could not leave politics and public service behind in order to do so most effectively.

Eight

Fulminations and Fulfillment

Daniel D'Oyley was born in Charleston around 1761, the son of Daniel D'Oyley and Charles Pinckney's aunt, Ann Pinckney. D'Oyley served in the Revolution as a lieutenant, and St. Bartholomew's Parish elected him to the South Carolina General Assembly in 1787. In 1799, he served again as a representative from the parishes of St. Philip's and St. Michael's. In less than a month after his election to the assembly, he became treasurer of the lower division of the state, assuming those responsibilities in December. All the while he continued handling the affairs of his second cousin in Spain. But in 1804 Pinckney relieved D'Oyley of his duties, and by 1806 impeachment proceedings had been drawn up against him for misusing funds while serving as treasurer. Almost immediately, Daniel D'Oyley began an all-out war against his cousin and former friend.[1]

Despite D'Oyley's endeavors and the opinion of some at the national level, Republican supporters at home elected Charles Pinckney to an unprecedented fourth term as governor within one year of his arrival back in the state. On 11 December, he stood before a joint session of the South Carolina legislature in the senate chambers of the statehouse and once again took the oath of office. Those assembled soon moved outside to the portico and publicly proclaimed him governor of the state. Beginning with this, his final term as governor, and during a subsequent term in the South Carolina House of Representatives, Pinckney saw many of his dreams for the state come to fruition in the culmination of his political career. His political philosophy and principles continued to ascend both in South Carolina and the nation. James Madison, Jefferson's handpicked successor, won the presidency in 1808, assuring that the executive branch of the government remained in Republican hands. Congress also became more influenced by Jeffersonians, many of them urging another war against Great Britain. Pinckney and his associates worked to see that South Carolina representatives to the national legislature reflected the state's rapidly growing Republican majority.[2]

Within the state, many of the reforms Pinckney had been advocating for more than twenty years began to be put in place. He suggested action on such issues as legislative reapportionment, penal reform, public education, and more widespread white male suffrage. Then he watched as the South Carolina legislature enacted many of his proposals into law. By following Pinckney's advice, the legislature took steps to unite the state in the manner Pinckney had long desired. And just as Jefferson had been replaced by his protégé, so now Pinckney began to step aside for a new generation of leaders. The revolutionary generation slowly began to fade from the scene. Pinckney sought to make sure that the new generation echoed and furthered his own ideas. In this manner and in motivating the legislature into action, Pinckney fulfilled his role as a transitional figure. Politically he had linked the state from its Federalist past to its Republican present and future. Economically he participated in the crowning of King Cotton and the implications that went along with that coronation. Geographically he helped move the power base in the state from its lowcountry origins to a more central region around the Columbia midlands. His election to a fourth term as governor indicated that his ideas, his philosophy, and his personality had won, despite much adversity.

He began his fourth term just as the legislature began impeachment proceedings against Daniel D'Oyley, his cousin and former attorney. D'Oyley paid Pinckney a visit the day he returned to Charleston from Spain in 1806. He urged Pinckney to forego the lawsuit filed by his new attorney, Peter Freneau, and, knowing Pinckney to be an advocate of the procedure, asked him to pursue arbitration. Pinckney refused. Later that year Pinckney swore affidavits against D'Oyley's conduct and filed an amended complaint against him. Part of the allegations concerned the misapplication of funds obtained from the sale of land on the Wateree River near the town of Stateburgh that once belonged to D'Oyley's father and on which the estate of Colonel Pinckney had a lien. Judgment was handed down in Pinckney's favor even after D'Oyley appealed the ruling. In December, the house of representatives presented four articles of impeachment to the senate alleging that D'Oyley, in his capacity of treasurer of the lower district, misappropriated funds in 1801 and 1802.[3]

Stinging from the court ruling and charges of unethical conduct while treasurer, D'Oyley turned to his pen for relief. In a pamphlet entitled *A Letter Addressed to His Excellency Charles Pinckney,* D'Oyley made charges and claims, some of them true, that tainted Pinckney's reputation even further among those who already disliked him and served as more fodder for many historians' subsequent assessments of the South Carolina statesman. The pamphlet traced a long line of financial difficulties and irregularities commencing in 1799. D'Oyley detailed these difficulties and the circumstances under which he came to be employed by his cousin:

> It is well known that in the year 1799, your embarrassments sir, became extremely oppressive, that the kindness of the house of Mr. John S. Cripps had long supported your credit in hand and out of doors, that their immense advances of money to you, combined with your conduct to them, had excited great uneasiness to that gentleman, to whom you made many promises of settlement, none of which you performed, and great dissatisfaction prevailed: Indeed, so reduced was your situation, that for many years your taxes remained unpaid and you were sued for low and pitiful debts, such as your arrears to charitable institutions, and for other trifling amounts, as well as for very considerable obligations—that your property was advertised for sale by the Sheriff, and threatened by several of your creditors; your crops at the Congaree, at Winyaw [*sic*] and at Ashepoo, were inconsiderable, when compared to the funds your necessities required, and that your whole estate was fast approximating ruin from your distress and total deficiency of management. It was in this condition I found you, and unwilling to see you torn to pieces (as you sir, wrote me you would be if I did not assist you).

Despite the vitriol, there were many truths in the pamphlet. For instance, both the Agricultural Society of South Carolina and the St. Cecilia Society filed suit against Pinckney for unpaid dues; the administrators of Elizabeth Brimner, a recently deceased former housekeeper, filed suit for wages owed but never paid; and, as D'Oyley pointed out elsewhere in the pamphlet, a carpenter, John Milligan, had filed suit for payment of the coffin used to bury Pinckney's mother.[4]

Despite the factual content of much of D'Oyley's publication, he omitted many of the reasons Pinckney found himself in the situation he described. Pinckney had inherited the debts of his father's estate, which was further encumbered by the debts of Pinckney's uncle Miles Brewton. And the estate, besides being attached to all sorts of previous debts, was reduced in size by twelve percent due to the postrevolutionary amercement levied by the Jacksonborough Assembly. In all likelihood, Pinckney did not pay as much attention to his financial affairs as he should have done. He failed to consolidate his landholdings into larger portions on which he could have profitable crop production. Instead, he held on to smaller plots in various places along the Ashepoo, Congaree, and Black Rivers. He preferred politics to planting and seemed unable to strike a happy medium between the two. He also enjoyed living far beyond his means, surrounding himself with thousands of books and fine art. He would probably have taken some comfort in the fact that someone he greatly admired, Thomas Jefferson, was similarly situated financially for comparable reasons.

The letter continued by describing how Pinckney had played a role in D'Oyley's own demise as treasurer of the lower district. He relayed how he had loaned Pinckney money and accepted large drafts from him and had never collected the money owed. "Traitor, thou has betrayed me," he disparaged Pinckney and then made scandalous charges that Pinckney had actually encouraged him to embezzle money from the South Carolina Treasury in order to relieve the future Spanish minister of at least a part of his debt before he departed South Carolina:

> Do you recollect sir, (perhaps it is not quite convenient) the 20th day of September 1800, when you sent a messenger in haste requesting me immediately to come to you. I attended; met you in your passage, incapable of utterance and bathed in tears; you took me by the hand and let me into your back parlour—there indeed was woe—your two principal house servants bound and in possession of the Sheriff—you introduced me with awe that became the gloom of death—you begged my interposition—you urged your own incapacity to pay the debt, and that ruin, certain ruin, must now befall you if the circumstances should be disclosed—invited my return to the passage—I told you I had not the money—you requested me to use it from the funds in the Treasury—I shuddered—you supplicated with tears—I surrendered. . . . Equally suitable would it be for you to dissipate into air the conversation when you urged me to pay to the Bank of South Carolina, the sum of one thousand dollars on your note. . . . I asked you for Heaven's sake where was I to find the money? You replied, if you can't find the money, make your clerk, Mr. Levy, (the clerk of the Treasury) find it.

One can only wonder at Pinckney's reaction to D'Oyley's charges when he read the pamphlet. He had struggled for so long to overcome the stigma placed on him by his father's seeking protection from the British, and his own cousin was now criticizing him in the most public manner possible for his most private actions and alleging the most unethical and perhaps illegal behavior against his beloved state of South Carolina. But D'Oyley's diatribe probably did more harm to himself than it did to Pinckney. It was not a politically savvy move to publicly attack the governor and one of the most influential politicians in the state. When the senate eventually considered the articles against him in December of 1807, they found D'Oyley guilty of the charges.[5]

Pinckney made no public comment regarding the D'Oyley pamphlet. He was busy serving as governor and chose to remain above the fray. However, he did inform Judge William H. Gibbes that he would send evidence regarding the Stateburgh lands in compliance with the court of equity order. The evidence would prove his claims, despite D'Oyley's protestations to the contrary. "Mr. D'Oyley has frequently declared he was content to be bound by my father's books," Pinckney informed the judge, "and you will have them!"[6]

Although D'Oyley did not succeed in drawing his cousin under suspicion for contributing to his own unethical behavior, allegations found in the pamphlet have haunted Pinckney through the years. Contemporary South Carolinians watched with detached amusement as Pinckney discarded the legal services of D'Oyley for those of Federalist William Loughton Smith, his political opponent, who eventually represented him in his suit. Joseph Manigault wrote to his brother Gabriel regarding the matter, stating that the situation reminded him of advice Lord Chesterfield had given to his son: "To keep in mind that his friend may become his enemy, and his enemy his friend."[7]

While D'Oyley hurled his insults, Pinckney busied himself with the affairs of the state of South Carolina. He was especially concerned, once again, with strengthening the state's militia in response to perceived threats by the slave population. In June he received correspondence from Jacob Read, brigadier general of the Seventh Brigade, apprising him of the situation. "There are spread everywhere in the state," he informed the governor, "religious and other enthusiasts who are preaching very dangerous doctrines and inciting our black population." Only a strong militia, he concluded, could save them.[8]

The threat of military attacks from without the state also confronted Pinckney. The British had detained and boarded the naval frigate *Chesapeake* off the coast of Virginia in June of 1807, capturing three and hanging one British naval deserter who had signed up for service on the ship. In the process, some Americans were killed and others wounded. As news of the incident spread, the cry for war arose up and down the seaboard. In December, Pinckney recommended to the senate that steps be taken to fortify port cities in case of war or similar attack by the British.[9]

The threat of war with Great Britain did not overshadow problems lingering within South Carolina. In a lengthy address to both houses in November of 1807, Pinckney touched on many areas of his concern regarding conditions in the state. South Carolina's judicial system still needed reform, including the creation of a court of appeals. He continued his cries for reform of the penal system, indicating his desire that reform, not punishment, be the main purpose of incarceration. He therefore advocated that the legislature repeal corporal punishment for all but the most severe crimes—just as he had done in his address to both houses nine years earlier. He also continued his support for public schooling and went so far as to call on the legislature to fund those who were eligible for but unable to afford a public education. "The poverty or loss of parents ought not to be the means of withholding from their country and burying in obscurity those who might have proved its most distinguished ornaments," he wrote. "Let me therefore earnestly recommend it to you as among your most sacred duties to adopt immediate and efficacious means for establishing public schools and generally diffusing the benefits of Education. You will thus be the instruments of rearing a grateful and valuable band of citizens who can never be unmindful of your liberality in extending to them the means of instruction and placing within the reach of their exertions whatever their genius or acquirements may entitle them to." Pinckney, ever the republican, realized the importance of an educated, virtuous citizenry, and he meant to establish such a citizenry in South Carolina via legislative support of public education.[10]

He also spent 1807 following the intrigue going on in the West caused by Aaron Burr. Burr's daughter had married South Carolina Republican politician Joseph Alston, one of the wealthiest men in the state. Alston financed much of his father-in-law's exploits in the West and actually traveled throughout the territory with Burr in 1806. Burr also had family connections with Revolutionary war hero Gen. Thomas Sumter, who had married Burr's adopted daughter, as well as political ties to both Wade Hampton and Pierce Butler, all of whom were also well known to Governor Pinckney. In January, as details of Burr's schemes in the West became public, Thomas Jefferson wrote his ally in South Carolina. Any questions about Pinckney's abilities seemed to have diminished. The president felt compelled to call upon his southern protégé in order to ascertain what, if anything, he knew about Burr's plans. Jefferson sent Pinckney sensitive information regarding the activities of Alston and Butler, leaving to the governor's discretion how best to use the information. "Nobody is a better judge than yourself whether any and what measures can be taken on this information," the president wrote, "but . . . if no use can be made of it, your own discretion and candor would lead you to keep it secret." Jefferson also revealed that an affidavit would soon be made public detailing some of Burr's activities.[11]

When the affidavit became public and word reached South Carolina, Joseph Alston realized the delicate position in which he found himself. He was close to being charged with treason for financing Burr's expeditions, which, according to allegations, sought to cleave the western part of the United States from the east, conquer Mexico, and create some sort of empire in the region. Alston was forced to act quickly and did so in the form of a letter to Governor Pinckney, published on 11 February in the *Georgetown Gazette*. He reminded Pinckney that "base" men would slander either of them in the furtherance of political gain. He denied the allegations that he was formally involved in the details of Burr's scheme, stating that he had no idea as to Burr's true intentions when he funded and accompanied a part of his enterprise in the West. He did not know what had led Burr to implicate him in the conspiracy, unless it was to induce men of other states to join it or a result of the familial relationship between the two.[12]

Alston also wrote a personal note to Pinckney, advising him that a published letter would soon be appearing. He stated that he had originally intended to send it to Pinckney prior to having it printed in the newspapers but decided that time was of the essence and he could not delay because of the allegations now leveled against him. While these events had been playing out, Pinckney had been away from Charleston examining the conditions in the upstate and midlands. When he arrived home on 16 February he found the correspondence from Jefferson, a copy of the *Georgetown Gazette,* and the private note from Alston. He wasted little time in sending a short letter to Jefferson defending his friend and assuring his discretion regarding the information he had received from the president. To prove his allegiance to Jefferson he enclosed copies of the published letter and the private note in his correspondence. Aided by Pinckney's assistance and defense of him to Jefferson, Alston was eventually exonerated from the charges and continued to serve South Carolina in local politics and eventually as governor.[13]

By the end of 1807 Jefferson had implemented the embargo that ultimately had a devastating effect on shipping and trade and hurt the financial benefits of southern agricultural pursuits. Hoping to avoid being drawn into war between Great Britain and France, he based his decision to employ an embargo on the idea that European powers would not be willing to tolerate lack of exports from the United States. In one of the biggest errors of his presidency, Jefferson underestimated the extent to which the embargo would hurt the nation he was trying to save from war. Charleston's southern planters, merchants, and traders were especially hurt by the strategy and never fully recovered from its effects. By early 1809 James Madison had repealed the embargo. He followed his Republican mentor as chief executive, winning against Charles Cotesworth Pinckney, who failed in another bid for the nation's highest office. In fact the Federalist candidate won only in New England. He lost his home state again and went on to lose in the electoral college by seventy-five votes. His cousin Charles, as governor, presided over the voting by the electors and forwarded congratulations to the president-elect. Despite the dissatisfaction with the embargo, the Federalists had fallen far and fast in the eight years since Jefferson became president.[14]

Perhaps the most important event that occurred during Pinckney's last term as governor centered around reapportionment of the state legislature to represent the upcountry more accurately. For years the republican ideologue had dreamed that his state would be more evenly represented in the house and senate. In December of 1808 he got his wish. The legislature passed the Compromise of 1808, which based representation in the house on population and wealth and gave each district within the state one senator. The exception was Charleston, which once again received two. As a result of the compromise, the backcountry controlled both the senate and the house. But the victory proved in many ways to be a hollow one, at least for the yeomen. The state was no longer geographically divided as it had once been. The wealth that once flourished along the coast had been steadily moving inland and, within a few years, the state's fall line marked the new division between upper and lower South Carolina. While the inhabitants of the old backcountry steadily gained power, the very nature of the backcountry's power base had changed drastically. Within a few years, midland cotton planters wielded their influence just as rice planters from the coast had in the past.[15]

It might seem surprising that one of the main forces behind the Compromise of 1808 was a wealthy planter from Georgetown, Joseph Alston. The same man who only a year earlier had been close to being charged with treason headed up the call for reapportionment. Alston and Pinckney had been friends and political allies long before Alston's troubles, and Pinckney had defended Alston to the president during the controversy. Alston worked diligently for reapportionment, in part because of the debt he owed the governor, who had espoused such equality for nearly twenty years. Alston also recognized the changes in the state's geographic economy that were occurring. In pleas to fellow legislative members he assured them they had little to fear from giving the backcountry more equal power. The backcountry was becoming more like the lowcountry in its view of the world as an organic, hierarchical society of master and slave. It was a major reason Pinckney's dream of uniting the state could finally come true.[16]

Pinckney's term ended, as did that of Thomas Jefferson, in 1809. He wasted little time writing the retired president to express his support for his implementation of the embargo. Perhaps somewhat disingenuously he assured that "you hear of no grumbling among us" with the exception of a few Federalists. He also wrote James Madison, extending his congratulations for winning the presidency. Over the next eleven years he retired from public life and set about putting his personal affairs in order. The latter part of 1809 found him at his home, Shell House, at Haddrell's Point, just across the Ashley River from Charleston. He wrote to Jefferson of the healthy effects of the "sea air." He also maintained his ties with fellow Republicans, attending and conducting political meetings and opposing Federalist allies "with all my might." He corresponded with the new president, informing him of breaks in the embargo around Amelia Island,

Georgia, "by which means all the effects intended by the Non-intercourse act, are in this Section of the Union, entirely prevented."[17]

Each Wednesday evening he and fellow Republicans Peter Freneau, an old friend, and Ebenezer Thomas, editor of the *Charleston City Gazette,* met in Charleston at Freneau's home on George Street to discuss politics. The Federalists sarcastically referred to them as Caesar, Pompey, and Lepidus, classic Roman republicans, and anxiously awaited the *City Gazette* each Thursday morning to determine the topic of discussion among the three. But scoff as they might, the group proved so successful in its endeavors that they "enabled the republican party . . . to bear down, most completely, all opposition." In fact, the three men, along with Col. Thomas Lehre, were instrumental in sending Langdon Cheves to the Unites States Congress. There, linking up with men such as John C. Calhoun, Cheves became one of a group of young advocates of a much more forceful policy against Great Britain, eventually becoming known as the War Hawks.[18]

The lure of more direct involvement in politics proved too strong for Pinckney, and in 1810 he was reelected to the South Carolina House of Representatives, where he served until 1813. During those three years he witnessed a major changing of the guard in South Carolina politics. A younger group of men like John C. Calhoun, Langdon Cheves, and other War Hawks gradually replaced the revolutionary generation in which Pinckney played such an important role. In the house, Charles Pinckney also encouraged going to war with England, and after fighting began in 1812 he was instrumental in passage of a resolution commending President James Madison for his handling of the affair. Pinckney apparently still did not realize the low regard with which Madison viewed him. Had he known he might never had worked so intensely, both personally and publicly, to encourage and support the Virginian's efforts both before and during the war. On the other hand, if he was in fact aware of Madison's attitude towards him, he never let it get in the way of his standing for his convictions.[19]

Also during his term in the house, South Carolina enacted major changes in the direction of republican democracy. The implementation of universal white manhood suffrage occurred in late 1810. If the yeomen of the upstate had not won completely in reapportionment, at least they had scored a major victory in obtaining suffrage. Pinckney also saw one of his most fervent dreams realized when, in December of 1811, the legislature voted to establish free schools throughout the state. It is perhaps not a coincidence the two events occurred less than a year apart. As Pinckney had written years before while governor, what better way to insure that a voting citizenry could be informed and educated than the establishment of public schools? Once white men throughout the state obtained the right to vote regardless of property ownership, the necessity of public education became even more obvious, especially in the eyes of republicans like Charles Pinckney.[20]

In 1814 his term expired and he did not seek reelection. He could no longer ignore his life's private concerns. In fact, the next several years would prove to be full of trials for the retired statesman. After years of service to South Carolina and the United States, sacrificing the attention needed towards his personal affairs, his desperate financial situation was about to catch up with him. He was in very real danger of losing everything he owned. And if his financial situation was not enough to give him sleepless nights, he would soon once again endure the one experience every parent dreads more than any other—the loss of a child.

Nine

Finis

Although Daniel D'Oyley had made unsubstantiated and inaccurate allegations about Charles Pinckney's role in his impeachment, the former treasurer proved to be correct about Pinckney's dire financial situation. In less than a year from his retirement from the house in 1814, a tremendous effort took place to save him and his children from financial ruin. Shortly thereafter, he suffered another emotional blow and turned once again to politics to help him deal with his loss. In doing so he would take the national stage one last time, expressing himself on the issues of slavery and states' rights in terms that eventually energized South Carolina as it took its first steps on the long road to secession. Pinckney's optimistic idea of republican government evolved to include, for the first time, a view of slavery as a prime force in the society he had helped create in his home state. He and others in South Carolina began espousing a more radical view on the subject than some in the South who maintained that abolition would eventually occur—a belief he himself had expressed during the Constitutional Convention. With the economic reign of King Cotton, the conviction developed that slavery was not something that should be regretted or removed from the continent. According to Pinckney, King Cotton had found its ideal working class in perpetual African slavery.

By early 1815, his debts were staggering, and the judgments against him continued to mount. In a last ditch effort to save what he could for his children, he called upon three friends, Charles Kershaw, Simon Magwood, and son-in-law Robert Y. Hayne, to assist him and become trustees of his property. Recognizing that his debts far outweighed his assets, but desiring to obtain the most he could from the sale of his properties, he entered into an agreement with the trustees and his creditors. He transferred all of his real property and his slaves to them and William H. Gibbes, attorney for his creditors. In return, they gave him time to sell portions of his land and fulfill the debts in a manner that allowed them to get the most out of the sale. This enabled Pinckney to obtain more for his property than he could at a sheriff's sale, while allowing his creditors the ability to collect more of the debt he owed.

When he signed the agreement on 1 November, he owned the following property in South Carolina: an unknown amount of acreage on both sides of the Congaree River, about five miles south of Columbia; 500 acres on the Black and Pee Dee Rivers near Georgetown; 1,200 acres on the Lynches River, probably in the Williamsburg District north of Georgetown; 815 acres at Snee Farm; Shell Hall, his house at Haddrell's Point; and his Charleston Meeting Street house. In addition he owned two tracts of land formerly belonging to Henry Laurens and coming into his possession as a result of his marriage to Mary Eleanor. One tract, Wright's Savannah, lay on the north side of the Savannah River about four miles from Savannah. The other tract, Mount Tacitus, lay on the Santee River just above the Santee Canal and contained a lumber mill and Pinckney's Ferry. He also owned 240 slaves, which were dispersed among his various landholdings.

The agreement gave the trustees full power to run the affairs of Pinckney's estate. It required that they assure that all rents or monies made from the lands' use were paid to creditors and authorized them to sell the land on the Lynches River, Wright's Savannah, Mount Tacitus, Snee Farm, Shell Hall, and even his home on Meeting Street. The cotton crops on the Congaree were to be sold to satisfy debts, but the land was to be replanted by the slaves the following year in order to insure future payments. The rice crop and the Georgetown land were to be treated similarly. Afterwards the plantations could be sold as needed to make payment. The trust also authorized the trustees to file complaints against his own debtors in order to recover monies needed to relieve him from his debts. Pinckney himself received two thousand dollars a year "for the support of himself and family."[1]

It must have been quite devastating to Charles Pinckney's honor and reputation to turn over complete control of his property to the trustees. He had proven himself completely incapable of managing his own financial affairs. Many of the allegations hurled at him a few years earlier had proven accurate. Daniel D'Oyley, still smarting from impeachment and conviction, probably took a great deal of satisfaction in the plight of his nemesis. Federalist opponents probably reveled in the news. It was not uncommon for one party to impugn the credibility of a member of the other by bringing to public view economic failure. For instance, Federalist Noah Webster sought to ruin the reputation of one of his Republican opponents by revealing that the Jeffersonian had overdrawn his account at the Bank of Pennsylvania. Pinckney's agreement went a long way towards bearing out D'Oyley's charges against him and Federalists' opinions of him.[2]

The enforced sale of his Meeting Street home prompted him to look for a new, less ostentatious, place to live. He even devised a plan to divide his Meeting Street property into lots consisting of the house in the front and the gardens in the rear, hoping the eventual sale would bring in more cash. But he could not pull himself away from politics. During 1816 he continued to do what he could to promote the cause of Jeffersonian Republicanism. Despite his financial difficulties and the damage caused to his reputation, he still believed his influence could be effective in the party. He spent several months drafting a pamphlet regarding the election of his old friend James Monroe to the presidency. Federalists and even some members of the Republican Party resented the possibility of having yet another Virginian in the White House. In response to such opinions appearing in North Carolina newspapers, Pinckney responded with the somewhat cumbersomely titled *Observations to Shew the Propriety of the Nomination of Colonel Monroe, to the Presidency of the United States by the Caucus at Washington. In which a full answer is given to the pamphlet entitled "Exposition of the motives for opposing the nomination of Mr. Monroe as President of the United States.*" He distributed it across the region and sent copies to both James Madison and Thomas Jefferson. Jefferson, upon receiving his copy, immediately gave it to Monroe, who had driven over to Monticello from Ash Lawn for dinner. Monroe had supported Pinckney ten years earlier during the doubts about his performance in Spain, and now Pinckney stood by his beleaguered Republican friend.[3]

Pinckney also supported and looked with pride on his son's decision to continue in the family tradition of public service. Having graduated valedictorian at South Carolina College in 1812, young Henry Laurens Pinckney toured the north in 1813, stopping to visit Jefferson, Madison, Monroe, and Albert Gallatin. Pinckney wrote of his son to President Madison, "He is destined to grow up in the pursuit of those principles which have so distinguished yourself and them [Jefferson, Monroe and Gallatin] and so much honoured and benefitted our country." Henry soon began studying in law at his brother-in-law Robert Y. Hayne's office. But even before he could enter the bar, he ran for the South Carolina house from Charleston. In 1816, at age twenty-two, forsaking the practice of law, he began a public career that, like his father before him, propelled him from the lowcountry of South Carolina onto the national stage in the halls of the United States Congress. He also began editing the *Charleston Mercury* in 1822. The influence of that paper and its states' rights and pro-slavery ideology helped coalesce the South into the Confederacy.[4]

Shortly after watching his son take office in late 1816, Pinckney faced a major blow. In 1813 his youngest daughter, Frances Henrietta, had married Robert Y. Hayne. The young lawyer's mentor was Langdon Cheves, one of the War Hawks Pinckney had helped win election to the United States Congress. Thus, the couple obviously enjoyed the blessing of her father at the prospect of their marriage. They produced three children: Robert, William Charles, and Frances. But in October, Henrietta became ill with some type of fever and died, throwing the family into turmoil. Pinckney was distraught. Early the next year he drew up a new will. In it he instructed that his body be interred, not at Mepkin where Polly was buried or at Saint Philip's Church where he worshiped, but next to Henrietta's grave at the Circular Congregational Church on Meeting Street in Charleston. It was also shortly after her death that Pinckney sent his recollections of the Pinckney draft to John Quincy Adams. Perhaps the distraction over the death of his daughter and the emotional stress produced thereby contributed to a faulty memory or caused him to send an inaccurate document to Adams.[5]

Charles Pinckney was sixty-one years old. He had outlived his wife, an infant son, and one adult daughter. Although an old man by the day's standards, he once again fought his grief by turning to politics and the public arena. The Charleston Federalists still enjoyed a commanding influence despite their party's decline in most parts of the country. Fearing they could elect a candidate of their choosing to the United States House of Representatives, Pinckney decided to run for public office yet again. The agreement between him, his trustees, and creditors of several years earlier had succeeded in rescuing him from bankruptcy, but it, as well as the charges leveled at him in 1807 by his cousin Daniel D'Oyley, served as fuel for his political opponents.

Despite the opposition, Pinckney won election to the House and entered in December of 1819. In doing so he wrote the prelude to what would be the final great episode in his life. This episode served not only as his own apotheosis but also as a bridge to the future and the rise of men like John C. Calhoun, along with an ideology that eventually divided the Union that Pinckney had striven all of his adult life to create, defend, and preserve. His final stand occurred during the controversy over the admission of Missouri to the union. The "Missouri question" divided the young nation as it had never quite been divided before: North versus South, slave states versus nonslave states. Even when the Federalists posed a viable threat to the Jeffersonians, the divide had not been strictly along such well-defined geographic lines. The Missouri Compromise became one of the first in a long line of agreements designed to heal this deepening wound between the North and the South over the issues of slavery and states' rights.

Pinckney presented his credentials to the sixteenth session of the House of Representatives on 6 December. The issue of Missouri had first been considered in the fifteenth session when the territory's population had reached the required number for statehood. Most of the population consisted of settlers from the South. When they moved into the territory, they brought their slaves with them. Upon the first application for statehood, Congressman James Talmadge from New York attempted to amend the petition submitted by the territory. His amendment would have prevented any further importation of slaves. It also required children of slaves then residing in the area to be freed upon reaching the age of twenty-five. Although the amendment passed in the House—along geographic sectional lines—it did not fare so well in the Senate.

In the Senate, South Carolinian William Smith went further than most of his southern allies may have wished in his address to that body regarding the controversy. He averred that slavery, far from being a necessary evil, was actually a positive good. It was one of the first times such an opinion had been made publicly, but it was an idea that would eventually flourish in the South. Unlike the more conservative Virginians who had long sought to excuse themselves from the evils of slavery by using Jefferson's metaphor and claiming they had "the wolf by the ears," Smith averred that slavery had been sanctioned by the Bible and classical republican civilizations. He asserted that the South treated its working class better than any other place in the world, feeding, clothing, and sheltering slaves throughout their lives.

The more conservative members of the South developed an alternate line of reasoning for opposing Talmadge's amendment. They argued that expansion of slavery would not contribute to its continuance but actually cause it to become more diffused, thereby weakening its hold on certain areas. Virginian John Tyler advocated such diffusion. He argued that continued confinement of an ever growing slave population into finite geographic regions would fan both the fires and fears of slave insurrections. Under such an increased threat, white attitudes towards control of the slave population would harden and forever destroy any chance of abolition or emancipation.[6]

When the Congress adjourned in March of 1819, the question of Missouri statehood remained up in the air. Until the proposed admission of Missouri as a slave state, the North had enjoyed a slight majority in both houses of Congress. Therefore it was imperative for the slaveholding South that Missouri be admitted as a southern slave state if they were not to lose even more influence in Congress. To compound the problem, northern Massachusetts had broken apart from the southern part of the state and was petitioning to enter as the new, free state of Maine, thus throwing the balance even further out of kilter. A compromise known as the Thomas Proviso after its sponsor, Sen. Jesse Thomas of Illinois, emerged, allowing Missouri to enter the Union as a slave state but henceforth prohibiting slavery in all states entering the Union north of Missouri's southern border—the infamous 36° 30' line. During the first months of 1820, debates ensued in both houses of Congress.[7]

On 24 February 1820, Charles Pinckney addressed his fellow congressmen in the well of the old House chamber, advocating similar ideology towards the institution of slavery as William Smith. Pinckney, however, had an advantage Smith lacked. He had intimate knowledge of the intent of the framers of the Constitution because he had been one of them. He began by asserting that, in agreeing to the three-fifths compromise during the Constitutional Convention, the North had not given up rights, as had been alleged recently by his fellow congressmen from that region. On the contrary, he averred, the South had been the loser. Because he was one of the few remaining members of the Convention and the only one in the House of Representatives, he felt it his duty to inform his colleagues that "the concession, on that occasion, was from the southern and not the northern states." As was his wont, he turned to history to help him make his point, detailing the role of slavery in the South from the Revolution to the present and defending the three-fifths clause based on the productivity inherent in the slaves' labor.

Once again he cited his role in the Convention in clarifying statements made by the amendment's backers who stated that the ninth article of the Constitution gave them the right to restrict the importation of slaves from one state to another after 1808. "The intention was to give to the Congress a power, after the year 1808, to prevent the importation of slaves either by land or water from other countries," he stated. "The word 'import' includes both and applies wholly to slaves. Without this limitation Congress might have stopped it sooner under their general power to regulate commerce and it was an agreed point, a solemnly understood compact, that on the southern states consenting to shut their ports against the importation of Africans, no power was to be delegated to Congress, nor were they ever to be authorized to touch the question of slavery; that the property of the southern states in slaves was to be as sacredly preserved, and protected to them, as that of land, or any other kind of property in the eastern states were to be to their citizens."

In addition to his experience in the Constitutional Convention, he recalled his ambassadorship to Spain and negotiations over the Louisiana Purchase. He noted that no special exceptions or exemptions were made in the treaty or otherwise regarding the extension of slavery into the territory itself or states arising therefrom. Missouri was on equal footing with Louisiana in this regard, because slaves had been freely brought into the former for years and because most of the inhabitants desired that slavery be allowed to continue therein and not prohibited further. Otherwise, he declared, territories would be subject to a sort of "colonial tyranny." He asked, "Where will you stop? May you not dictate to her the nature of the government she shall have? May you not give her plural executive, a legislature for six, and judges for one year? If you say there shall be no slavery, may you not say there shall be no marriage? May you not insist on her being different in every respect from the others? Sir, if you are determined to break the Constitution in this important point you may ever proceed to do so in the essences of the very form you are bound to guarantee to them!"

Then, using a states' rights ideology that would find its way into many issues in the coming years, he continued, "Instead of endeavoring to lessen or injure the force and spirit of the state governments, every true friend of his country ought to endeavor, as far as he can, to strengthen them. For be assured, it will be to the strength and increase of our state governments, more than any other, that the American republic will owe its firmness and duration." Some Europeans, he stated, looked forward to the demise of the American republic once its population became too numerous. They expected it to become more like Europe, and break up into many smaller governments. He had heard such ideas while he served in Spain. The only way to prevent such an occurrence was to empower the states as much as possible "for municipal or individual purposes," but "leaving the central government at leisure and in a situation solely to devote itself to the exercise of the great powers of war and peace, commerce and our connections with foreigners, and all the natural authorities delegated by the Constitution." Only in this manner would the central government be able to remain strong and viable.[8]

He also expressed his opinion that the danger of factions would be lessened when a central government was vested with only the most necessary and strictly stated powers. Here he badly miscalculated, stating that it would be nearly impossible for a group of states to form a faction that would threaten the Union. He believed that "even in cases where doubts may arise as to the wisdom or policy of the measures, all factious measures will be made to wait constitutional redress, in the peaceable manner prescribed by the Constitution." He could not foresee that his ideas regarding states' rights would be picked up and used to justify some of the most invective rhetoric and actions against his beloved Union and that a faction led by his own state would one day refuse to "wait constitutional redress" and would break the country wide open.

After reemphasizing his opinion that both the Constitution and the treaty regarding the Louisiana Purchase prohibited the restriction of slavery in such a manner as the Thomas Proviso desired, he then enumerated additional reasons. He recalled the Northwest Ordinance, which outlawed slavery in the old Northwest Territory, and his role in creating it in the Confederation Congress. But he cast it aside as precedent because it had been the product of "a body literally in the very agonies of political death" and, as such, was usurped by the Constitution. He turned to the Bible and, although he did not mention his own participation in its creation, some of his critics who portrayed him as arrogant and vain probably expected him to do so. Instead he cited a passage that sanctioned slavery. Next he justified the South's treatment of its slaves by discussing the treatment of the "lower classes" by other countries. "Let him then go to England," he suggested, "the comforts, if they have any, of the lower classes of inhabitants are far inferior to those of our slaves." He chastised the North for its treatment of free blacks. "Then let him come nearer home and examine into the situation of the free Negroes now resident in New York and Philadelphia and compare them with the situation of our slaves." He described his own experience in the City of Brotherly Love. "I saw their streets crowded with idle, drunken Negroes at every corner and, on visiting their penitentiary, found, to my astonishment, that out of the five hundred convicts there confined, more than one half were blacks and as all the convicts throughout that state are sent to that penitentiary and, if Pennsylvania contains eight hundred thousand white inhabitants and only twenty-six thousand blacks, of course the crimes and vices of the blacks in those states are, comparatively, twenty times greater than those of the whites in the same states and clearly proves that a state of freedom is one of the greatest curses you can inflict on them."

He concluded the speech stating his belief that, for the sake of the Union, no compromise on the Constitution could ever be made. "I cannot on any ground think of agreeing to a compromise on this subject," he stated. "However we all may wish to see Missouri admitted, as she ought, on equal terms with the other states, this is a very unimportant object to her compared with keeping the Constitution inviolate, with keeping the hands of Congress from touching the question of slavery." He emphatically declared, "On the subject of the Constitution, no compromise ought ever be made! Neither can any be made on the national faith, so seriously involved in the treaty which gives to all Louisiana, to every part of it, a right to be incorporated into the union on equal terms with the other states."[9]

Despite Pinckney's zeal and role in the creation of the Constitution, he did not convince enough of his fellow representatives. On 1 March, the House voted to admit Missouri as a free state. Pinckney, of course, voted in the minority. The Senate, however, consisted of a stronger southern contingent and refused to go along with the lower house. A conference committee removed the restriction on slavery in Missouri and replaced it with the Thomas Proviso, putting both issues before the House for a vote. By doing so, Speaker of the House Henry Clay knew that at least the less offensive portion of the bill would pass in the South, thereby securing eventual passage on the compromise. On 2 March, the House voted to strike the slave restriction. Pinckney voted in the affirmative. A few minutes later, with Pinckney voting "nay," the House voted for the Thomas amendment, passed the final compromise, and admitted Missouri as a slave state, Maine as a free state, and prohibited slavery above Missouri's southern border.[10]

During the debates on the Missouri question, tensions rose, new enemies were made, and old disagreements exacerbated. When Pinckney compared the plight of slaves in the South to those of free blacks in the North, he insulted many of his northern allies. An old enemy he may have succeeded in offending even further was Harrison Gray Otis of Massachusetts. Otis, an ardent Federalist, had supported Pinckney's cousin Charles Cotesworth Pinckney in the election of 1800. In late March, after all the debate had ended, he wrote to his wife, Sally, informing her of life in Washington and gossip around town. One of those pieces of gossip concerned Congressman Pinckney, who had allegedly been caught in an abandoned house with a "mulatto wench." A butcher, the victim of a robbery, claimed that he saw Pinckney go into the house and mistook him for the robber looking for a place to hide. A group of men surrounded the building and called on the "thief" to come forward. Pinckney, in a state of panic, jumped from a window and attempted to flee. However, his age slowed him down and he fell. The group apprehended him, but once they recognized the representative from South Carolina they allowed him to leave. Humiliation over the incident may explain why he chose not to run for reelection the following year. Whether the story promulgated by one of his political opponents was true or not, it dealt another blow to his already less-than-exemplary reputation.[11]

When Congress adjourned in 1820, Pinckney returned once again to Charleston. In late September he wrote Jefferson seeking his opinion on the Missouri question. Although the compromise had been approved in March, Congress had not yet received or approved the new state's constitution. Pinckney foresaw problems. Referring Jefferson to *Nile's Register,* which had published his February address to the House, he once again reiterated his states' rights belief. Of those who had opposed his views, he wrote, "I hope they will not trouble us any more on this subject although I should not be surprised if they attempted it when the Constitution of Missouri comes to be laid before Congress." He also informed Jefferson that his health and the climate in Washington prevented him from running for reelection, although he assured the former president that he could probably run again unopposed for the seat if he so desired.[12]

Sometime in October, he once again left Charleston for Washington, where he arrived in November. If he suffered lingering effects from the humiliation of Otis' allegations, he rose above them to address the House once more when Missouri submitted its constitution early the next year. The constitution, as submitted, called for the exclusion of free blacks and mulattoes from the state.

Despite Pinckney's hopes to the contrary, vigorous debate ensued. In the Senate, William Smith justified the right of the state to excuse whatever inhabitants it so chose. In the House, Pinckney addressed the issue early in the spring. Almost a year to the day from his speech on the compromise itself, he once again addressed states' rights. He rallied support for the constitution of the state, calling it "the very best republican constitution" he had ever seen, going so far as to say it was even better than the national one he had helped create. To prove his point he compared it to constitutions of Virginia, Maryland, and New York, pointing out deficiencies within each when compared to that submitted by Missouri, which he believed seemed to have taken lessons from errors contained in constitutions created before it.

He addressed the meaning of the word "citizen" in the United States Constitution. While doing so, he made one of the few public statements regarding his contribution in Philadelphia in 1787, publicly taking credit for both the only complete plan of government submitted by one person and the very language of such an important portion:

> It appears by the journal of the Convention that formed the Constitution of the United States that I was the only member of that body that ever submitted the plan of a constitution completely drawn in articles and sections. And this having been done at a very early stage of their proceedings, the article on which now so much stress is laid and on the meaning of which the whole of this question is made to turn and which is in these words: "the citizens of each State shall be entitled to all privileges and immunities in every State," having been made by me, it is supposed I must know, or perfectly recollect, what I meant by it. In answer I say that at the time I drew that constitution I perfectly knew that there did not then exist such a thing in the Union as a black or colored citizen, nor could I then have conceived it possible such a thing could ever have existed in it.

Surely he would not have spoken so boldly and emphatically on such an important matter had he thought that such a claim could or would be questioned.

He went on to discuss what should be meant by the term "citizen" but did so using the laws of the state of South Carolina. He probably immediately alienated many from the North who could not agree with the South's treatment of blacks. His definition may be summed up as follows: a free white male above the age of twenty-one eligible to vote within the state. Females, blacks, and those under twenty-one were not citizens and, according to his logic, not subject to the privileges and immunities clause for which he claimed authorship. He stated that it was pure hypocrisy on the part of northern states to suggest citizenship extended to people of color, especially in light of the way they were treated in that region. He also spent a great deal of his speech averring that Africans as they existed on their own continent were savages and intellectually inferior to Europeans.

He concluded by expressing hope that the compromise of the previous year would insure harmony throughout the Union. But he was pessimistic about that chance as long as northern and eastern interests could impede on the interests of the South and slavery. Then he offered his public career's swan song:

> These, sir, are the sentiments which my duty to the Union of these States, to my constituents, and to myself, have made it incumbent upon me to express on this momentous question. Our ancestors, with those gone and a few, very few, of our Revolutionary heroes and statesmen still left, by the noblest effort which ever adorned the pages of history, have erected such a monument to rational liberty as the world has never before seen. . . . And shall we . . . destroy the work for which its illustrious founders have received the thanks and gratitude of every friend of freedom throughout the globe and draw down deservedly upon ourselves not only their contempt but imprecations? In a word, shall we destroy that Union on which not alone depend our own existence as a free, a powerful, or a happy people, but the only example left to prove to succeeding generations what real patriotism, firmness, and prudence might realize in the cause of liberty and self-government? I hope, I pray not.

Because none of the benefits touted by Charles Pinckney in his depiction of the American republic extended to African Americans and because white heirs to that republic magnified and extended his own rhetoric, the answer to his last question would become "yes." Congress finally passed the Missouri constitution after agreeing that nothing therein would violate the privileges and immunities clause. But the question of whom the clause protected would remain unanswered for years to come.[13]

In early April, recovering from a brief illness, Charles Pinckney left Washington for the last time. He traveled north to New York where he met with old friends from earlier days in national politics. On the fifteenth he, Langdon Cheves, and others from the South Carolina delegation sailed for Charleston. By August he had arrived in Charleston at his new residence on Church Street. Hearing of and anxiously awaiting the impending publication of New York delegate Robert Yates' proceedings of the Constitutional Convention, he wrote a friend in New York and requested that a copy be mailed to him as soon as it was available.[14]

Over the next three years, Pinckney's health continued to decline. Although he wrote to old friends like Rufus King of traveling again to New York, in all likelihood he never did. Towards the end of 1824 he developed edema—"dropsy," as it was known then—possibly from heart or kidney disease. His long time friend Dr. David Ramsay attended him to no avail. He died on 29 October, just three days after turning sixty-seven. He had last changed his will in 1819. As indicated earlier, it freed a handful of his slaves. It also indicated his desire that one of his two grandsons change his name to Charles Pinckney Hayne. This was a fairly common practice at the time among men without namesakes, but it is an indicator that he did not want to be forgotten by his progeny. He also left instructions that his body be laid out until decomposition should start to set in. This, too, was a somewhat common practice, caused by the fear of being buried alive. Despite his instructions, the funeral took place at four o'clock the next day after a wake at son Henry's home. He was buried in St. Philip's churchyard—another violation of a request in his will—where he and his family had worshiped for years. He left behind his son, surviving daughter, their families, and a state and nation grateful for his nearly fifty years of service.[15]

Conclusion

Final Assessments

When W. E. Bowen arrived in Charleston on 19 April 1928, he made his way to St. Philip's Church. He spoke with the rector, the Reverend Samuel Cary Beckwith, who confirmed that Charles Pinckney had been buried there in 1824 according to the church's funeral records, even though a subsequent survey of the graveyard made in 1835 did not show a location for Pinckney's final resting place. The colonel was in the yard, and a grave was located beside his with a slab that had been defaced and was unreadable. Could this have been the grave of Charles Pinckney? Bowen had come to the end of the trail. According to most evidence, Pinckney's remains were at St. Philip's, but there was no documentation attesting to the exact location.

Twenty years passed before A. S. Salley finally affirmed his opinion that the grave next to the colonel's was "the logical place" for Charles Pinckney to be buried. Eventually, Dr. Thornwell Jacobs, a South Carolina novelist, donated a stone to mark the plot. On 6 December 1949, local dignitaries and Pinckney's descendants gathered at St. Philip's to attend a ceremony dedicating the stone. Pinckney's great-great-granddaughter Emma Pinckney and his great-great-great-great-grandson Charles Pinckney Roberts unveiled the marker that listed some of Pinckney's achievements.[1]

Despite the manner in which Charles Pinckney's physical legacy has been nearly obliterated, his role in the founding of the nation cannot be similarly erased. Although his exact contributions to the final version of the United States Constitution may never be known, his function within the Constitutional Convention was important and substantial, especially his espousal of a new vision for the nation being created. Within twenty years of that role, he succeeded in building a Jeffersonian coalition in South Carolina, siphoning power from conservatives who had been entrenched in power there for nearly a century. That coalition resulted in the "Revolution of 1800," in which the nation took a decided turn towards classic liberal enlightenment ideals. As a reward, he was appointed minister to Spain during a formative time in the nation's diplomatic history. Almost without exception, and contemporary and historical assessments to the contrary, he distinguished himself and accomplished nearly everything with which he had been charged.

Those contemporary assessments, beginning almost immediately when he emerged on the public stage for the first time in the Confederation Congress, contributed to a historical eclipse of Pinckney. A letter to his friend James Monroe, written in haste and without the benefit of mature experience, cast him in a negative light to James Madison. Adding to the initial pejorative opinions occasioned by the missive, Pinckney arrived at the Constitutional Convention a few years later in 1787 intending to play an important role therein. This ambition caused resentment in Madison, who had already staked out his own position. Madison viewed it as an attempt to upstage him when Pinckney laid before the delegates the only completed draft of a governing document authored by one man. Pinckney, totally oblivious to Madison's disdain for him, blithely ignored the danger of placing confidence in the Virginian and considered him a trusted ally, going so far as to hang his portrait in his drawing room in Charleston. Madison's scorn, however, continued to build and was once again supported, at least in his own mind, by the opinion of his protégé John Graham, when Pinckney arrived in Spain. Graham wasted little time letting Madison know how ill prepared he believed Pinckney was for the task. The seriousness with which Madison took Graham's opinions is evident in Madison's description of his protégé as "among the most worthy of men, and most estimable citizens; as adding to a sound and discriminating judgement."[2]

After all of the aforementioned incidents, Pinckney committed what Madison probably viewed as a disingenuous, last-ditch attempt by his rival to establish himself in the pantheon of American founders: Pinckney overstated his own contributions to the Constitution. The draft he submitted to John Quincy Adams could not possibly have contained the original plan as given to the Convention on its third day. Madison never confronted Pinckney with the discrepancies, preferring to wait until Pinckney was dead, precluding any chance he may have had to defend himself.

Whether James Madison purposely set about to undermine Charles Pinckney's reputation is unclear. But it is clear that, after obtaining an unfavorable first impression of the young delegate to the Confederation Congress, misunderstanding piled atop misconception to taint permanently the reputation of the South Carolinian in the Virginian's eyes. When Pinckney became successful in delivering the state of South Carolina for Madison's mentor, Thomas Jefferson, in 1800, he posed an even more viable threat to Madison's influence with the president and within the Republican Party. From that point on, it appears that Madison did as much as he could to diminish Pinckney within the eyes of Jefferson. He also continued to impugn Pinckney's reputation even after he died in 1824.

But Madison alone cannot be blamed for Pinckney's ill fortune. Pinckney's behavior was at times arrogant and vain as he strove to overcome the inferiority he felt as a result of his father's actions towards the close of the Revolution. His less-than-stellar personal behavior provided ammunition for his Federalist critics and for those within his own party, like Madison, who may have considered him to be a rival. His mismanagement of his own business affairs contributed to the shame of having all of his assets placed in the hands of younger and more able men at a time when he should have been a more established and financially solvent planter. Daniel D'Oyley's mismanagement of his finances may have been a culminating event, but a lifetime of inattention was the main cause of his disastrous economic condition. His own shortcomings combined with lethal political enemies, which included lowcountry Federalists and James Madison, virtually assured that his role as a major founder of the United States would be forgotten.

If those weaknesses were not enough, nearly all physical traces of his existence were wiped out also. His house in Charleston was torn down. His plantation south of Columbia, Greenwich, fell into disrepair and disappeared. His impressive library was burned or scattered, with a few volumes eventually turning up in the general stacks at the University of South Carolina Thomas Cooper library. Even his "home" at Snee Farm, saved by a group of concerned citizens and purchased by the federal government to be administered by the National Park Service, turned out to postdate his death. Only recently have archaeological discoveries at the site in Mount Pleasant turned up the original footings of his family's eighteenth-century home where George Washington stopped in 1791. His grave was unknown for over a hundred years, and even now there is no definite verification that his stone marks the proper plot.[3]

Both political friends and foes have overshadowed Charles Pinckney in the annals of United States history. Cousins Charles Cotesworth and Thomas are considered Revolutionary War heroes, and many of their homes and belongings have survived. Their families have been documented by historians and their contributions to the founding of the nation preserved. Few college survey courses of the first half of United States history omit the XYZ affair in which Charles Cotesworth played a major role, uttering the immortal words, "No! No! Not a sixpence!" His political cohorts have also gained more attention. Madison is routinely championed as the "Father of the Constitution" and his writing of the Kentucky Resolution in response to the Alien and Sedition Acts is much more recognized than anything Pinckney did to further the cause of Jeffersonian Republicanism.

Pinckney is truly a forgotten founder. Despite the major roles he played in the establishment of the United States, the development of republican ideology that informed that founding, and his successes in nearly every public political office he held, he has been overlooked by most. At a personal level he was a product of the time and place in which he lived. He supported slavery and held humans in bondage just as did most of his friends and acquaintances in the South. He recognized a role for women in the founding of the new nation but limited that involvement to the domestic arenas and the raising and influencing of children, instilling in them republican virtues and their own place as their gender dictated. And the impact of gender also influenced Pinckney's attitude towards the rest of society, both locally and nationally. But he did resist certain aspects of his own society, rejecting certain notions of the South Carolina lowcountry elite and embracing the middling classes in the backcountry, winning elections, securing republican and Republican victories, and uniting the state.

This unification crossed many lines. He linked the lowcountry elite with an emerging political force in the backcountry, forsaking his own largely Federalist family and embracing the republican ideology that would come to dominate the early years of the nation. He also spanned the economic differences that developed in the state as the financial locus shifted from the profitability of coastal rice to that of the interior's King Cotton. By seeking to insure fairness in the judicial process as well as education and upward mobility for the less wealthy, he sought to stabilize the state's class differences and mold them into a harmonious society. In this he also acted as a link to a more democratic age personified by Andrew Jackson's presidency. And in being one of the youngest delegates to the Constitutional Convention, he lived further than many of his colleagues into his country's adolescence and served as a bridge to younger political figures like his son, Henry Laurens Pinckney, his son-in-law, Robert Y. Haynes, and others like Langdon Cheves and John C. Calhoun. As one of the last survivors of that August Philadelphia body and a major contributor to the document that came out of it, Charles Pinckney could assert that he was one of the few who actually knew what the framers had in mind. And in one of his last public acts, he espoused rhetoric that the succeeding generations of South Carolinians would develop into an ideology that would drive a near-fatal wedge in the country he had worked so hard to create.

Just as W. E. Bowen searched for the grave in the 1920s, anyone interested in Charles Pinckney's life has had to search through a variety of sources to put together some semblance of a story. Perhaps now he is more accessible and will no longer be a forgotten founder.

Notes

ABBREVIATIONS

AHR	*American Historical Review*
APS	American Philosophical Society, Philadelphia, Pa.
BDHR	*Biographical Directory of the South Carolina House of Representatives*
CLS	Charleston Library Society, Charleston, S.C.
JCC	*Journals of the Continental Congress*
JHR	*Journal of the House of Representatives*
LDC	*Letters of Delegates to Congress*
LOC	Library of Congress, Washington, D.C.
NYHS	New York Historical Society, New York, N.Y.
NYPL	New York Public Library, New York, N.Y.
PHS	Pennsylvania Historical Society, Philadelphia, Pa.
RFC	*Records of the Federal Convention*
SCDAH	South Carolina Department of Archives and History
SCHM	*South Carolina Historical (and Genealogical) Magazine*
SCL	South Caroliniana Library, Columbia, S.C.
SDDDS	State Department Diplomatic Despatches, Spain
WMQ	*William and Mary Quarterly*

Introduction

1. See *The Unveiling of the Memorial Ledger to Charles Pinckney* (Atlanta: Westminster Publishers, 1949).

2. Joseph J. Ellis, *Founding Brothers: The Revolutionary Generation* (New York: Alfred A. Knopf, 2000), 13.

3. Mark D. Kaplanoff, "Charles Pinckney and the American Republican Tradition," in *Intellectual Life in Antebellum Charleston,* ed. Michael O'Brien and David Moltke-Hansen (Knoxville: University of Tennessee Press, 1986), 86n. 8; speech on Charles Pinckney by George C. Rogers, given on Charles Pinckney Day, 28 August 1987, in the Charleston Exchange at A Bicentennial Commemoration celebration sponsored by Americans United for Separation of Church and State and the Charleston Commission on the bicentennial of the United States Constitution. Major portions of this biography are influenced by ideas originally espoused by Rogers and Kaplanoff.

4. Gary B. Nash et al., *The American People: Creating a Nation and a Society,* brief 3d ed. (New York: Longman, 2000), 851.

Prelude

1. Much of the information on the family preceding Charles Pinckney is taken from the most complete assessment of them written: Frances Leigh Williams, *A Founding Family: The Pinckneys of South Carolina* (New York: Harcourt Brace Jovanovich, 1978),

3–6. See also Mabel L. Webber, "The Thomas Pinckney Family of South Carolina," *SCHM* 39 (1938): 128–52.

2. Williams, *Founding Family,* 6–12. This branch of the family, including matriarch Eliza Lucas, has received much attention from historians and others. See, for example, *The Letterbook of Eliza Lucas Pinckney,* edited by Elise Pinckney and Marvin L. Zahniser (Chapel Hill: University of North Carolina Press, 1972); the entire issue of the July 1998 edition of *SCHM,* vol. 99; Marvin L. Zahniser, *Charles Cotesworth Pinckney, Founding Father* (Chapel Hill: University of North Carolina Press, 1967); Merrill G. Christopherson, *Biography of an Island: General C. C. Pinckney's Sea Island Plantation* (Fennimore, Wis.: Westburg Associates, 1972); and Charles Cotesworth Pinckney, *Life of General Thomas Pinckney* (Boston: Houghton Mifflin and Company, 1895). There are also numerous accounts in various historic works of the roles of both Charles Cotesworth and Thomas in Revolutionary and early national periods of United States history.

3. Williams, *Founding Family,* 9; A. S. Salley, "Col. Miles Brewton and Some of His Descendants," *SCHM* 2 (1901): 33; Walter Edgar and N. Louise Bailey, *BDHR, The Commons House of Assembly, 1692–1775* (Columbia: University of South Carolina Press, 1977), 2:95–97; George C. Rogers Jr., *Charleston in the Age of the Pinckneys* (Columbia: University of South Carolina Press, 1969), 9.

4. Quoted in Rogers, *Charleston in the Age of the Pinckneys,* 126; Edgar and Bailey, *BDHR,* 2:523.

5. Williams, *Founding Family,* 13; Susan Hart Vincent, *Charles Pinckney National Historic Site Cultural Landscape Report* (Atlanta: National Park Service, 1998), 7; Edgar and Bailey, *BDHR,* 2:523.

6. Robert M. Weir, "'The Harmony We Were Famous For': An Interpretation of Pre-Revolutionary South Carolina Politics," *WMQ* 18 (October 1969): 473–501.

Chapter 1

1. Rogers, *Charleston in the Age of the Pinckneys,* 3; Richard Walsh, *Charleston's Sons of Liberty: A Study of the Artisans, 1763–1789* (Columbia: University of South Carolina Press, 1959); Robert M. Weir, *Colonial South Carolina: A History* (Millwood, N.Y.: KTO Press, 1983; reprint, Columbia: University of South Carolina Press, 1997), quote on 105, see also 265–66.

2. The seminal work on the influence and contributions of African slaves to the lowcountry remains Peter H. Wood, *Black Majority: Negroes in Colonial South Carolina from 1670 through the Stono Rebellion* (New York: W. W. Norton and Company, 1974). See also Robert Olwell, *Masters, Slaves, and Subjects: The Culture of Power in the South Carolina Low Country, 1740–1790* (Ithaca, N.Y.: Cornell University Press, 1998), which takes up where Wood leaves off in 1740, asserting that slaves were instrumental in creating and maintaining the southern colonial society of Charles Town; and Philip Morgan, *Slave Counterpoint: Black Culture in the Eighteenth-Century Chesapeake and Lowcountry* (Chapel Hill: University of North Carolina Press, 1998), a comparative survey of the two slave cultures. Regarding other religions and ethnicities, see Walter Edgar, *South Carolina: A History* (Columbia: University of South Carolina Press, 1998), 63, and chapter 9,

155–203, which provides excellent insight into "Everyday Life in Colonial South Carolina."

3. Quote from Rogers, *Charleston in the Age of the Pinckneys,* 99; see also James Raven, *London Booksellers and American Customers: Transatlantic Literary Community and the Charleston Library Society, 1748–1811* (Columbia: University of South Carolina Press, 2002), 69; Terry W. Lipscomb, "In Search of the Charles Pinckney Library," *Ex Libris* (1998–99): 2–7; Walter Edgar, "The Libraries of Colonial South Carolina" (master's thesis, University of South Carolina, 1969).

4. Edgar and Bailey, *BDHR,* 2:522–23.

5. Weir, *Colonial South Carolina,* 232–34; Edgar, *South Carolina,* 168–69. See also Julia Cherry Spruill, *Women's Life and Work in the Southern Colonies* (Chapel Hill: University of North Carolina Press, 1938); Mary Beth Norton, *Liberty's Daughters: The Revolutionary Experience of American Women, 1750–1800* (Ithaca, N.Y.: Cornell University Press, 1980); Linda Kerber, *Women of the Republic: Intellect and Ideology in Revolutionary America* (Chapel Hill: University of North Carolina Press, 1980).

6. Edgar and Bailey, *BDHR,* 2:523–24.

7. James Haw, *John and Edward Rutledge of South Carolina* (Athens: University of Georgia Press, 1997), 29–32; David Duncan Wallace, *South Carolina: A Short History, 1520–1948* (Columbia: University of South Carolina Press, 1961), 229–34; Edgar, *South Carolina,* 209–10; Weir, *Colonial South Carolina,* 294–97. Regarding the Stamp Act Crisis in general, see Edmund S. and Helen M. Morgan, *The Stamp Act Crisis: Prologue to Revolution* (New York: Macmillan, 1963).

8. Williams, *Founding Family,* 32.

9. Regarding geographical effects on the history of South Carolina, see Charles F. Kovacik and John J. Winberry, *South Carolina: A Geography* (Boulder, Colo.: Westview Press, 1987). Regarding Woodmason, see Richard J. Hooker, ed., *The Carolina Backcountry on the Eve of the Revolution: The Journal and Other Writings of Charles Woodmason, Anglican Itinerant* (Chapel Hill: University of North Carolina Press, 1953) and Rachel Klein, *Unification of a Slave State: The Rise of the Planter Class in the South Carolina Backcountry, 1760–1808* (Chapel Hill: University of North Carolina Press, 1990).

10. Edgar, *South Carolina,* 212–16; Klein, *Unification of a Slave State,* 47–77; Hooker, *Charles Woodmason,* xi–xxx.

11. Haw, *John and Edward Rutledge,* 58–62; Williams, *Founding Family,* 34–35.

12. Wallace, *Short History,* 234; *Pennsylvania Gazette,* 19 July 1770.

13. Walsh, *Charleston's Sons of Liberty,* 61–64.

14. Edgar, *South Carolina,* 221–22; Walsh, *Charleston's Sons of Liberty,* 68; *Pennsylvania Gazette,* 23 June 1775; Rogers, *Charleston in the Age of the Pinckneys,* 126. Wallace's *Short History,* 262, also indicates Pinckney was "suspected, however, of veering toward moderation."

15. Edgar, *South Carolina,* 226–27; Williams, *Founding Family,* 87–88.

16. Williams, *Founding Family,* 96–97.

17. N. Louise Bailey and Elizabeth Ivey Cooper, *BDHR, House of Representatives, 1775–1790* (Columbia: University of South Carolina Press, 1981), 3:555–56; Edgar and Bailey, *BDHR,* 2:494–95; Williams, *Founding Family,* 41.

18. David Ramsay to Benjamin Rush, 6 August 1776, "David Ramsay, 1749–1815, Selections from His Writings," ed. Robert L. Brunhouse, *Transactions of the American Philosophical Society* 55 (1965): 53.

19. Col. Charles Pinckney to Robert Brewton, 7 August 1776, Manuscripts Division, SCL; Edgar and Bailey, *BDHR,* 2:95–98. Regarding smallpox and early attempts at its treatment, see Nicolau Barquet and Pere Domingo, "Smallpox: The Triumph over the Most Terrible Ministers of Death," *Annals of Internal Medicine* 127 (15 October 1997): 635–42; Joel N. Shurkin, *The Invisible Fire: The Story of Mankind's Victory over the Ancient Scourge of Smallpox* (New York: Putnam, 1979). Although smallpox inoculations did not become more common until later in the eighteenth century, experiments had taken place much earlier. Both the Pinckneys and the Brewtons appear to have been familiar with the practice, including Charles' great aunt Eliza Lucas. See Constance B. Schulz, "Eliza Lucas Pinckney," in *Portraits of American Women from Settlement to the Civil War,* ed. G. J. Barker-Benfield and Catherine Clinton (New York: St. Martin's Press, 1991), 69.

20. Quoted in Edgar, *South Carolina,* 229–30; Jerome J. Nadelhaft, *The Disorders of War: The Revolution in South Carolina* (Orono: University of Maine at Orono, 1981), 27–43; Weir, *Colonial South Carolina,* 332–34. Nadelhaft argues that the Revolution in South Carolina and the constitution it produced, although conservative in the short term, set the stage for the gradual movement of power from the lowcountry toward the western portion of the state.

21. Quoted in Walter J. Fraser Jr., *Charleston! Charleston! The History of a Southern City* (Columbia: University of South Carolina Press, 1989), 157. See also Harriott Horry Rutledge Ravenel, *Charleston: The Place and the People* (New York: Macmillan Company, 1906), 253–54; Williams, *Founding Family,* 113.

22. Wallace, *Short History,* 280–86; Williams, *Founding Family,* 114–15; Edgar, *South Carolina,* 230.

23. Ebenezer Smith Thomas, *Reminiscences of the Last Sixty-Five Years, Commencing with the Battle of Lexington; Also Sketches of His Own Life and Times* (Hartford, Conn.: Case, Tiffany, and Burhnam, 1840), 1:37; Williams, *Founding Family,* 123.

24. Haw, *John and Edward Rutledge,* 88–90, 117–18; Edgar and Bailey, *BDHR,* 2:579.

25. Williams, *Founding Family,* 123–25. Williams discovered in her research that the printers of General Moultrie's memoirs of 1802 had mistakenly credited several portions of this correspondence to Col. Charles Cotesworth Pinckney of the regular army and not Col. Charles Pinckney of the Charlestown militia. Regarding contributions made by the militia volunteers in general, see Don Higginbotham, "The American Militia: A Traditional Institution with Revolutionary Responsibilities," in *War and Society in Revolutionary America: The Wider Dimension of Conflict* (Columbia: University of South Carolina Press, 1988), 106–31.

26. Williams, *Founding Family,* 139–40; Wallace, *Short History,* 291–92; David Ramsay, *The History of the American Revolution* (Philadelphia: R. Aitken, 1789), 447–48.

27. Williams, *Founding Family,* 141–42; Charles Cotesworth Pinckney to Eliza Lucas Pinckney, 9 October 1779, quoted in *Founding Family,* 143; Ramsay, *American Revolution,* 448–49.

28. Ramsay, *American Revolution,* 448–49.

29. Williams, *Founding Family,* 145–46; Haw, *John and Edward Rutledge,* 130–31; Wallace, *Short History,* 293.

30. Quoted in Haw, *John and Edward Rutledge,* 131; Ramsay, *American Revolution,* 477–79; Williams, *Founding Family,* 152–55.

31. *Charleston (S.C.) City Gazette,* 23 July 1818; Williams, *Founding Family,* 153.

32. Ramsay, *American Revolution,* 480; Wallace, *Short History,* 294; quoted in Ravenel, *Charleston,* 273.

33. Edward McCrady, *The History of South Carolina in the Revolution, 1775–1780* (New York: Macmillan Company, 1901), 533.

34. George C. Rogers and C. James Taylor, *A South Carolina Chronology 1497–1992,* 2d ed. (Columbia: University of South Carolina Press, 1994), 55–56; McCrady, *South Carolina in the Revolution,* 358–59; Philip Renlet, "In the Hands of the British: The Treatment of American POWs during the War of Independence," in *The Historian* 62 (summer 2000): 731–58; Mabel L. Webber, ed., "Josiah Smith's Diary," *SCHM* 33 (1932) 34 (1933); Franklin Hough, ed. *The Siege of Charleston by the British Fleet and Army under the Command of Admiral Arbuthnot and Sir Henry Clinton Which Terminated with the Surrender of That Place on the Twelfth of May, 1780* (Albany: J. Munsell, 1867), 204.

35. McCrady, *South Carolina in the Revolution,* 360–64.

36. Arthur Middleton to Charles Pinckney, 30 October 1782, "The Correspondence of Honorable Arthur Middleton," *SCHM* 27 (1926): 26–27.

37. Bailey and Cooper, *BDHR,* 3:110; Robert M. Weir, "'The Violent Spirit,' the Reestablishment of Order, and the Continuity of Leadership in Post-Revolutionary South Carolina," in *An Uncivil War: The Southern Backcountry during the American Revolution,* ed. Ronald Hoffman et al. (Charlottesville: University Press of Virginia for the U.S. Capitol Historical Society, 1985), 70–98.

38. Fraser, *Charleston! Charleston!,* 166.

39. First quote from Williams, *Founding Family,* 185; second from Edgar and Bailey, *BDHR,* 2:261.

40. Charles Cotesworth Pinckney to Arthur Middleton, 24 June 1782, *SCHM* 27 (1926): 63.

41. Thomas Cooper and David J. McCord, ed. , *The Statutes at Large of South Carolina* (Columbia, S.C.: A. S. Johnston, 1836–41), 6:633.

42. Charles Pinckney to Charles Cotesworth Pinckney, 15 July 1782, Pinckney Family Papers, series 1, box 1, LOC.

43. Charles Cotesworth Pinckney to Harriott Pinckney Horry, 22 September 1782, quoted in Williams, *Founding Family,* 188.

44. Quoted in Arthur Middleton to Charles Pinckney, 30 October 1782, *SCHM* 27 (1926): 27.

45. *South Carolina Gazette,* 16 April 1783 and 24 June 1783. Frances Leigh Williams indicates that Charles was too ashamed to return to South Carolina and face the problem of his father's taking protection. See *Founding Family,* 188. But according to an advertisement he placed in the *Gazette* requesting his father's creditors contact him, he was probably back in Charlestown by the end of April. It is also interesting to note that in January, his mother, Frances, gave Charles land that originally had belonged to her brother Miles Brewton on the Congaree just south of Columbia. Had she been upset because she

believed Charles was delaying his return home, she may have delayed conveying this property to him. That she did could indicate she had received word he was on his way home. See Brent Holcombe, ed., *South Carolina Deed Abstracts, 1783–1788* (Columbia: South Carolina Magazine of Ancestral Research, 1996), 457.

Chapter 2

1. Will of Charles Pinckney, 18 April 1770, will book A (1783–86), 431, SCDAH.

2. Petition of Frances Pinckney in Theodora J. Thompson, ed., *Journal of the House of Representatives, 1783–1784* (Columbia: University of South Carolina Press for the South Carolina Department of Archives and History, 1977), 177–78, 180.

3. Frances Pinckney to Robert Brewton, 30 March 1783, Pinckney Family Papers, series 1, box 1, LOC.

4. Walsh, *Sons of Liberty,* 114–23; Nadelhaft, *Disorders of War,* 97–99; Edgar, *South Carolina,* 245–46; Fraser, *Charleston! Charleston!,* 169.

5. Nadelhaft, *Disorders of War,* 102–3; Edgar, *South Carolina,* 247.

6. David Ramsay, *The History of South Carolina from its First Settlement in 1670, to the Year 1808* (Charleston: David Longworth for David Ramsay, 1809), 2:238.

7. Petition of Charles Pinckney in Thompson, *JHR, 1783–1784,* ix–x, 383; Cooper and McCord, *Statutes,* 4:699–701, 756–59.

8. Bailey and Cooper, *BDHR,* 3:367–68; Thompson, *JHR, 1783–1784,* 515.

9. Charles Pinckney, *Three Letters Addressed to the Public Chiefly in Defense of a Permanent Revenue for the Constitutional Congress of Confederation* (Charleston: n.p., 1783); *South Carolina Gazette and Public Advertiser,* 24–27 March 1784; Bailey and Cooper, *BDHR,* 3:268–72; John Lewis Gervais to Henry Laurens, 15 April 1784, Manuscripts Division, SCL.

10. Charles Pinckney to Jacob Read, 8 August 1784, Gratz Collection, PHS; Richard P. McCormick, *Experiment in Independence: New Jersey in the Critical Period, 1781–1789* (New Brunswick: Rutgers University Press, 1950), 247; Fraser, *Charleston! Charleston!,* 88.

11. Pinckney to Benjamin Guerard, 22 November 1784 and 2 December 1784, Paul H. Smith, ed., *LDC* (Washington, D.C.: Library of Congress, 1976–2000), 22:30, 41; *JCC,* ed. Worthington C. Ford et al. (Washington, D.C., 1904–37), 27:641–42, 647–49; McCrady, *South Carolina in the Revolution,* 359.

12. Pinckney to Guerard, *LDC,* 22:74.

13. *JCC,* 27:694–95.

14. Merrill D. Peterson, *Thomas Jefferson and the New Nation: A Biography* (New York: Oxford University Press, 1970), 280–83; Harry Ammon, *James Monroe: The Quest for National Identity* (Charlottesville: University Press of Virginia, 1990), 41–45.

15. Ammon, *James Monroe,* 45–49.

16. *JCC,* 27:705–6.

17. Ibid., 706–8.

18. Pinckney to Guerard, 2 January 1785, *LDC,* 22:98–102; Ammon, *James Monroe,* 42.

19. South Carolina delegates to Guerard, 25 January 1785, *LDC,* 22:136; Pinckney to Guerard, 25 January 1785, *LDC,* 22:132. See Gordon S. Wood, *The Creation of the American Republic, 1776–1787* (Chapel Hill: University of North Carolina Press, 1969),

58, 356. By 1795, Jefferson was taking exception to the notion that smaller republics were better. In a letter to Monsieur D'Ivernois, he wrote, "I suspect that the doctrine that small States alone are fitted to be republics, will be exploded by experience, with some other brilliant fallacies accredited by Montesquieu and other political writers." See Jefferson to D'Ivernois, 6 February 1795, Andrew A. Lipscomb and Albert Ellery Bergh, ed., *The Writings of Thomas Jefferson* (Washington, D.C.: Thomas Jefferson Memorial Foundation, 1903), 9:297–301.

20. *JCC,* 28:375–81; Ammon, *James Monroe,* 53–54.

21. *JCC,* 28:164–65, 31:669–73.

22. Ibid., 28:25, 98; Haw, *John and Edward Rutledge,* 182–97; Edgar and Bailey, *BDHR,* 2:577–81; John Ferling, *John Adams: A Life* (New York: Henry Holt and Company, 1996), 274–75.

23. Pinckney to Guerard, 14 February 1785, *LDC,* 22:199.

24. Lark Emerson Adams and Rosa Stoney Lumpkin, ed., *JHR, 1785–1786* (Columbia: University of South Carolina Press for the *South Carolina Department of Archives and History,* 1979), 80, 85, 601; Bailey and Cooper, *BDHR,* 3:591, 393–95.

25. McCormick, *Experiment in Independence,* 240–44.

26. Committee of Congress to William Livingston, *LDC,* 23:184, 188–89, 194–95n. 2; Matthew Carey, ed., *American Museum* 2 (July 1787): 153–59.

27. *New Jersey Gazette,* 20 March 1786, quoted in *LDC,* 21:194n. 8; *JCC,* 30:122.

28. Andrew C. McLaughlin, "The Articles of Confederation," in *Essays on the Making of the Constitution,* ed. Leonard W. Levy, 2d ed. (New York: Oxford University Press, 1987), 54, 59; *JCC* 26:318–22; Page Smith, *John Adams, 1784–1826* (Garden City, N.Y.: Doubleday and Company, 1962), 2:634–37; Julian P. Boyd, *Number 7: Alexander Hamilton's Secret Attempt to Control Foreign Policy,* quoted in Richard B. Morris, *The Forging of the Union, 1781–1789* (New York: Harper and Row Publishers, 1987), 206.

29. David Ramsay to Benjamin Rush, 3 May 1786, *Transactions of the American Philosophical Society,* 101; Ammon, *James Monroe,* 57.

30. *JCC,* 26:355; Frank Monaghan, *John Jay: Defender of Liberty* (New York: Bobbs-Merrill Company, 1935), 244.

31. Monaghan, *John Jay,* 255–61; Morris, *Forging of the Union,* 235–40; Ammon, *James Monroe,* 54–57.

32. Ammon, *James Monroe,* 56.

33. Pinckney's speech is found at *JCC,* 31:933–48. See also *JCC,* 31:595.

34. *JCC,* 31:597–600; Ammon, *James Monroe,* 58.

35. Pinckney to John Jay, draft, *LDC,* 23:548–49; Monroe to James Madison, 3 September 1786, *LDC,* 23:544; Ralph Ketcham, *James Madison: A Biography* (Charlottesville: University Press of Virginia, 1990), 184–85.

36. *JCC,* 30:230; David Ramsay to John Adams, 14 May 1786, *Transactions of the American Philosophical Society,* 102; Morris, *Forging of the Union,* 253–57. See also Jack Rakove, *The Beginnings of National Politics: An Interpretive History of the Continental Congress* (New York: Alfred A. Knopf, 1979), 370. Rakove cites a letter from William Grayson to James Madison stating a motion had been made in Congress regarding a convention as early as March. Rakove goes on to assert that its author was probably Pinckney. However,

there is no mention of such a motion in the congressional journals, and Grayson wrote Madison again on 28 May 1786 informing him of Pinckney's motion earlier in the month. See *LDC,* 23:318.

37. Morris, *Forging of the Union,* 253–57; *JCC,* 31:494–98. See also South Carolina delegates to William Moultrie, 6 November 1786, *LDC,* 24:7–8; and *Pennsylvania Gazette,* 17 November 1786, which printed the report more than three months after the articles were originally presented to Congress.

38. *JCC,* 32:71–72, 33:719; Morris, *Forging of the Union,* 253, 256–57; *LDC,* 24:14n. 12.

Chapter 3

1. Gilbert Stuart, *Charles Pinckney (1757–1824),* oil on canvas, no date, New York State Office of Parks, Recreation, and Historic Preservation; Wilbourn E. Benton, ed., *1787: Drafting the Constitution* (College Station: Texas A&M University Press, 1986), 1:37; Christopher and James Lincoln Collier, *Decision in Philadelphia: The Constitutional Convention of 1787* (New York: Ballantine Books, 1986), 93; J. B. O'Neall, *Biographical Sketches of the Bench and Bar of South Carolina* (Charleston, S.C.: S. G. Courtenay and Company, 1859; reprint, Spartanburg, S.C.: Reprint Company Publishers, 1975), 2:140.

2. Irving Brant, *James Madison, Father of the Constitution, 1787–1800* (Indianapolis: Bobbs-Merrill Company, 1950), 16–17, 29; Donald Jackson and Dorothy Twohig, ed., *The Diaries of George Washington* (Charlottesville: University Press of Virginia, 1979), 5:236.

3. Max Farrand, ed., *RFC,* rev. ed. (New Haven: Yale University Press, 1937; reprint, 1966), 1:1, 4–6.

4. Ibid., 7–14.

5. Ibid., 15–16.

6. Ibid., 20–24.

7. *Pennsylvania Gazette,* 24 October 1787.

8. Pinckney to John Quincy Adams, 30 December 1818, *RFC,* 3:427, 479–80.

9. Ibid., 604–9; Michael Kammen, ed., *The Origins of the American Constitution* (New York: Penguin Books, 1986), 25–30; Pinckney to Matthew Carey, 10 August 1788, Pinckney Family Papers, LOC.

10. James Madison to George Washington, 14 October 1787, *LDC,* 24:479.

11. Washington to Madison, 22 October 1787, *RFC,* 3:131.

12. Charles C. Nott, "The Mystery of the Pinckney Draft" (New York: Century Company, 1908). For a good recent overview of "The Puzzle of Charles Pinckney," see Collier and Collier, *Decision in Philadelphia,* 87–101. For contemporary accounts of the discoveries, see J. Franklin Jameson, "Portions of Charles Pinckney's Plan for a Constitution, 1787," *AHR* 8 (April 1903): 509–11 and Andrew C. McLaughlin, "Sketch of Charles Pinckney's Plan for a Constitution," *AHR* 9 (July 1904): 735–47. For Farrand's account, see *RFC,* 3:595–605. See also Andrew J. Bethea, *The Contribution of Charles Pinckney to the Formation of the American Union* (Richmond: Garrett and Massie, 1937); Shirley Sidney Ulmer, "The South Carolina Delegates to the Constitutional Convention of 1787" (Ph.D. diss., Duke University, 1956); and Ulmer, "Charles Pinckney: Father of the Constitution?" *South Carolina Law Quarterly* 10 (winter 1958).

13. All article numbers taken from Kammen, *Origins,* 25–30; Clinton Rossiter, *The Grand Convention* (New York: W. W. Norton and Company, 1966), 173; *RFC,* 2:342.

14. *RFC,* 2:616.

15. Jacques Necker, *A Treatise on the Administration of the Finances of France,* transl. Thomas Mortimer (London: Logographic Press, 1785), Special Collections Division, Thomas Cooper Library, University of South Carolina, Columbia, S.C.

16. *RFC,* 2:171, 1:33–34.

17. Collier and Collier, *Decision in Philadelphia,* 98.

18. *RFC,* 1:398–403.

19. Pinckney to John Jay, draft, *LDC,* 23:548; Pinckney to Guerard, 14 December 1784, ibid., 22:74.

20. Pinckney to Edward Carrington, 12 July 1790, Manuscripts Division, New York Public Library, New York, N.Y.

21. Kaplanoff, "Charles Pinckney and the American Republican Tradition," 98.

22. *RFC,* 1:132, 154.

23. Ibid., 2:370.

24. Kenneth S. Greenberg, *Masters and Statesmen: The Political Culture of Slavery* (Baltimore: Johns Hopkins University Press, 1985), 88–90.

25. Charles Pinckney, "Missouri Question: Speech of Mr. Pinckney of S. Carolina in the House of Representatives," *Niles Register,* 15 July 1820.

26. Pinckney to Charles Bellenger and Anthony Hughes, 14 August 1791, Miscellaneous manuscripts, NYPL.

27. *RFC,* 2:420; Max Farrand, *The Framing of the Constitution of the United States* (New Haven: Yale University Press, 1913), 148–53; Thornton Anderson, *Creating the Constitution: The Convention of 1787 and the First Congress* (University Park, Penn.: Pennsylvania State University Press, 1993), 102–6; Rossiter, *The Grand Convention,* 217; Collier and Collier, *Decision in Philadelphia,* 223–40; William Lee Miller, *The Business of May Next: James Madison and the Founding* (Charlottesville: University Press of Virginia, 1992), 127–32.

28. *RFC,* 2:340–44.

29. Ibid., 551.

30. Ibid., 628.

31. Ibid., 632.

32. Ibid., 641–44.

Chapter 4

1. W. S. Elliott, "Honorable Charles Pinckney, LL.D.," *DeBow's Review* 33 (1864): 66; Benjamin Franklin to Abbés Chalet and Arnoux, M. Leroy, and Ferdinand Grand, 19 October 1787, unpublished CD-ROM PH1, APS; Franklin to Grand, 22 October 1787, *The Writings of Benjamin Franklin,* ed. Albert Henry Smyth (New York: Haskell House Publishers, 1970), 9:619.

2. Michael E. Stevens and Christine M. Allen, *JHR, 1787–1788* (Columbia: University of South Carolina Press, 1981), 318, xx.

3. Jonathan Elliot, *The Debates in the Several State Conventions, on the Adoption of the Federal Constitution, as Recommended by the General Convention at Philadelphia, in 1787* (Washington, D.C.: Library of Congress, 1836), 4:254–62.

4. Ibid., 265–77.

5. Ibid., 277–317.

6. Henry Laurens to Lachlan McIntosh, 10 May 1770, *The Papers of Henry Laurens,* ed. George C. Rogers et al. (Columbia: University of South Carolina Press, 1979), 7:290–91.

7. See Joanna Bowen Gillespie, *The Life and Times of Martha Laurens Ramsay, 1759–1811* (Columbia: University of South Carolina Press, 2001), 69.

8. Ibid., 71, 95–97; Henry Laurens to Martha Laurens, 17 August 1776, Rogers et al., *Papers of Henry Laurens,* 11:256; John Laurens to Henry Laurens, 26 April 1776, ibid., 11:204.

9. Pinckney to Rufus King, 15 June 1788, Rufus King Papers, NYHS.

10. John Sanford Dart to "Colonel," 1 April 1788, Papers of John Sanford Dart, SCL; *State Gazette of South Carolina,* 1 May 1788.

11. George C. Rogers, *Evolution of a Federalist: William Loughton Smith of Charleston (1758–1812)* (Columbia: University of South Carolina Press, 1962), 150–51.

12. Ibid., 152–53; Klein, *Unification of a Slave State,* 168–69; Jerome Nadelhaft, "South Carolina: A Conservative Revolution," in *The Constitution and the States: The Role of the Original Thirteen in the Framing and Adoption of the Federal Constitution,* ed. Patrick T. Conley and John P. Kaminski (Madison, Wis.: Madison House, 1988), 173. See also Michael E. Stevens, "Their Liberties, Properties, and Privileges: Civil Liberties in South Carolina, 1663–1791," in *The Bill of Rights and the States: The Colonial and Revolutionary Origins of American Liberties,* ed. Patrick T. Conley and John P. Kaminski (Madison, Wis.: Madison House, 1992), 398–423.

13. Stevens and Allen, *JHR, 1787–1788,* xxv–xxvi.

14. Elliot, *Debates,* 4:320–21; Weir, *Colonial South Carolina,* 230.

15. Elliot, *Debates,* 4:322–23.

16. There are numerous works on republican ideology and its influence across the cultural, social, and political spectrum. Three major groundbreaking works deserve mention: Bernard Bailyn, *The Ideological Origins of the American Revolution* (Cambridge: Harvard University Press, 1967); Wood, *Creation of the American Republic;* and J. G. A. Pocock, *The Machiavellian Moment: Florentine Political Thought and the Atlantic Republican Tradition* (Princeton: Princeton University Press, 1975). For a good overview of the topic, see Daniel T. Rodgers, "Republicanism: The Career of a Concept," *Journal of American History* 79 (June 1992): 11–38.

17. Elliot, *Debates,* 4:329.

18. Ibid., 331.

19. Ibid., 335–36.

20. Ibid., 338–41.

21. Pinckney to Rufus King, 15 June 1788, Rufus King Papers, NYHS.

22. Michael E. Stevens and Christine M. Allen, *JHR, 1789–1790* (Columbia: University of South Carolina Press, 1984), 71; *Pennsylvania Gazette,* 25 February 1789; James Madison to George Washington, 2 December 1788, *LDC,* 25:460.

23. Wallace, *Short History,* 345; Adams, *JHR, 1785–1786,* viii, 595–96.

24. Stevens and Allen, *JHR, 1789–1790,* xv–xvi, 291.

25. Pinckney to Madison, 28 March 1789, Madison Papers, LOC. This letter is perhaps the only evidence that a male child was born to the Pinckneys in early 1789. That he was named after his father is based on Pinckney's desire expressed in his will that one of his nephews take his name, thus indicating a regret at not having a son who bore it. The couple would eventually name their only surviving son after Henry Laurens, who would die two years before the child was born.

26. Rebecca and Jacob Motte to Charles and Frances Pinckney, 9 September 1777, SCDAH, Dower Renunciations, no. 1775, 41; Holcombe, *South Carolina Deed Abstracts,* 457; Edward Hooker Papers, SCL; Edwin L. Green, *A History of Richland County,* vol. 1, *1732–1805* (1832; reprint, Baltimore: Regional Publishing Company, 1974), 165.

27. Edgar, *South Carolina,* 254–57; Haw, *James and Edward Rutledge,* 216–20; Klein, *Unification of a Slave State,* 144–48; Wallace, *Short History,* 340–45; Nadelhaft, *Disorders of War,* 202–13. Nadelhaft argues that the convention and constitution, although appearing to give little to the backcountry, actually proved to be a boon to them in the long run, especially over the next ten years. See also *Journal of the South Carolina Constitutional Convention, May 10–June 3, 1790* (Columbia: Historical Commission of South Carolina, 1946).

Chapter 5

1. Charleston Judgement Rolls, 1798, 788-A, SCDAH.

2. See Joyce Chaplin, *An Anxious Pursuit: Agricultural Innovation and Modernity in the Lower South, 1730–1815* (Chapel Hill: University of North Carolina Press, 1993), especially 277–329; also Edgar, *South Carolina,* 265–75; Lacy K. Ford, *Origins of Southern Radicalism: The South Carolina Upcountry, 1800–1860* (New York: Oxford University Press, 1988), 255–57; Wallace, *Short History,* 355.

3. Pinckney to Edward Carrington, 12 July 1790, Miscellaneous manuscripts, NYPL.

4. Klein, *Unification of a Slave State,* 178–202. Although Klein's is the most comprehensive study of South Carolina between the Revolution and the turn of the century, she does not give credit to Pinckney for his role as unifier of the state. She makes the argument that Pierce Butler was the driving force behind the empowerment of the backcountry, basing much of her argument on his letter books. Although she does recognize Pinckney's role at the Constitutional Convention, she almost completely ignores him during the decade in which he played perhaps his most important role in the state's history. Charleston Judgement Rolls, 1805, 97-A and 99-A, SCDAH; *The Statutes at Large of South Carolina,* 9:187–89, 371.

5. Pinckney to Madison, 14 June 1790, Madison Papers, LOC.

6. Pinckney to Gen. Andrew Pickens, 4 July 1790, Andrew Pickens Papers, CLS.

7. D. E. Huger Smith and A. S. Salley Jr., ed. , *Register of St. Philip's Parish Charles Town or Charleston, S.C. 1754–1810* (Columbia: University of South Carolina Press, 1971), 115.

8. Pinckney to the South Carolina House and Senate, 10 January 1791, Governor's Messages, Records of the General Assembly, no. 528, SCDAH; Klein, *Unification of a Slave State,* 176.

9. Pinckney to the South Carolina House and Senate, 2 February 1791, Governor's Messages, no. 532, SCDAH.

10. Governor's Messages, Pinckney to the South Carolina House and Senate, 28 November 1791, no. 523, SCDAH. See also John A. Hall, "A Rigour of Confinement That Violates Humanity: Jail Conditions in South Carolina during the 1790s," *Southern Studies: An Interdisciplinary Journal of the South* 24 (1985): 284–305; John C. Meleney, *The Public Life of Aedanus Burke* (Columbia: University of South Carolina Press, 1989), 252–54.

11. Jackson and Twohig, *Diaries of George Washington,* 6:96, 123–24, 126, 134; Washington to Pinckney, 29 March 1791, Washington Papers, LOC; Terry Lipscomb, *George Washington's Southern Tour* (Columbia: South Carolina Department of Archives and History, 1991); A. S. Salley, " President Washington's Tour through South Carolina in 1791," *Bulletins of the Historical Commission of South Carolina,* no. 12 (Columbia, S.C.: The State Company, 1932).

12. Pinckney to Washington, 26 April 1791, Washington Papers, LOC.

13. Jackson and Twohig, *Diaries of George Washington,* 6:126–31.

14. Washington to Pinckney, 8 November 1791, Washington Papers, LOC; Lipscomb, *Washington's Southern Tour,* 67.

15. Jackson and Twohig, *Diaries of George Washington,* 6:132–34.

16. Laurens to Washington, 20 August 1791, Washington Papers, LOC.

17. Pinckney to Madison, 6 August 1791, Madison Papers, LOC.

18. Laurens to Washington, 20 August 1791, Washington Papers, LOC; see Stanley Elkins and Eric McKitrick, *The Age of Federalism: The Early American Republic, 1788–1800* (New York: Oxford University Press, 1993), 742, and John Harold Wolfe, *Jeffersonian Democracy in South Carolina* (Chapel Hill: University of North Carolina Press, 1940), 63–64.

19. See George D. Terry, "A Study of the Impact of the French Revolution and the Insurrections in Saint-Dominque upon South Carolina: 1790–1805" (master's thesis, University of South Carolina, 1975), upon which much of this discussion is based. Regarding the toast, see page 13. See also Thomas O. Ott, *The Haitian Revolution: 1789–1804* (Knoxville: University of Tennessee Press, 1973).

20. President of the Saint-Dominque General Assembly to Pinckney, 20 August 1791 and Resolution of the Saint-Dominque General Assembly, 24 August 1791, Governor's Messages, no. 522, SCDAH.

21. Wallace, *Short History,* 340; Wood, *Black Majority,* 308–26; Terry, "Impact of the French Revolution," 39; Pinckney to President of the Saint-Dominque General Assembly, September 1791, Governor's Messages, no. 522, SCDAH; Pinckney to Washington, 12 September 1791, quoted in Rogers, *Evolution of a Federalist,* 249.

22. Pinckney to the South Carolina House, 14 December 1791, Governor's Messages, no. 522, SCDAH.

23. Terry, "Impact of the French Revolution," 43–45.

24. Jefferson to Pinckney, 1 April 1792, Jefferson Papers, LOC; Pinckney to the South Carolina Senate, 2 December 1792, Governor's Messages, no. 554, SCDAH.

25. See the 1790 South Carolina census, SCDAH. Two mid-nineteenth-century articles for *DeBow's Review* stated that Pinckney owned as many as two thousand slaves. See Elliott, "Honorable Charles Pinckney," *DeBow's Review* 33 (1864): 59–71, and W. S. Elliott, "Founder of the American Union: Charles Pinckney," *DeBow's Review* 1 (1866): 372–78. But this is an unrealistic number for a planter of Pinckney's means. Even the wealthiest planters rarely had one thousand slaves. See Kenneth Stampp, *The Peculiar Institution: Slavery in the Ante-bellum South* (New York: Random House, 1956), 30–31; Ulrich B. Phillips, *Life and Labor in the Old South* (Boston: Little, Brown and Company, 1929), 255; and Wallace, *Short History,* 434–35. Regarding slave autonomy and the task system, see Charles W. Joyner, *Down by the Riverside: A South Carolina Slave Community* (Urbana: University of Illinois Press, 1984); Morgan, *Slave Counterpoint;* and Wood, *Black Majority.*

26. Eugene V. Genovese, *Roll, Jordan, Roll: The World the Slaves Made* (New York: Random House, 1972), 322.

27. Ira Berlin, *Slaves Without Masters: The Free Negro in the Antebellum South* (New York: Pantheon Books, 1974), 218–19; Morgan, *Slave Counterpoint,* 236–44.

28. *Cripps v Pinckney,* Charleston Judgement Rolls, 1805, 99-A, SCDAH; Genovese, *Roll, Jordan, Roll,* 578, 641–42.

29. Genovese, *Roll, Jordan, Roll,* 329–30.

30. Ibid., 413–31; will book F, 1818–26, 609, SCDAH.

31. See Fawn Brodie, *Thomas Jefferson: An Intimate Biography* (New York: W. W. Norton, 1974); Annette Gordon-Reed, *Thomas Jefferson and Sally Hemings: An American Controversy* (Charlottesville: University Press of Virginia, 1997); Eugene Foster et al., "Jefferson Fathered Slave's Last Child," *Nature* 196 (5 November 1998): 27–28; Jan Ellen Lewis and Peter Onuf, ed., *Sally Hemings and Thomas Jefferson: History, Memory, and Civic Culture* (Charlottesville: University Press of Virginia, 1999).

32. Charleston Judgement Rolls, 1798, 788-A, SCDAH; Edgar, *South Carolina,* 266.

33. Pinckney to Thomas Pinckney, 8 October 1792, Manuscripts Division, SCL.

34. Pinckney to Washington, 14 October 1792, Washington Papers, LOC.

35. Pinckney to Benjamin Waring, 22 October 1792, Manuscripts Division, SCL.

36. Edgar and Bailey, *BDHR,* 2:698–99; *Annals of Congress,* 2d Cong., 1st sess., 435; Pinckney to the South Carolina Senate, 26 November 1792, Governor's Messages, no. 551, SCDAH.

37. Edgar and Bailey, *BDHR,* 2:393.

38. Charleston Judgement Rolls, 1793, 38-A, 188-A, 222-A, 272-A; 1794, 148-A, 181-A, SCDAH; Pinckney to John Grimke, 10 February 1797, Manuscripts Division, SCL.

39. Bertram Wyatt-Brown, *Southern Honor: Ethics and Behavior in the Old South* (New York: Oxford University Press, 1982), 113–324.

40. Ruth Bloch, "The Gendered Meanings of Virtue in Revolutionary America," *Signs: Journal of Women in Culture and Society* 13, no. 1 (1987): 53–54; Rosemary Zagarri, "The Rights of Man and Woman in Post-Revolutionary America," *WMQ* 55, no. 2 (April 1998): 203–30; Linda Kerber, *Women of the Republic.*

41. Stephanie McCurry, *Masters of Small Worlds: Yeomen Households, Gender Relations, and the Antebellum South Carolina Low Country* (New York: Oxford University Press, 1995), 18–19.

42. Pinckney, "Missouri Question," 356–57.

Chapter 6

1. Quote from Klein, *Unification of a Slave State,* 210. See also George C. Rogers, *Evolution of a Federalist,* 247–48; Harry Ammon, *The Genet Mission* (New York: W. W. Norton, 1973), 44–45; Terry, "Impact of the French Revolution," 35–36.

2. Klein, *Unification of a Slave State,* 204–5; Ammon, *Genet Mission,* 132–46.

3. There are many excellent studies of national politics in the 1790s. Perhaps the best and most complete is Elkins and McKitrick, *Age of Federalism.* See also John C. Miller, *The Federalist Era, 1789–1801* (New York: Harper and Row, 1960). Regarding the opposing sides, see Joyce Appleby, *Capitalism and a New Social Order: The Republican Vision of the 1790s* (New York: New York University Press, 1984); Lance Banning, *The Jeffersonian Persuasion: Evolution of a Party Ideology* (Ithaca, N.Y.: Cornell University Press, 1978); David Hackett Fisher, *The Revolution of American Conservatism: The Federalist Party in the Era of Jeffersonian Democracy* (New York: Harper and Row, 1965); and Linda K. Kerber, *Federalists in Dissent: Imagery and Ideology in Jeffersonian America* (Ithaca, N.Y.: Cornell University Press, 1970). Regarding the relationship between Jefferson and Hamilton, see Claude G. Bowers, *Jefferson and Hamilton: The Struggle for Democracy in America* (New York: Harper and Row, 1925); Dumas Malone, *Jefferson and the Ordeal of Liberty* (Boston: Little, Brown and Company, 1962); and Forrest McDonald, *Alexander Hamilton: A Biography* (New York: W. W. Norton, 1979). Regarding the South, see Lisle A. Rose, *Prologue to Democracy: The Federalists in the South, 1789–1800* (Lexington: University of Kentucky Press, 1968).

4. Edgar, *South Carolina,* 253; Jerald A. Combs, *The Jay Treaty: Political Battleground of the Founding Fathers* (Berkeley: University of California Press, 1970).

5. Rogers, *Evolution of a Federalist,* 276–77; Thomas, *Reminiscences,* 35; Henry Tuckniss, ed., *The American Remembrancer, or an Impartial Collection of Essays, Resolves, Speeches, Relative or Having Affinity to the Treaty with Great Britain* (Philadelphia, 1795), 1:5.

6. Tuckniss, *American Remembrancer,* 1:7, 9.

7. Ibid.,16–19.

8. Ibid., 17, 20; Thomas, *Reminiscences,* 35.

9. Ralph Izard to Jacob Read, 12 October 1795, quoted in Rogers, *Evolution of a Federalist,* 278; Tuckniss, *American Remembrancer,* 1:200; Terry, "Impact of the French Revolution," 88–90.

10. Edgar, *South Carolina,* 253–54.

11. See Albert Hall Bowman, *The Struggle for Democracy: Franco-American Diplomacy during the Federalist Era* (Knoxville: University of Tennessee Press, 1974); Alexander DeConde, *The Quasi-War: The Politics and Diplomacy of the Undeclared War with France, 1797–1801* (New York: Charles Scribner's Sons, 1966); Elkins and McKitrick, *Age of Federalism,* 529–690; William Stinchcombe, *The XYZ Affair* (Westport, Conn.: Greenwood Press, 1980).

12. Pinckney to John Gabriel, 16 May 1798, Manuscripts Division, SCL; Wallace, *Short History,* 373.

13. Pinckney to South Carolina Senate, 28 November 1798, Governor's Messages, no. 721, SCDAH; Pinckney to Abraham Rumph, 24 July 1798, Manuscripts Division, SCL; Terry, "Impact of the French Revolution," 120.

14. Pinckney to South Carolina Senate, 28 November 1798, Governor's Messages, no. 721, SCDAH.

15. Quoted in Bailey and Cooper, *BDHR,* 3:362; *Senate Journal,* 6th Cong., 1st sess., 16 February 1799, 586.

16. Pinckney to Jefferson, 12 October 1800 and 6 December 1800, in "South Carolina in the Presidential Election of 1800," *AHR* 4 (October 1898): 114, 123–24.

17. Charles Pinckney, *Pinckney Speeches* (1800), 19–32; Ferling, *John Adams,* 380.

18. David Ramsay to Rufus King, 28 January 1800, in Brunhouse, "David Ramsay, 1749–1815," 150.

19. Pinckney, *Speeches,* 7, 13–14.

20. Ibid., 87, 101.

21. Pinckney to Madison, 30 September 1799, *The Papers of James Madison,* ed. David B. Mattern et al. (Chicago: University of Chicago Press, 1962–1991), 17:272; Noble E. Cunningham, *The Jeffersonian Republicans: The Formation of Party Organizations, 1789–1801* (Chapel Hill: University of North Carolina Press, 1957), 144–45. See also Klein, *Unification of a Slave State,* 260; Wallace, *Short History,* 348–49; and Wolfe, *Jeffersonian Democracy,* 161.

22. Pinckney, *Speeches,* 46, 83–84.

23. *Philadelphia Aurora,* 19 February 1800; *Pennsylvania Gazette,* 5 March 1800.

24. Pinckney, *Speeches,* 102–4, 106, 119–20, 122, 134.

25. Pinckney to Jefferson, 12 October 1800, "South Carolina in the Presidential Election of 1800," 113–16.

26. Pinckney to Madison, 26 October 1800, ibid., 116; Pinckney, *Speeches,* I; Pinckney to Joseph Nicholson, 13 August 1800, Joseph H. Nicholson Papers, vol. 2, Manuscripts Division, LOC.

27. The election of 1800 revolved around other issues as well and contained a great deal of intrigue. See Elkins and McKitrick, *The Age of Federalism,* 691–754, and Stephen Kurtz, *The Presidency of John Adams: The Collapse of Federalism* (Philadelphia: University of Pennsylvania Press, 1957). It was during the campaign that the allegations regarding Jefferson and his slave Sally Hemings first arose. See Brodie, *Thomas Jefferson,* 15.

28. Pinckney to John Bynum, undated, Miscellaneous manuscripts, NYPL; Pinckney to Andrew Norris, 28 August 1800, Miscellaneous manuscripts, NYPL; Pinckney to Jefferson, 22 November 1800, "South Carolina in the Presidential Election of 1800," 119.

29. Pinckney to Madison, 26 October 1800, "South Carolina in the Presidential Election of 1800," 117.

30. Pinckney to Jefferson, 12 October 1800, ibid., 114–15.

31. Pinckney to Jefferson, 22 November 1800, ibid., 118–19; Marvin R. Zahniser, *Charles Cotesworth Pinckney: Founding Father,* 240.

32. Pinckney to Jefferson, December 1800, ibid., 121–22.

33. Ibid. See also Elkins and McKitrick, *Age of Federalism,* 735, 743. The authors assert that Charles Cotesworth's inaction played more of a role in Jefferson's winning of the state than Charles Pinckney's efforts. But from the time his name was placed on the ticket, Cotesworth became limited in what he could or could not do. Even if he had desired the office—and Elkins and McKitrick allege he did not—he could have worked behind the scenes, but he could never have been as visible as his cousin. There is no way to tell what could have happened had Cotesworth attempted to orchestrate a behind-the-scenes campaign. He enjoyed popularity in the state, but as a Federalist, he could not have been as popular in the backcountry. His cousin enjoyed as much popularity and, by some accounts, even more. He had won the governor's office three times. He had been elected to both the Confederation Congress and the senate. Cotesworth was a hero and had received much acclaim from his role in the XYZ affair, but he had only been elected to one office after his attendance at the South Carolina Constitutional Convention in 1790—when he adamantly opposed relocating the capital to Columbia.

34. Ibid., 746–50; Forrest McDonald, *Alexander Hamilton: A Biography,* 352–53; Pinckney to Jefferson, 9 February 1801, Jefferson Papers, LOC.

35. Pinckney to Jefferson, 5 March 1801, "South Carolina in the Presidential Election of 1800," 128.

36. *Senate Journal,* 6th Cong., 2d sess., 23 February 1801, 4 March 1801.

37. Pinckney to Jefferson, undated, Jefferson Papers, LOC.

38. *Senate Executive Journal,* 7th Cong., 1st sess., 6 January 1802.

39. Daniel D'Oyley, *A Letter Addressed to His Excellency Charles Pinckney* (South Carolina, 1807), 11; Pinckney to Jefferson, 26 May 1801, Jefferson Papers, LOC; Bailey and Cooper, *BDHR,* 3:192–93; Consolidated Index, SCDAH; *Adam Tunno v Pinckney,* 4 January 1799, *Adam and William Tunno v Pinckney,* 15 August 1800, *Administrators of Elizabeth Brimner v Pinckney,* 26 September 1799, Charleston Judgement Rolls, SCDAH.

Chapter 7

1. See Edward Hooker's 1805 diary quoted in Green, *History of Richland County,* 165. Hooker speaks of a ride south of Columbia along the Congaree River where he passed Pinckney's property. Hooker stated the house looked "neglected" and spoke of the property being "very much embarrassed by debt." Hooker also reported that, on the day he arrived in Columbia, the sheriff sold several of Pinckney's slaves at auction to satisfy his debts. Pinckney to Thomas Jefferson, 12 January 1806, Jefferson Papers, LOC.

2. Jefferson to James Monroe, January 1804, in *Writings of Thomas Jefferson,* ed. Paul L. Ford (New York: G. P. Putnam's Sons, 1892–99), 8:289.

3. Irving Brant, *James Madison, Secretary of State, 1800–1809* (Indianapolis: Bobbs-Merrill Company, 1953), 208; Nathan Schachner, *Thomas Jefferson: A Biography* (New York: Appleton-Century-Crofts, 1951), 2:787–88.

4. John E. Findling, *Dictionary of American Diplomatic History* (Westport, Conn.: Greenwood Press, 1980), 387.

5. Pinckney to Jefferson, 8 September 1801 and 6 October 1801, Jefferson Papers, LOC; Pinckney to Madison, 22 September 1801, Madison Papers, LOC; Pinckney to

Madison, 11 November 1801, SDDDS, vol. 6., Rare Book, Manuscript, and Special Collections Library, Duke University, Durham, N.C.; David Humphrey to Madison, 6 November 1801 and 18 December 1801, SDDDS; Neville Wyndham, *Travels Through Europe* (London: H. D. Symonds, ca. 1790), Special Collections, Thomas Cooper Library, University of South Carolina, Columbia, S.C.

6. John Graham to James Madison, 9 September 1802, quoted in Brant, *James Madison, Secretary of State,* 106; Findling, *Dictionary of American Diplomatic History,* 194–95; Madison quoted in "John Graham" in *Dictionary of American Biography* (New York: Charles Scribner's Sons, 1931–32), 4:477–78; Collier and Collier, *Decision in Philadelphia,* 94–95. See also Ketcham, *James Madison,* which is probably the most complete recent study of Madison. Lending support to the impression that even Madison's biographers have dismissed Pinckney's contributions to the founding of the republic is that Ketcham only mentions Pinckney once in the entire 671 pages of text.

7. Pinckney to Madison, 28 March 1802, Madison Papers, LOC; Pinckney to Madison, 6 and 7 November 1802, SDDDS.

8. See Klein, *Unification of a Slave State,* 244–46.

9. In 1787, while Pinckney served in the Constitutional Convention, Thomas Jefferson toured the south of France. He, too, traveled the Canal du Languedoc but in the opposite direction from Pinckney. Since the two had much in common in the way of politics, they may have discussed traveling in southern Europe, with Jefferson, the seasoned traveler, giving Pinckney advice. See Roy and Alma Moore, *Thomas Jefferson's Journey to the South of France* (New York: Stewart, Tabori, and Chang, 1999), especially 100–131. See also Wendell D. Garrett, *Thomas Jefferson Redivivus* (Barre, Mass.: Barre Publishers, 1971) 110–16 .

10. Graham to Madison, 28 November 1802, SDDDS.

11. Pinckney to Madison, 28 November 1802, ibid.

12. The letter to his daughter has not survived. Pinckney to Madison, 20 December 1802, Madison Papers, LOC; Graham to Madison, 1 February 1803, Pinckney to Madison, 22 February 1803, SDDDS.

13. Madison to Pinckey, 8 March 1803, in Mattern, *The Papers of James Madison,* 4:398–401.

14. Monroe to Pinckney, 14 April 1804, ibid., 166; Monroe to Madison, 26 May 1805, quoted in Ammon, *James Monroe,* 238.

15. Pinckney to Madison, 6 July 1802, SDDDS.

16. Ibid., 15 August 1802.

17. *Annals of Congress,* 7th Cong., 2d sess., 23, 270; *Senate Executive Journal,* 8th Cong., 1st sess., 21 December 1803, 9 January 1804.

18. Charles E. Hill, "James Madison," in *The American Secretaries of State and Their Diplomacy*, ed. Samuel Flagg Bemis (New York: Pageant Book Company, 1958), 50.

19. Paul C. Nagel, *John Quincy Adams: A Public Life, A Private Life* (New York: Alfred A. Knopf, 1997), 249–51. Although it can be argued that the settlement of the claims was instrumental in obtaining Florida in the treaty, some historians have contended that Andrew Jackson's actions in the territory caused Spain to see "the handwriting on

the wall," aiding in John Quincy Adams' diplomatic efforts. Thus, had the claims been settled in 1803 as Pinckney suggested, the Adams-Onis treaty nearly twenty years later might have worked even more to the advantage of United States interests. See Thomas A. Bailey, *A Diplomatic History of the American People* (Englewood Cliffs, N.J.: Prentice-Hall, 1980), 172–73.

20. Pinckney to Madison, 4 May 1803, SDDDS; Bailey, *Diplomatic History,* 113–14.

21. Pinckney to Madison, 10 January 1804, SDDDS; Hill, "James Madison," 44–46.

22. Hill, "James Madison," 50; Pinckney to Madison, 23 and 24 January 1804, SDDDS; Madison to Jefferson, 9 April 1804, James Norton Smith, *The Republic of Letters: The Correspondence between Thomas Jefferson and James Madison, 1776–1826* (New York: W. W. Norton and Company, 1995), 2:1305–6; Brant, *James Madison: Secretary of State,* 260.

23. Ammon, *James Monroe,* 238; Monroe to John Armstrong, 2 July 1805, in *The Writings of James Monroe,* ed. Stanislaus Murray Hamilton (New York: G. P. Putnam's Sons, 1898–1903), 4:299–301.

24. Ammon, *James Monroe,* 238–40; Hill, "James Madison," 53–56.

25. Hill, "James Madison," 56; Monroe to Madison, 6 August 1805, *The Writings of James Monroe,* 4:303–9; Pinckney to Madison, 28 May 1805, SDDDS.

26. Pinckney to Madison, 14 and 24 July 1805, 22 September 1805, undated letter of September 1805, and 22 October 1805, SDDDS.

27. Alice Izard to Mrs. Manigault, 3 October 1805, Manigault Family Papers, Manuscripts Division, SCL; D'Oyley, *A Letter Addressed to His Excellency Charles Pinckney,* 11–13; Consolidated Index, Charleston Judgement Rolls, SCDAH; South Carolina Judgement Rolls, no. CH 175, 1806, SCDAH; *Journals of the Senate,* 5 December 1807, SCDAH; Bailey and Cooper, *BDHR,* 3:192–93.

Chapter 8

1. Edgar and Bailey, *BDHR,* 2:196–97; Bailey and Cooper, *BDHR,* 3:192–93; Williams, *Founding Family,* 15.

2. *Journals of the Senate,* 9 and 11 December 1806, SCDAH.

3. Joseph Manigault to Gabriel Manigault, 24 May 1807, Manigault Family Papers, Manuscripts Division, SCL; South Carolina Judgement Rolls, no. CH 175, 1806, SCDAH; Pinckney to William H. Gibbes, 1 June 1807, Manuscripts Division, SCL; Charleston Court of Equity Decrees, 1807, 11–13, 16–17, SCDAH; *Journals of the Senate,* 10 December 1806, SCDAH.

4. D'Oyley, *A Letter Addressed to His Excellency Charles Pinckney,* 5, 15; *The Agricultural Society of South Carolina v Charles Pinckney,* 1 September 1798, Charleston Judgement Rolls, no. 754-A, SCDAH; *St. Cecilia Society v Charles Pinckney,* 22 March 1809, ibid., no. 161-A; *Administrators of Elizabeth Brimner v Charles Pinckney,* 26 September 1799, ibid., no. 423-A; *James Milligan v Charles Pinckney,* 1 September 1797, ibid., no. 777-A.

5. D'Oyley, *A Letter Addressed to His Excellency Charles Pinckney,* 8; *Journals of the Senate,* 18 December 1807, SCDAH.

6. Pinckney to William H. Gibbes, 1 June 1807, Manuscripts Division, SCL.

7. Joseph Manigault to Gabriel Manigault, 24 May 1807, ibid.

8. Jacob Read to Pinckney, 10 June 1807, ibid.; Bailey and Cooper, *BDHR,* 3:597–98.

9. Pinckney to South Carolina Senate, 17 December 1807, Governor's Messages, no. 982, SCDAH.

10. See Pinckney to the South Carolina Senate, 28 November 1798, Governor's Messages, no. 721, SCDAH, discussed in chapter 6. Pinckney to the South Carolina House and Senate, 17 November 1807, Governor's Messages, no. 976, SCDAH.

11. See Roger Kennedy, *Burr, Hamilton, and Jefferson: A Study in Character* (New York: Oxford University Press, 2000); Milton Lomask, *Aaron Burr: The Conspiracy and Years of Exile, 1805–1835* (New York: Farrar, Straus, and Giroux, 1982); Nathan Schachner, *Aaron Burr: A Biography* (New York: Frederick A. Stokes Company, 1937); N. Louise Bailey, *BDHR,* volume 4, 1791–1815 (Columbia: University of South Carolina Press, 1984), 32–35; Jefferson to Pinckney, 20 January 1807, Jefferson Papers, LOC.

12. *Georgetown Gazette,* 11 February 1807.

13. Alston to Pinckney, 6 February 1807, Pinckney to Jefferson, 16 February 1807, Jefferson Papers, LOC; Bailey, *BDHR,* 4:34–35.

14. Pinckney to Madison, 6 December 1808, Madison Papers, LOC; Ketcham, *James Madison,* 468.

15. Wallace, *Short History,* 356–60; Edgar, *South Carolina,* 261–62.

16. Klein, *Unification of a Slave State,* 264–66.

17. Pinckney to Jefferson, 2 January 1809 and 30 September 1809, Jefferson Papers, LOC; Pinckney to Madison, 2 January 1809 and 18 November 1809, Madison Papers, LOC.

18. See Col. Thomas Lehre to Ebenezer Smith Thomas, 30 January 1819, in Thomas, *Reminiscences,* 54–55; Rogers, *Evolution of a Federalist,* 393; Edgar, *South Carolina,* 325.

19. Pinckney to Madison, 18 December 1811, Madison Papers, LOC; Williams, *Founding Family,* 355; Rogers, *Evolution of a Federalist,* 392.

20. Wallace, *Short History,* 360, 460.

Chapter 9

1. Charleston County Equity Bills, 1827, no. 85, SCDAH.

2. Bruce H. Mann, *Republic of Debtors: Bankruptcy in the Age of American Independence* (Cambridge: Harvard University Press, 2002), 8.

3. Pinckney to William H. Gibbes, circa 1816, Pinckney to Madison, 21 August 1816, Manuscripts Division, SCL; Jefferson to Pinckney, 3 September 1816, Jefferson Papers, LOC; Ammon, *James Monroe,* 352–57.

4. Theodore D. Jervey, *Robert Y. Hayne and His Times* (New York: Macmillan Company, 1909), 47; Pinckney to Madison, 16 January 1813, Madison Papers, LOC; Alexander Moore, *BDHR,* volume 5, 1816–1828 (Columbia: South Carolina Department of Archives and History, 1992), 206–8. See also Lacy K. Ford, *Origins of Southern Radicalism,* 114, regarding the factionalism occurring in South Carolina; Rogers, *Evolution of a Federalist,* 393–94.

5. Bailey, *BDHR,* 4:272–73.

6. William W. Freehling, *The Road to Disunion: Secessionists at Bay, 1774–1854* (New York: Oxford University Press, 1990), 150–51.

7. See Glover Moore, *The Missouri Controversy, 1819–1821* (Lexington: University of Kentucky Press: 1953); George Dangerfield, *The Awakening American Nationalism, 1815–1828* (New York: Harper and Row, 1965), 97–140.

8. See Pinckney to Jefferson, 6 September 1820, Jefferson Papers, LOC.

9. Pinckney, "Missouri Question," 349–57.

10. *House Journal,* 16th Cong., 1st sess., 1 and 2 March 1820, 269; Dangerfield, *Awakening of American Nationalism,* 122–24.

11. Elkins and McKitrick, *Age of Federalism,* 734–35; Cynthia Diane Earman, "Boardinghouses, Parties, and the Creation of a Political Society in Washington City, 1800–1830" (master's thesis, Louisiana State University, 1992), 72–73.

12. Pinckney to Jefferson, 6 September 1820, Jefferson Papers, LOC.

13. Dangerfield, *Awakening of American Nationalism,* 130–36; *Annals of Congress,* 16th Cong., 2d sess., 1130–45.

14. Pinckney to Robert Y. Hayne, 31 March 1821, NYPL, Miscellaneous manuscripts; Pinckney to James Anderson, 28 August 1821, PHS.

15. Pinckney to Rufus King, 20 March 1822, Rufus King Papers, NYHS; *Charleston (S.C.) City Gazette,* 30 October 1824; regarding dropsy, see Williams, *Founding Family,* 360; will of Charles Pinckney, SCDAH; *Charleston Mercury,* 30 October 1824.

Conclusion

1. *Unveiling of the Memorial Ledger,* 7–8, 21.

2. *Dictionary of American Biography,* 4:478; Pinckney to Madison, 27 October 1800, "South Carolina in the Presidential Election of 1800," 118.

3. Terry W. Lipscomb, "In Search of the Charles Pinckney Library," 2–7.

Bibliography

Primary Sources

NEWSPAPERS

Charleston (S.C.) City Gazette

Charleston (S.C.) Mercury

(Charleston, S.C.) City Gazette

South Carolina Gazette

South Carolina Gazette and Public Advertiser

State Gazette of South Carolina

Georgetown (S.C.) Gazette

Pennsylvania Gazette

Pennsylvania Journal

Philadelphia Aurora

MANUSCRIPTS

American Philosophical Society. Unpublished CD-ROM PH1. American Philosophical Society, Philadelphia, Pa.

Library of Congress. Jefferson Papers. Madison Papers. Joseph H. Nicholson Papers. Pinckney Family Papers. Washington Papers.

New York Historical Society. Rufus King Papers.

New York Public Library. Miscellaneous manuscripts.

Pennsylvania Historical Society. Gratz Collection. Miscellaneous manuscripts.

South Caroliniana Library, University of South Carolina, Columbia. Edward Hooker Papers. John Sanford Dart Papers. Manigault Family Papers. Pinckney Papers.

PUBLIC DOCUMENTS

Adams, Lark Emerson, and Rosa Stoney Lumpkin, ed. *Journal of the House of Representatives, 1785–1786.* Columbia: University of South Carolina Press for the South Carolina Department of Archives and History, 1979.

Annals of the Congress of the United States, 1789–1824. 18 vols. Washington, D.C., 1834–1856.

Charleston Court of Equity Decrees. South Carolina Department of Archives and History, Columbia, S.C.

Charleston County Equity Bills. South Carolina Department of Archives and History, Columbia, S.C.

Charleston Judgement Rolls. South Carolina Department of Archives and History, Columbia, S.C.

Consolidated Index. South Carolina Department of Archives and History, Columbia, S.C.

Cooper, Thomas, and David J. McCord, ed. *The Statutes at Large of South Carolina.* Columbia, S.C.: A. S. Johnston, 1836–41.

Elliot, Jonathan. *The Debates in the Several State Conventions, on the Adoption of the Federal Constitution, as Recommended by the General Convention at Philadelphia, in 1787.* 5 vols. Washington, D.C.: Library of Congress, 1836.

Governor's Messages, 1783–1830. South Carolina Department of Archives and History, Columbia, S.C.

Hamilton, Stanislaus Murray. *The Writings of James Monroe.* New York: G. P. Putnam's Sons, 1898–1903.

Holcombe, Brent, ed. *South Carolina Deed Abstracts, 1783–1788.* Columbia: South Carolina Magazine of Ancestral Research, 1996.

Journal of the South Carolina Constitutional Convention, May 10–June 3, 1790. Columbia: Historical Commission of South Carolina, 1946.

Journals of the Senate. South Carolina Department of Archives and History, Columbia, S.C.

Pinckney, Charles. 18 April 1770. Will book A (1783–1786), South Carolina Department of Archives and History, Columbia, S.C.

Renunciation of Dower Books, Court of Common Pleas, 1726–1787. South Carolina Department of Archives and History, Columbia, S.C.

Smith, D. E. Huger, and A. S. Salley Jr., ed. *Register of St. Philip's Parish Charles Town or Charleston, S.C. 1754–1810.* Columbia: University of South Carolina Press, 1971.

Smith, Paul H., ed. *Letters of the Delegates to Congress.* Washington, D.C.: Library of Congress, 1976–2000.

South Carolina Judgement Rolls. South Carolina Department of Archives and History, Columbia, S.C.

State Department Diplomatic Despatches, Spain. Vol. 6. Rare Book, Manuscript, and Special Collections Library, Duke University, Durham, N.C.

Stevens, Michael E., and Christine M. Allen. *Journal of the House of Representatives, 1787–1788.* Columbia: University of South Carolina Press, 1981.

Stevens, Michael E., and Christine M. Allen. *Journal of the House of Representatives, 1789–1790.* Columbia: University of South Carolina Press, 1984.

Thompson, Theodora J., ed. *Journal of the House of Representatives, 1783–1784.* Columbia: University of South Carolina Press for the South Carolina Department of Archives and History, 1977.

U.S. Congress. *House Journal.* 16th Cong., 1st sess.

———. *Senate Executive Journal.* 8th Cong., 1st sess.

———. *Senate Journal.* 6th Cong., 1st sess.

Vincent, Susan Hart. *Charles Pinckney National Historic Site Cultural Landscape Report.* Atlanta: National Park Service, 1998.

PUBLISHED PAMPHLETS, MEMOIRS, DIARIES, AND OTHER PRIMARY SOURCES

Brunhouse, Robert L., ed. "David Ramsay, 1749–1815, Selections from His Writings." *Transactions of the American Philosophical Society* 55 (1965): 1–16.

Carey, Matthew, ed. *American Museum* 2 (July 1787): 153–59.

Continental Congress. *Journals of the Continental Congress, 1774 -1789.* Edited by Worthington C. Ford et al. 34 vols. Washington, D.C., 1904–37.

D'Oyley, Daniel. *A Letter Addressed to His Excellency Charles Pinckney.* South Carolina: 1807, LOC.

Farrand, Max, ed. *Records of the Federal Convention of 1787.* Rev. ed. New Haven: Yale University Press, 1937. Reprint, 1966.

Ford, Paul L., ed. *Writings of Thomas Jefferson.* 10 vols. New York: G. P. Putnam's Sons, 1892–99.

Hooker, Richard J., ed. *The Carolina Backcountry on the Eve of the Revolution: The Journal and Other Writings of Charles Woodmason, Anglican Itinerant.* Chapel Hill: University of North Carolina Press, 1953.

Jackson, Donald, and Dorothy Twohig, ed. *The Diaries of George Washington.* 6 vols. Charlottesville: University Press of Virginia, 1979.

Kammen, Michael, ed. *The Origins of the American Constitution.* New York: Penguin Books, 1986.

Lipscomb, Andrew A., and Albert Ellery Bergh, ed. *The Writings of Thomas Jefferson.* Washington, D.C.: Thomas Jefferson Memorial Foundation, 1903.

Mattern, David B. et al., ed. *The Papers of James Madison.* 17 vols. Chicago: University of Chicago Press, 1962–1991.

Middleton, Arthur. "The Correspondence of Honorable Arthur Middleton." *South Carolina Historical (and Genealogical) Magazine* 27 (1926).

Necker, Jacques. *A Treatise on the Administration of the Finances of France.* Translated by Thomas Mortimer. London: Logographic Press, 1785. Special Collections Division. Thomas Cooper Library, University of South Carolina, Columbia, S.C.

O'Neall, J. B. *Biographical Sketches of the Bench and Bar of South Carolina.* 20 vols. Charleston, S.C.: S. G. Courtenay and Company, 1859. Reprint, Spartanburg, S.C.: Reprint Company Publishers, 1975.

Pinckney, Charles. "Missouri Question: Speech of Mr. Pinckey of S. Carolina in the House of Representatives." *Nile's Register,* 15 July 1820.

———. *Pinckney Speeches.* 1800.

———. *Three Letters Addressed to the Public Chiefly in Defense of a Permanent Revenue for the Constitutional Congress of Confederation.* Charleston, n.p., 1783.

Pinckney, Elise, and Marvin L. Zahniser, ed. *The Letterbook of Eliza Lucas Pinckney.* Chapel Hill: University of North Carolina Press, 1972.

Ramsay, David. *The History of South Carolina, from its First Settlement in 1670, to the Year 1808.* 2 vols. Charleston: David Longworth for David Ramsay, 1809.

———. *The History of the American Revolution.* Philadelphia: R. Aitkin, 1789.

Rogers, George C., et al., ed. *The Papers of Henry Laurens.* Vol. 7. Columbia: University of South Carolina Press, 1979.

Smyth, Albert Henry, ed. *The Writings of Benjamin Franklin.* 10 vols. New York: Haskell House Publishers, 1970.

Thomas, Ebenezer Smith. *Reminiscences of the Last Sixty-Five Years, Commencing with the Battle of Lexington; Also Sketches of His Own Life and Times.* Hartford, Conn.: Case, Tiffany, and Burnham, 1840.

Tuckniss, Henry, ed. *The American Remembrancer or an Impartial Collection of Essays, Resolves, Speeches, Relative or Having Affinity to the Treaty with Great Britain.* Philadelphia: H. Tuckniss, for M. Carey, 1795.

The Unveiling of the Memorial Ledger to Charles Pinckney. Atlanta: Westminster Publishers, 1949.

Warren, Mercy Otis. *History of the Rise, Progress, and Termination of the American Revolution.* Boston: Manning and Loring for E. Larking, 1805.

Webber, Mabel L., ed. "Josiah Smith's Diary." *South Carolina Historical (and Genealogical) Magazine* 33 (1932), 34 (1933).

Wyndham, Neville. *Travels through Europe* London: H. D. Symonds, ca. 1790. Special Collections Division, Thomas Cooper Library, University of South Carolina, Columbia, S.C.

Secondary Sources

BOOKS

Alden, John R. *A History of the American Revolution.* New York: Alfred Knopf, 1969.

Ammon, Harry. *The Genet Mission.* New York: W. W. Norton, 1973.

———. *James Monroe: The Quest for National Identity.* Charlottesville: University Press of Virginia, 1990.

Anderson, Thornton. *Creating the Constitution: The Convention of 1787 and the First Congress.* University Park, Penn.: Pennsylvania State University Press, 1993.

Appleby, Joyce. *Capitalism and a New Social Order: The Republican Vision of the 1790s.* New York: New York University Press, 1984.

Bailey, N. Louise. *Biographical Directory of the South Carolina House of Representatives.* Vol. 4, *1791–1815.* Columbia: University of South Carolina Press, 1984.

Bailey, N. Louise, and Elizabeth Ivey Cooper. *Biographical Directory of the South Carolina House of Representatives.* Vol. 3, *House of Representatives, 1775–1790.* Columbia: University of South Carolina Press, 1981.

Bailey, Thomas A. *A Diplomatic History of the American People.* Englewood Cliffs, N.J.: Prentice-Hall, 1980.

Bailyn, Bernard. *The Ideological Origins of the American Revolution.* Cambridge: Harvard University Press, 1967.

Banning, Lance. *The Jeffersonian Persuasion: Evolution of a Party Ideology.* Ithaca, N.Y.: Cornell University Press, 1978.

Benton, Wilbourn E., ed. *1787: Drafting the Constitution.* 2 vols. College Station, Tex.: Texas A&M University Press, 1986.

Berlin, Ira. *Slaves Without Masters: The Free Negro in the Antebellum South.* New York: Pantheon Books, 1974.

Bethea, Andrew J. *The Contribution of Charles Pinckney to the Formation of the American Union.* Richmond: Garrett and Massie, 1937.

Bowers, Claude G. *Jefferson and Hamilton: The Struggle for Democracy in America.* New York: Harper and Row, 1925.

Bowling, Kenneth R. *The Creation of Washington, D.C.: The Idea and Location of the American Capital.* Fairfax, Va.: George Mason University Press, 1991.

Bowman, Albert Hall. *The Struggle for Diplomacy: Franco-American Diplomacy during the Federalist Era.* Knoxville: University of Tennessee Press, 1974.

Brant, Irving. *James Madison, Father of the Constitution, 1787–1800.* Indianapolis: Bobbs-Merrill Company, 1950.

———. *James Madison, Secretary of State, 1800–1809.* Indianapolis: Bobbs-Merrill Company, 1953.

Brodie, Fawn. *Thomas Jefferson: An Intimate Biography.* New York: W. W. Norton, 1974.

Chaplin, Joyce E. *An Anxious Pursuit: Agricultural Innovation and Modernity in the Lower South, 1730–1815.* Chapel Hill: University of North Carolina Press, 1993.

Christopherson, Merrill G. *Biography of an Island: General C. C. Pinckney's Sea Island Plantation.* Fennimore, Wis.: Westburg Associates, 1972.

Collier, Christopher, and James Lincoln Collier. *Decision in Philadelphia: The Constitutional Convention of 1787.* New York: Ballantine Books, 1986.

Combs, Jerald A. *The Jay Treaty: Political Battleground of the Founding Fathers.* Berkeley: University of California Press, 1970.

Countryman, Edward. *The American Revolution.* New York: Norton and Company, 1976.

Cunningham, Noble E. *The Jeffersonian Republicans: The Formation of Party Organizations, 1789–1801.* Chapel Hill: University of North Carolina Press, 1957.

Dangerfield, George. *The Awakening of American Nationalism, 1815–1828.* New York: Harper and Row, 1965.

DeConde, Alexander. *The Quasi-War: The Politics and Diplomacy of the Undeclared War with France, 1797–1801.* New York: Charles Scribner's Sons, 1966.

Dictionary of American Biography. New York: Charles Scribner's Sons, 1931–32.

Edgar, Walter. *South Carolina: A History.* Columbia: University of South Carolina Press, 1998.

Edgar, Walter, and N. Louise Bailey. *Biographical Directory of the South Carolina House of Representatives.* Vol. 2, *The Commons House of Assembly, 1692–1775.* Columbia: University of South Carolina Press, 1977.

Elkins, Stanley, and Eric McKitrick. *The Age of Federalism: The Early American Republic, 1788–1800.* New York: Oxford University Press, 1993.

Ellis, Joseph T. *Founding Brothers: The Revolutionary Generation.* New York: Alfred A. Knopf, 2000.

Farrand, Max. *The Framing of the Constitution of the United States.* New Haven: Yale University Press, 1913.

Ferling, John. *John Adams: A Life.* New York: Henry Holt and Company, 1996.

Findling, John E. *Dictionary of American Diplomatic History.* Westport, Conn.: Greenwood Press, 1980.

Fisher, David Hackett. *The Revolution of American Conservatism: The Federalist Party in the Era of Jeffersonian Democracy.* New York: Harper and Row, 1965.

Ford, Lacy K. *Origins of Southern Radicalism: The South Carolina Upcountry, 1800–1860.* New York: Oxford University Press, 1988.

Fraser, Walter J. Jr. *Charleston! Charleston! The History of a Southern City.* Columbia: University of South Carolina Press, 1989.

Freehling, William W. *The Road to Disunion: Secessionists at Bay, 1774–1854.* New York: Oxford University Press, 1990.

Frey, Sylvia R. *Water from the Rock: Black Resistance in a Revolutionary Age.* Princeton: Princeton University Press, 1991.

Garraty, John A., and Mark C. Carnes, ed. *American National Biography.* New York: Oxford University Press, 1999.

Garrett, Wendell D. *Thomas Jefferson Redivivus.* Barre, Mass.: Barre Publishers, 1971.

Genovese, Eugene G. *Roll, Jordan, Roll: The World the Slaves Made.* New York: Random House, 1972.

Gillespie, Joanna Bowen. *The Life and Times of Martha Laurens Ramsay, 1759–1811.* Columbia: University of South Carolina Press, 2001.

Gordon, Asa. *Sketches of Negro Life and History in South Carolina.* Columbia: University of South Carolina Press, 1928.

Gordon-Reed, Annette. *Thomas Jefferson and Sally Hemings: An American Controversy.* Charlottesville: University Press of Virginia, 1997.

Green, Edwin L. *A History of Richland County.* Vol. 1, 1732–1805. 1832. Reprint, Baltimore: Regional Publishing Company, 1974.

Greenberg, Kenneth S. *Masters and Statesmen: The Political Culture of American Slavery.* Baltimore: Johns Hopkins University Press, 1985.

Haw, James. *John and Edward Rutledge of South Carolina.* Athens: University of Georgia Press, 1997.

Higginbotham, Don. *The War of American Independence: Military Attitudes, Policies, and Practice, 1763–1789.* New York: Macmillan, 1971.

Hough, Franklin. *The Siege of Charleston by the British Fleet and Army, under the Command of Admiral Arbuthnot and Sir Henry Clinton, Which Terminated with the Surrender of That Place on the Twelfth of May, 1780.* Albany: J. Munsell, 1867.

Jameson, J. Franklin. *The American Revolution Considered as a Social Movement.* Princeton: Princeton University Press, 1926.

Jensen, Merrill. *The Founding of A Nation: A History of the American Revolution, 1763–1776.* New York: Oxford University Press, 1968.

Jervey, Theodore D. *Robert Y. Hayne and His Time.* New York: Macmillan Company, 1909.

Joyner, Charles W. *Down by the Riverside: A South Carolina Slave Community.* Urbana: University of Illinois Press, 1984.

Kennedy, Roger. *Burr, Hamilton, and Jefferson: A Study in Character.* New York: Oxford University Press, 2000.

Kerber, Linda K. *Federalists in Dissent: Imagery and Ideology in Jeffersonian America.* Ithaca, N.Y.: Cornell University Press, 1970.

———. *Women of the Republic: Intellect and Ideology in Revolutionary America.* Chapel Hill: University of North Carolina Press, 1980.

Ketcham, Ralph. *James Madison: A Biography.* Charlottesville: University Press of Virginia, 1990.

Klein, Rachel N. *Unification of a Slave State: The Rise of the Planter Class in the South Carolina Backcountry, 1760–1808.* Chapel Hill: University of North Carolina Press, 1990.

Kovacik Charles F., and John J. Winberry. *South Carolina: A Geography.* Boulder, Colo.: Westview Press, 1987.

Kurtz, Stephen. *The Presidency of John Adams: The Collapse of Federalism.* Philadelphia: University of Pennsylvania Press, 1957.

Lewis, Jan Ellen, and Peter S. Onuf, ed. *Sally Hemings and Thomas Jefferson: History, Memory, and Civic Culture.* Charlottesville: University Press of Virginia, 1999.

Lipscomb, Terry. *George Washington's Southern Tour.* Columbia: South Carolina Department of Archives and History, 1991.

Lomask, Milton. *Aaron Burr: The Conspiracy and Years of Exile, 1805–1835.* New York: Farrar, Straus, and Giroux, 1982.

Malone, Dumas. *Jefferson and the Ordeal of Liberty.* Boston: Little, Brown and Company, 1962.

Mann, Bruce. *Republic of Debtors: Bankruptcy in the Age of American Independence.* Cambridge: Harvard University Press, 2002.

Martin, James Kirby, and Mark Edward Lender. *A Respectable Army: The Military Origins of the Republic, 1763–1789.* Arlington Heights, Ill.: Harlan Davidson, 1982.

Matson, Cathy D., and Peter S. Onuf. *A Union of Interests: Political and Economic Thought in Revolutionary America.* Lawrence, Kans.: University Press of Kansas, 1990.

McCormick, Richard P. *Experiment in Independence: New Jersey in the Critical Period, 1781–1789.* New Brunswick: Rutgers University Press, 1950.

McCrady, Edward. *The History of South Carolina in the Revolution, 1775–1780.* New York: Macmillan Company, 1901.

———. *South Carolina in the Revolution, 1780–1783.* New York: Macmillan Company, 1902.

McCurry, Stephanie. *Masters of Small Worlds: Yeomen Households, Gender Relations, and the Antebellum South Carolina Low Country.* New York: Oxford University Press, 1995.

McDonald, Forrest. *Alexander Hamilton: A Biography.* New York: W. W. Norton, 1979.

———. *E Pluribus Unum: The Formation of the American Republic, 1776–1790.* Indianapolis: Liberty Press, 1979.

Meleney, John C. *The Public Life of Aedanus Burke.* Columbia: University of South Carolina Press, 1989.

Miller, John C. *The Federalist Era, 1789–1801.* New York: Harper and Row, 1960.

Miller, William Lee. *The Business of May Next: James Madison and the Founding.* Charlottesville: University Press of Virginia, 1992.

Monaghan, Frank. *John Jay: Defender of Liberty.* New York: Bobbs-Merrill Company, 1935.

Moore, Alexander. *Biographical Directory of the South Carolina House of Representatives.* Vol. 5, 1816–1828. Columbia: South Carolina Department of Archives and History, 1992.

Moore, Glover. *The Missouri Controversy, 1819–1921.* Lexington: University of Kentucky Press, 1953.

Moore, Roy, and Alma Moore. *Thomas Jefferson's Journey to the South of France.* New York: Stewart, Tabori, and Chang, 1999.

Morgan, Edmund S. *The Birth of the Republic, 1763–1789.* Chicago: University of Chicago Press, 1977.

Morgan, Edmund S., and Helen M. Morgan. *The Stamp Act Crisis: Prologue to Revolution.* New York: Macmillan, 1963.

Morgan, Philip. *Slave Counterpoint: Black Culture in the Eighteenth-Century Chesapeake and Lowcountry.* Chapel Hill: University of North Carolina Press, 1998.

Morris, Richard B. *The Forging of the Union, 1781–1789.* New York: Harper and Row Publishers, 1987.

Nadelhaft, Jerome J. *The Disorders of War: The Revolution in South Carolina.* Orono, Maine: University of Maine at Orono, 1981.

Nagel, Paul C. *John Quincy Adams: A Public Life, A Private Life.* New York: Alfred A. Knopf, 1997.

Nash, Gary B., et al. *The American People: Creating a Nation and a Society.* Brief 3d ed. New York: Longman, 2000.

Neimeyer, Charles. *America Goes To War: A Social History of the Continental Army.* New York: New York University Press, 1996.

Norton, Mary Beth. *Liberty's Daughters: The Revolutionary Experience of American Women, 1750–1800.* Ithaca, N.Y.: Cornell University Press, 1980.

Nott, Charles C. *The Mystery of the Pinckney Draft.* New York: Century Company, 1908.

Olwell, Robert. *Masters, Slaves, and Subjects: The Culture of Power in the South Carolina Low Country, 1740–1790.* Ithaca, N.Y.: Cornell University Press, 1998.

Ott, Thomas O. *The Haitian Revolution: 1789–1804.* Knoxville: University of Tennessee Press, 1973.

Peterson, Merrill D. *Thomas Jefferson and the New Nation: A Biography.* New York: Oxford University Press, 1970.

Phillips, Ulrich B. *Life and Labor in the Old South.* Boston: Little, Brown and Company, 1929.

Pinckney, Charles Cotesworth. *Life of General Thomas Pinckney.* Boston: Houghton Mifflin and Company, 1895.

Pocock, J. G. A. *The Machiavellian Moment: Florentine Political Thought and the Atlantic Republican Tradition.* Princeton: Princeton University Press, 1975.

Rakove, Jack. *The Beginnings of National Politics: An Interpretive History of the Continental Congress.* New York: Alfred A. Knopf, 1979.

Raven, James. *London Booksellers and American Customers: Transatlantic Literary Community and the Charleston Library Society, 1798–1811.* Columbia: University of South Carolina Press, 2002.

Ravenel, Harriott Horry Rutledge. *Charleston: The Place and the People.* New York: Macmillan Company, 1906.

Rogers, George C. Jr. *Charleston in the Age of the Pinckneys.* Columbia: University of South Carolina Press, 1969.

———. *Evolution of a Federalist: William Loughton Smith of Charleston (1758–1812).* Columbia: University of South Carolina Press, 1962.

Rogers, George C. Jr., and C. James Taylor. *A South Carolina Chronology, 1497–1992.* 2d ed. Columbia: University of South Carolina Press, 1994.

Rose, Lisle A. *Prologue to Democracy: The Federalists in the South, 1789–1800.* Lexington: University of Kentucky Press, 1968.

Rossiter, Clinton. *The Grand Convention.* New York: W. W. Norton and Company, 1966.

Royster, Charles. *A Revolutionary People at War: The Continental Army and American Character.* Chapel Hill: University of North Carolina Press, 1979.

Schachner, Nathan. *Aaron Burr: A Biography.* New York: Frederick A. Stokes Company, 1937.

———. *Thomas Jefferson: A Biography.* Vol. 2. New York: Appleton-Century-Crofts, 1951.

Shurkin, Joel N. *The Invisible Fire: The Story of Mankind's Victory over the Ancient Scourge of Smallpox.* New York: Putnam, 1979.

Shy, John. *A People Numerous and Armed: Reflections on the Military Struggle for American Independence.* New York: Oxford University Press, 1976.

Smith, James Norton. *The Republic of Letters: The Correspondence between Thomas Jefferson and James Madison, 1776–1826.* Vol. 2. New York: W. W. Norton and Company, 1995.

Smith, Page. *John Adams, 1784–1826.* Vol. 2. Garden City, N.Y.: Doubleday and Company, 1962.

Spruill, Julia Cherry. *Women's Life and Work in the Southern Colonies.* Chapel Hill: University of North Carolina Press, 1938.

Stampp, Kenneth M. *The Peculiar Institution: Slavery in the Ante-bellum South.* New York: Random House, 1956.

Stinchcombe, William. *The XYZ Affair.* Westport, Conn.: Greenwood Press, 1980.

Vipperman, Carl J. *The Rise of Rawlin Lowndes, 1721–1800.* Columbia: University of South Carolina Press, 1978.

Wallace, David Duncan. *South Carolina: A Short History, 1520–1948.* Columbia: University of South Carolina Press, 1961.

Walsh, Richard. *Charleston's Sons of Liberty: A Study of the Artisans, 1763–1789.* Columbia: University of South Carolina Press, 1959.

Weir, Robert M. *Colonial South Carolina: A History.* Millwood, N.Y.: KTO Press, 1983; reprint, Columbia: University of South Carolina Press, 1997.

Williams, Frances Leigh. *A Founding Family: The Pinckneys of South Carolina.* New York: Harcourt Brace Jovanovich, 1978.

Wolfe, John Harold. *Jeffersonian Democracy in South Carolina.* Chapel Hill: University of North Carolina Press, 1940.

Wood, Gordon. *The Creation of the American Republic, 1776–1787.* Chapel Hill: University of North Carolina Press, 1969.

Wood, Peter H. *Black Majority: Negroes in Colonial South Carolina from 1670 through the Stono Rebellion.* New York: W. W. Norton and Company, 1974.

Wyatt-Brown, Bertram. *Southern Honor: Ethics and Behavior in the Old South.* New York: Oxford University Press, 1982.

Zahniser, Marvin L. *Charles Cotesworth Pinckney, Founding Father.* Chapel Hill: University of North Carolina Press, 1967.

ARTICLES

Barquet, Nicolau, and Pere Domingo. "Smallpox: The Triumph over the Most Terrible Ministers of Death." *Annals of Internal Medicine* 127 (15 October 1997): 635–42.

Bloch, Ruth. "The Gendered Meanings of Virtue in Revolutionary America." *Signs: Journal of Women in Culture and Society* 13, no. 1 (1987): 48–57.

Elliott, W. S. "Honorable Charles Pinkney, LL.D." *DeBow's Review* 33 (1864): 66–69.

———. "Founder of the American Union: Charles Pinckney." *Debow's Review* 1 (1866): 372–78.

Foster, Eugene, et al. "Jefferson Fathered Slave's Last Child." *Nature* 196 (5 November 1998): 27–28.

Hall, John A. "A Rigour of Confinement That Violates Humanity: Jail Conditions in South Carolina during the 1790s." *Southern Studies: An Interdisciplinary Journal of the South* 24 (1985): 284–305.

Higginbotham, Don. "The American Militia: A Traditional Institution with Revolutionary Responsibilities." In *War and Society in Revolutionary America: The Wider Dimensions of Conflict.* Columbia: University of South Carolina Press, 1988.

Hill, Charles E. "James Madison." In *The American Secretaries of State and Their Diplomacy,* ed. Samuel Flagg Bemis. New York: Pageant Book Company, 1958.

Jameson, J. Franklin. "Portions of Charles Pinckney's Plan for a Constitution, 1787." *American Historical Review* 8 (April 1903): 509–11.

Kaplanoff, Mark D. "Charles Pinckney and the American Republican Tradition." In *Intellectual Life in Antebellum Charleston,* ed. Michael O'Brien and David Moltke-Hansen, 85–122. Knoxville: University of Tennessee Press, 1986.

Lipscomb, Terry W. "In Search of the Charles Pinckney Library." *Ex Libris* (1998–99): 2–7.

McLaughlin, Andrew C. "The Articles of Confederation." In *Essays on the Making of the Constitution,* ed. Leonard W. Levy, 44–60. 2d ed. New York: Oxford University Press, 1987.

———. "Sketch of Charles Pinckney's Plan for a Constitution." *American Historical Review* 9 (July 1904): 735–47.

Nadelhaft, Jerome J. "South Carolina: A Conservative Revolution." In *The Constitution and the States: The Role of the Original Thirteen in the Framing and Adoption of the Federal Constitution,* ed. Patrick T. Conley and John P. Kaminski, 156–84. Madison, Wis.: Madison House, 1988.

Renlet, Philip. "In the Hands of the British: The Treatment of American POWs during the War of Independence." *The Historian* 62 (summer 2000): 731–58.

Rodgers, Daniel T. "Republicanism: The Career of a Concept." *Journal of American History* 79 (June 1992): 11–38.

Salley, A. S. "Col. Miles Brewton and Some of His Descendants." *South Carolina Historical and Genealogical Magazine* 2 (April 1901): 15–35.

———. "President Washington's Tour through South Carolina in 1791." *Bulletins of the Historical Commission of South Carolina,* no. 12. Columbia, S.C.: The State Company, 1932.

Schulz, Constance B. "Eliza Lucas Pinckney." In *Portraits of American Women from Settlement to the Civil War,* ed. G. J. Barker-Benfield and Catherine Clinton, 65–82. New York: St. Martin's Press, 1991.

South Carolina Historical Magazine 99 (July 1998).

"South Carolina in the Presidential Election of 1800." *American Historical Review* 4 (October 1898): 114–24.

Stevens, Michael E. "Their Liberties, Properties, and Privileges: Civil Liberties in South Carolina, 1663–1791." In *The Bill of Rights and the States: The Colonial and Revolutionary Origins of American Liberties,* ed. Patrick T. Conley and John P. Kaminski, 398–423. Madison, Wis.: Madison House, 1992.

Ulmer, Shirley Sidney. "Charles Pinckney: Father of the Constitution?" *South Carolina Law Quarterly* 10 (winter 1958).

———. "James Madison and the Pinckney Plan." *South Carolina Law Quarterly* 9 (spring 1957).

Webber, Mabel L., ed. "Josiah Smith's Diary." *South Carolina Historical and Genealogical Magazine* 3 (1932): 1–28, 79–116, 197–207, 281–89; 34 (1933): 31–39, 67–84, 138–48, 194–210.

———. "The Thomas Pinckney Family of South Carolina." *South Carolina Historical and Genealogical Magazine* 39 (1938): 128–52.

Weir, Robert M. "'The Harmony We Were Famous For': An Interpretation of Pre-Revolutionary South Carolina Politics." *William and Mary Quarterly* 18 (October 1969): 473–501.

———. "'The Violent Spirit,' the Reestablishment of Order, and the Continuity of Leadership in Post-Revolutionary South Carolina." In *An Uncivil War: The Southern Backcountry during the American Revolution,* ed. Ronald Hoffman et al., 70–98. Charlottesville: University Press of Virginia for the U.S. Capitol Historical Society, 1985.

Zagarri, Rosemary. "The Rights of Man and Woman in Post-Revolutionary America." *William and Mary Quarterly* 55, no. 2 (April 1998): 203–30.

UNPUBLISHED SECONDARY SOURCES

Earman, Cynthia Diane. "Boardinghouses, Parties, and the Creation of a Political Society in Washington City, 1800–1830." Master's thesis, Louisiana State University, 1992.

Edgar, Walter "The Libraries of Colonial South Carolina." Masters thesis, University of South Carolina, 1969.

Matthews, Marty D. "'To Save the Republic . . .': The Influence of Natural Law on Thomas Jefferson's Attitudes towards Native and African Americans." Master's thesis, North Carolina State University, 1995.

Rogers, George C. "Speech on Charles Pinckney Day," 28 August 1987, in the Charleston Exchange at "A Bicentennial Commemoration" sponsored by Americans United for Separation of Church and State and the Charleston Commission on the Bicentennial of the United States Constitution.

Terry, George D. "A Study of the Impact of the French Revolution and the Insurrections in Saint-Dominque upon South Carolina: 1790–1805." Master's thesis, University of South Carolina, 1975.

Ulmer, Shirley Sidney. "The South Carolina Delegates to the Constitutional Convention of 1787: An Analytical Study." Ph.D. diss., Duke University, 1956.

Index